World's Best
Origami

Nick Robinson

ALPHA

A member of Penguin Group (USA) Inc.

ALPHA BOOKS

Published by the Penguin Group

Penguin Group (USA) Inc., 375 Hudson Street, New York, New York 10014, USA

Penguin Group (Canada), 90 Eglinton Avenue East, Suite 700, Toronto, Ontario M4P 2Y3, Canada (a division of Pearson Penguin Canada Inc.)

Penguin Books Ltd., 80 Strand, London WC2R 0RL, England

Penguin Ireland, 25 St. Stephen's Green, Dublin 2, Ireland (a division of Penguin Books Ltd.)

Penguin Group (Australia), 250 Camberwell Road, Camberwell, Victoria 3124, Australia (a division of Pearson Australia Group Pty. Ltd.)

Penguin Books India Pvt. Ltd., 11 Community Centre, Panchsheel Park, New Delhi—110 017, India

Penguin Group (NZ), 67 Apollo Drive, Rosedale, North Shore, Auckland 1311, New Zealand (a division of Pearson New Zealand Ltd.)

Penguin Books (South Africa) (Pty.) Ltd., 24 Sturdee Avenue, Rosebank, Johannesburg 2196, South Africa

Penguin Books Ltd., Registered Offices: 80 Strand, London WC2R 0RL, England

International Standard Book Number: 978-1-61564-053-9
Library of Congress Catalog Card Number: 2010926625

12   8 7 6 5 4 3 2

Interpretation of the printing code: The rightmost number of the first series of numbers is the year of the book's printing; the rightmost number of the second series of numbers is the number of the book's printing. For example, a printing code of 10-1 shows that the first printing occurred in 2010.

Printed in the United States of America

Note: This publication contains the opinions and ideas of its author. It is intended to provide helpful and informative material on the subject matter covered. It is sold with the understanding that the author and publisher are not engaged in rendering professional services in the book. If the reader requires personal assistance or advice, a competent professional should be consulted.

The author and publisher specifically disclaim any responsibility for any liability, loss, or risk, personal or otherwise, which is incurred as a consequence, directly or indirectly, of the use and application of any of the contents of this book.

Trademarks: All terms mentioned in this book that are known to be or are suspected of being trademarks or service marks have been appropriately capitalized. Alpha Books and Penguin Group (USA) Inc. cannot attest to the accuracy of this information. Use of a term in this book should not be regarded as affecting the validity of any trademark or service mark.

Most Alpha books are available at special quantity discounts for bulk purchases for sales promotions, premiums, fund-raising, or educational use. Special books, or book excerpts, can also be created to fit specific needs.

For details, write: Special Markets, Alpha Books, 375 Hudson Street, New York, NY 10014.

Contents

Chapter 1: Origami Basics **1**

How to Fold 2

Tips for Perfect Folding 3

Set Up Your Environment 3

Origami Likes Company 3

Go Online 3

Find Your Style 3

Get Creative 4

Join a Club 4

Teach Others 4

Choosing Your Paper 4

Origami Symbols 5

The Valley Fold 5

The Valley Fold and Unfold 6

The Mountain Fold 6

The Pleat 6

Turn the Paper Over 7

Rotate the Paper 90 Degrees 7

Rotate the Paper 180 Degrees 7

Fold to the Dotted Line 7

Pull Out the Paper 8

Push In the Paper 8

The Crimp 8

The Repeat Arrow 8

Making Shapes 9

The A4 Rectangle 9

Creating Hexagons 11

Creating Triangles and Octagons 12

Creating Pentagons 13

Creating Divisions 14

Folding Thirds 14

Folding Fifths 15

Techniques 16

The Rabbit's Ear 16

Making Reverse Folds 17

Making a Sink 18

Creating Bases 19

The Preliminary Base 19

The Waterbomb Base 21

The Kite/Fish Base 23

The Blintz Base 25

The Multiform Base 26

The Bird Base 27

Chapter 2: Birds **29**

Pecking Bird 30

Swan 31

Peacock 33

Hungry Chick 35

Perched Owl 36

Songbird 38

Great-Horned Owl 40

Mother and Baby Penguin 43

Fat Bird 46

Bowing Bird 48

Fancy Swan 52

Chapter 3: Animals **57**

Cricket 58

Pig 59

Cat's Head 61

Frog's Head 63

Whale's Tail 65

Fantail Goldfish 67

Horse 69

Mad March Hare 71

Dolphin 73

Frog on a Window 76

Howling at the Moon 79

Elephant 83

Puma's Head 86

Squarosaurus 90

Koala 94

Chapter 4: Flowers 97

Water Lily 98

Tulip and Stem 99

    Tulip 99

    Stem 100

Long-Stemmed Rose 101

Boutonniere Blossom 102

Sunflower 104

Snowdrop 106

Camellia 108

Orchid 110

Bluebell 111

Desert Flower 114

Chapter 5: People 119

Girl's Head 1 120

Girl's Head 2 121

Simple Santa 123

Napoleon 125

Grumpy Alien 127

Vampyra 129

Crying Baby 132

Robot's Head 135

Human Face 138

Mr. Muppet 142

Angel 146

Chapter 6: Containers 151

Simple Tray 152

Square Bowl 154

Spanish Box 156

Poppy Dish 158

Triangular Box 161

    Desk Tidy 164

Fox Dish 165

Star Box 168

Curly Box 171

Lidded Box 173

Classic Bowl 176

Bristol Box 179

Chapter 7: Geometric 181

Tessellating Cross 182

Squared Square 183

Proving Pythagoras 185

    Module 1A 185

    Module 1B 186

    Module 2 187

    Module 3 188

    The Proof 188

Flexagon 189

Tower 191

8-Point Star 193

Tri-Puzzle 195

    Module 1 195

    Module 2 197

    Module 3 198

Pinwheel Tato 199

Cross Puzzle 201

Classic Cube 204

Double Cube 207

Tri-Coaster 210

DNA Strand 213

Umulius Rectangulum 216

Tri-Puzzle and Cross Puzzle Solutions 220

Chapter 8: Modular. 221

Hexahedron 222

Squared Square Cube 223

Modular Twist. 224

    Module 224

    Assembly 225

Pyramid. 226

Windmill Cube 228

Tri-Module Unit. 230

    Hexahedron 230

    Tetrahedron 231

    Spiked Models 232

    Four-Sided Pyramid. 232

    For Real Enthusiasts 232

Snowflake Module 233

Snow Cube 235

Goldfinch Star. 237

Octahedron 240

Chapter 9: Practical 241

Wallet. 242

Cup 243

Booklet 245

Envelope from Bonn 246

Party Hat 247

French Fries Bag. 249

Set Square 250

Pocket Fan. 252

Classic Cap 254

Sailboat Envelope 256

Elforia Envelope 258

Holiday Card. 260

Ring 262

Chapter 10: Fun. 265

Gliding Hoop. 266

Crown 267

Sheffield Sailboat. 269

Word Dominoes 271

Freising Plane 272

Cart 274

Standing Heart 276

Popsicle. 278

Bug-Eye Glider 280

3D Heart 283

Candle 285

Reverse Pinwheel 288

Kettle 291

Tent 295

Trees on a Hillside 298

Apple. 302

Index of Models 307

Foreword

Whatever your experience with origami, you've picked up the right book. Perhaps you've never folded paper except for a few airplanes, waterbombs, or fortune-tellers (a.k.a. cootie catchers) as a child, or maybe not even that. Perhaps you're a seasoned origami expert, very familiar with what's been created for centuries all over the world. You may consider yourself talented in arts and crafts or somewhat lacking in aesthetic capacities. You may be very old or very young. Regardless of your reasons for coming here, you've come to the right place. Of course, I am pleased to be able to explain why: Nick Robinson.

Nick has been involved in paper-folding for nearly 30 years. He has created hundreds of original models. He's an experienced and accomplished teacher of origami. He's a clear and wise origami illustrator. And as an active leader in the wide world of origami, Nick is in touch with what folders all over the world are creating. Oh yes, he also wrote many origami books before publishing this one. So who would I choose to write and draw a book for top instruction? Select a great variety of models, traditional and new, from international masters of the craft, mostly unpublished, and exhibiting fine aesthetic sensibility? Nick Robinson.

Page through this book, and you'll quickly discover some of its features. In the beginning, Nick offers the basics of folding paper and provides clear and simple instructions for beginners—and a reminder to the experienced about how to teach. The model chapters are divided into several fun categories. You'll see models that are objects of nature, such as flowers, birds, animals, and people. You'll also see a variety of geometric products, such as boxes and dishes, action toys, and purely abstract constructions. You can begin with any chapter that appeals to you. Each is organized to begin with the simplest model and process to the more complex. But note that the simplest to fold can be the most elegant.

Nick Robinson is a musician and composer. Perhaps this has influenced his creative paper-folding and selection of models for this book. He has a respect for simple beauty and a good eye for it in origami. He's also very funny, and his delight in life is revealed in some of his own models and those of others he's chosen for this book.

In short: dip into this book and have fun.

Robert Neale

Robert Neale is a retired teacher of the psychology of religion and has served as president of The Friends of the Origami Center of America. He created his first origami design in 1958 and has assembled a highly impressive catalog of work since then. His designs are usually fairly simple but possess life and wit that lift them into the "classic" category. As a magician, he also enjoys working on the presentation side of origami. His followers include many origami designers who are able to recognize the true genius of his work. Neale lives in Vermont.

Introduction

Origami is the act of creative paper-folding. It inhabits many points on the spectrum between high art and traditional craft and can be abstract, representational, stylized, geometric, free-form, and much, much more. It's used daily throughout the world as recreation, therapy, entertainment, problem-solving, engineering, and education. Yet despite all these varied possibilities, most people do origami for fun and relaxation.

All you need to do origami is a sheet of paper, a few spare minutes, and a set of instructions. There's a common misconception that you need to be artistic and patient to succeed with origami. As you'll see once you've started working through this book, that's purely a myth.

Origami can be a solitary activity, allowing you to focus your mind on making a perfect example of a design, or it can be enjoyed in company, where it acts as a perfect means of uniting a small group of strangers. Origami devotees can be found all around the world, and the Internet enables us to freely exchange new ideas, models, and photos and get almost instant help with "problem" models!

In this book, I present a wide range of subjects and styles by origami creators from all around the world. Each chapter starts with relatively simple models, moving smoothly toward more-challenging works. By the time you've folded the entire book, you'll be in a position to tackle origami at any level of complexity.

Acknowledgments

Over my more than 25 years in the wonderful world of origami, far too many people have helped me arrive at where I am today to thank them all individually. So a massive communal thanks to you all, especially the British Origami Society. (Join today!) I'd also like to mention my agent, Marilyn Allen, and editors, Karyn Gerhard, Randy Ladenheim-Gil, Christy Wagner, and Jan Zoya. Anne LaVin did sterling and thorough work checking my diagrams from an origami perspective. Thanks to Paulo Mulatinho, who drew the hands. For creative inspiration, I'd like to thank Philip Shen, Dave Brill, Paul Jackson, Edwin Corrie, Salz und Pfeffer, Francis Ow, Kuni Kasahara, Mick Guy, Thoki Yenn, Vicente Palacios, and Robert Neale. For lasting friendship, endless patience, and sage advice ("That's rubbish!"), thanks to the truly wonderful Wayne Brown. For musical accompaniment, thank you Dave, John, Chris, Rich and Aidan from Muttley Crew, Claude Debussy, Maurice Ravel, David Torn, and Bill Frisell. For de-stressing, thanks to my inner-city allotment, helped by Ant, Janice, and Kon. Hello to my recently discovered extended family Aunty Viv and Uncle Terry, plus their children—where have the last 30 years gone? Most importantly, thank you to my wife and best friend, Alison; children, Nick and Daisy; and cats Rhubarb and Matilda.

Special Thanks to the Technical Reviewer

World's Best Origami was reviewed by an artist who double-checked the accuracy of what you'll learn here, to help us ensure that this book gives you everything you need to know about the art and craft of origami. Special thanks are extended to Kurt Owens.

Kurt Owens is a designer and artist who enjoys playing with all forms of paper, from tissue to corrugated. He frequently confounds miniaturists with his minute pieces that require many delicate, miniscule cuts and has created very large pieces for theater productions and Mardi Gras costumes.

Chapter 1
Origami Basics

It's always tempting to leap into a new hobby and try the most challenging or exciting project you can find. Often, however, that route leads to frustration and, in the case of origami, lots of wadded-up pieces of paper! It's far better to begin with the basics and practice them as much as you can before moving on to the more difficult models. In this first chapter, we go over everything you need to know to start folding, from choosing your paper, to reading an origami diagram, to making your first folds.

Even when you've progressed past those first models, don't forget to revisit the techniques you learned in those early pieces from time to time. You can refresh your technique and maybe improve on some of the folds you're not quite up to par on. And as you reexamine the basics, you may be inspired to adapt them and even create your own models using them!

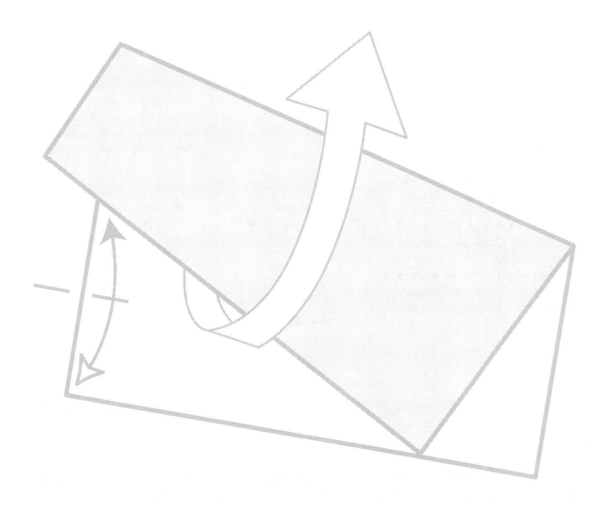

How to Fold

The most important thing to remember when creating origami is to take your time. Origami isn't a race, a competition, or an all-out battle with the paper. It's a relaxing and introspective activity. Rushing a fold almost inevitably results in an inaccurate crease. You can usually make simple models with a few inaccuracies and they'll still "work," but more complex folds require precision. A sloppy first fold may even result in your not being able to finish the model! Flattening a crease is a quick process; but do spend time lining up the paper, ensuring it's in *exactly* the right place, before flattening it.

There are no rules in folding paper, just different methods. Any method that gets results is fine, but some ways of folding are more reliable and, therefore, better for beginners. When you know how to fold, you can try some of the other methods if you want to.

Following is a typical sequence for folding a square in half. It may feel more natural to fold the paper toward you, but then your hands obscure the edges, so I recommend you fold the paper *away* from your body.

1. Begin with the paper flat on a table. More experienced folders may fold "in the air," but it's certainly a lot harder that way. Your hands should be on either side of the paper, pointing naturally in, your arms relaxed.

2. Put your thumbs under the paper, and hold it between first finger and thumb. Depending on how big the sheet is, your other fingers may support the paper or curl into your palms. Fold the paper toward the opposite side. Do not put any creases in yet.

3. Slide the upper edge past the lower edge and back, keeping the lower edge still. Make your movements smaller and smaller until you're certain the two edges are lined up. Don't concentrate on the corners because they might be too far apart to easily keep an eye on both. Instead, choose two points along the edge.

4. When the edges are in place, hold the paper firmly with your stronger hand, and swivel your other hand around on your thumb, keeping your thumb in place. You can then spread and use the rest of your fingers to hold the paper while you release your first hand. Slide your finger down the middle and to either side, forming the crease with your index finger. Then reinforce the crease by sliding both index fingers out from the center.

After folding, always check your accuracy. If things didn't line up perfectly, take more time and care the next time you make a fold. Eventually, accuracy will become easier to achieve.

Tips for Perfect Folding

Apart from folding slowly, a number of other things can help you progress in origami including where you fold, who you fold with, and more.

Set Up Your Environment

Folding on a table is the best way to enjoy it. Be sure the surface is clean and you've got plenty of room to place your paper, the instructions, and a cup of tea or coffee. A comfy chair helps, too.

Origami is best enjoyed in a peaceful environment, so find somewhere quiet where you won't be disturbed. Some folders like music while they fold, while others prefer silence. Try both to see what works for you.

Be sure you have either natural daylight or a suitable lamp. Without decent lighting, it can be hard to see where the creases are, and your eyes will get tired.

Origami Likes Company

Origami is essentially a solitary pastime, but the social side of folding can be tremendous. In addition to helping each other complete a tricky model, working together means you can discuss origami with a friend. Some more experienced folders even tend to do the talking instead of folding.

Like any hobby, the more background knowledge you have, the broader your perspective will be, and it all helps toward improving your standards. Most origami societies have regular national and local meetings where you can learn new folds and make new friends. (See the "Join a Club" section, later in this chapter, for more on locating clubs and societies near you.)

Go Online

The Internet has probably done more to further the spread of origami than anything else in recent years. Because they're independent of language, origami diagrams are perfectly suited to posting on websites all over the world, and thousands of them are currently available—mostly for free.

You can also join mailing lists to discuss anything origami-related, poke around in forums to share new models and techniques, read book review sites, and peruse thousands of other sites devoted to the many different styles of origami.

Find Your Style

Beginners to origami should try as many different styles and approaches as possible. Each has something to offer and helps you decide which types of origami you enjoy most. As with music, folders tend to have distinct preferences for what they like folding. For example, some love ultra-complex designs that can take several hours to fold, while others won't make anything with more than 12 or so steps.

The beauty of origami is that these styles are perfectly compatible with each other. It's not a matter of one being better than the other.

Get Creative

You may think origami creators are a special breed, but the truth is, almost anyone can create origami. It just takes the right attitude. Begin by adapting existing designs, fold a wide variety of styles, and eventually you'll begin to produce original work. It can be a slow process, but believe me, it's immensely rewarding. If you can learn to make diagrams of your new work, you'll be able to share your work easily with fellow folders.

Join a Club

Origami societies or clubs exist in almost every part of the world, and a quick Internet search will give you all the details.

Larger clubs often have a regular magazine and conventions open to all. Smaller clubs might meet in someone's house or at a local library. Whatever your folding abilities, you'll be made very welcome.

Teach Others

Showing others how to make a model can bring as much pleasure as folding it yourself. Sharing your talents, however small you might feel they are, is a great way to socialize, and all ages enjoy origami, from children to senior citizens.

Be sure you choose simple designs and practice them thoroughly before trying to teach. As one veteran lady folder in the United Kingdom always says, "You need to know the model backward!"

Choosing Your Paper

Put very simply, paper is made from tiny chips of wood (and other material such as grass or leaves), held together with a type of glue called sizing. Some folders take their origami so seriously that they make individual sheets of paper for specific models, choosing the color and content of the paper depending on how it will be folded. Michael LaFosse has been creating fine-art origami from his handmade papers since 1974, and his models show a level of artistry quite rare in origami.

Given the amazing variety of paper types available to you, where should you start? Ultimately, you need to try as many different types as you can find and discover which ones suit your folding style.

Here are some of the options worth checking out:

Origami paper   Countless different patterns and colors of origami paper are available, in a variety of sizes. It is (or should be!) perfectly square and has a pattern or color on one side only. The other side is white. Origami paper is also known as *kami,* the Japanese word for "paper."

Duo paper   Duo paper is like standard origami paper, but with a different color on either side. It's great to use when both sides of the paper will be exposed in the final model.

Photocopy paper   Don't overlook this humble paper! It's usually the cheapest paper you can buy, and it's generally crisp and easy to fold. Yes, you'll need to cut it into squares, but many geometric designs make use of rectangular paper, as do plenty of folds for children. Photocopy paper is available in lots of colors, the same on both sides.

Art paper   Thicker art papers, such as Canson or Ingres, are perfect for a technique called "wet-folding," where the paper is dampened before folding. This process enables you to make very expressive curves that "set" upon drying.

Washi paper   This is traditional Japanese paper, usually thicker and stronger than ordinary origami paper. It's generally made with different types of plant fiber. The pattern is usually on one side and the other side is a plain, solid color. Due to the thickness of the paper, it's best suited for simpler designs.

Chiyogami   Another traditional Japanese paper, chiyogami is available in a wide variety of beautiful patterns.

Newspaper   Although not ideally suited to complex models, newspaper can produce lots of fun folds. Think hats and baseball gloves. It's also very easy to find!

Paper currency   Dollar bills and most other paper currencies are made from very strong paper, perfect for simple models. In fact, there's an entire dollar-bill-folding genre. Origami folded with currency make perfect impromptu gifts.

Foil-backed paper   As the name suggests, this paper has thin metallic foil on one side. You can make thin points such as insect legs with this paper. But foil-backed paper is unforgiving to fold, and some feel it produces unattractive results.

"Poo" paper   Surprisingly enough, animal poo can make paper for folding with, although it's only suitable for very simple designs. It's basically dung washed and boiled for many hours, chopped up, colored, squashed, and dried in the sun. You can buy brands with the unique contributions of sheep, elephant, bison, reindeer, kangaroo, and many other species. These are best folded in the open air.

Origami Symbols

Over the past 50 years, origami diagrams, or folding instructions, have been refined and expanded, but they still use a core set of 15 or so symbols. These symbols are universally recognized and give enough information that you can follow diagrams regardless of the language the instructions are written in. After a while, the diagrams will become second nature to you, and you'll easily be able to follow them.

Experts can read diagrams like musical notes and even fold the model in their heads without a sheet of paper, mentally working out the difficult steps before trying it with paper. Then, the actual folding is much easier. Experts rarely read the accompanying words, but as a beginner, you should so you don't miss any of the information.

The Valley Fold

If you fold your piece of paper corner to opposite corner, you're making a valley fold. Unfold it, and you can see the sides rise slightly on either side of the crease, forming a valley in the center. The paper is even slightly V shaped. The symbol for a valley crease is a series of dashes.

You can also see the fold arrow. This is a solid line with an arrowhead at one end that shows the direction of the fold. Where it helps to clarify, a small circle identifies relevant corners or positions.

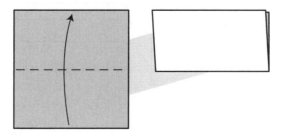

The Valley Fold and Unfold

On many occasions, you'll need to make a crease and then unfold it. This is known as precreasing, and with it, you create a crease for later use.

The fold and unfold arrow has an arrowhead at both ends. If it doesn't matter which direction you fold (such as a basic diagonal crease), both arrowheads are solid. Where it's better or easier to fold from a specific corner, the arrowhead at that end is hollow. An unfolded crease is shown by a very thin, solid line.

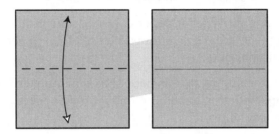

The Mountain Fold

If you turn an opened valley crease upside down, it becomes a mountain crease. The two are always formed at the same time. The symbol for a mountain crease is a dash followed by two dots. The mountain fold arrow is a solid line with a hollow, half-arrow head.

You can make a mountain fold by lifting up the paper and physically folding it behind/underneath, or by turning the paper over and treating it as a valley fold.

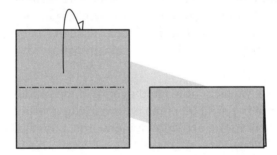

The Pleat

The pleat, a combination of both valley and mountain fold, usually parallel to each other, is a very common fold. It doesn't matter in which order you make the two creases, but do check carefully to see which is which.

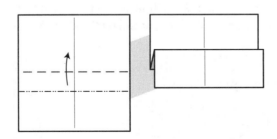

Turn the Paper Over

This is perhaps the simplest origami move of all: pick up the paper, and turn it over from side to side, as if you were flipping a pancake. At the start of a model, the different colors of the paper shown in the diagram indicate a turnover, but later on, the paper may be the same color on both sides.

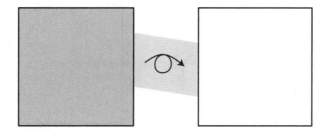

Rotate the Paper 90 Degrees

This symbol tells you to turn the paper around by—usually—90 degrees in the direction of the arrows. It may be used to indicate a slight rotation used to make the step clearer.

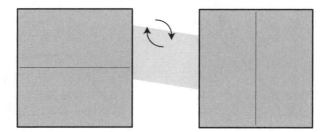

Rotate the Paper 180 Degrees

This symbol tells you to rotate the paper by 180 degrees. After a while, you'll just see this orientation change from the pictures themselves, but the symbol is a useful reminder.

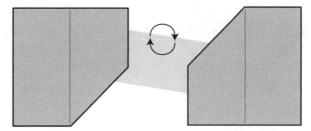

Fold to the Dotted Line

When you're folding a flap away from the main body of the paper, it can sometimes be difficult to see exactly where it's going. Checking the next picture in any design is always a good idea, but in this book, a dotted line will show you where to fold to.

Pull Out the Paper

Often you are asked to pull out trapped paper inside, or unfold a layer. I could use an ordinary fold arrow to signify this, but it's clearer with a larger, solid white arrow, showing where the paper comes from or goes to.

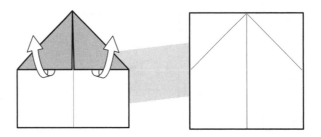

Push In the Paper

A black triangle indicates you need to apply gentle pressure in a given direction to complete the step. You'll see it on all reverse folds (as shown here) and sinks (see the "Sinks" section later in this chapter). Always try to use existing creases and persuade the paper into place rather than force it.

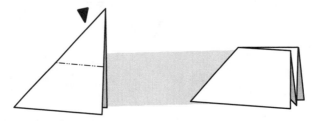

The Crimp

This is like a double reverse fold—you reverse it inside and then reverse part of it back out. It can also be seen as a pleat applied to a folded edge. The two creases may be parallel, or they may start from a single point and come out at an angle.

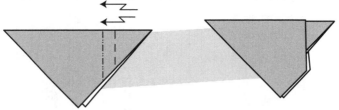

The Repeat Arrow

An arrow with a line through it indicates the fold shown should be repeated. Some people add extra dashes to the arrow to indicate how many times the move is repeated, but in this book, I use just the one and explain further in the text.

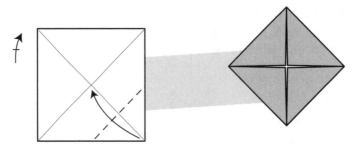

Making Shapes

Although origami is traditionally made from square paper, many variations use three-, five-, and six-sided paper; A4 rectangles; 2×1 rectangles; and even more obscure proportions. Most of these methods leave unwanted creases on the paper, but you can use them as a template to cut out "clean" shapes.

The following sections offer some guidelines to obtaining the most common shapes you may need.

The A4 Rectangle

A4 is the chosen paper size for Europe and the East. Its proportions are very elegant. To understand where the shape comes from requires a little math (but you don't need this to fold!).

Measure the length of a diagonal within a square and then extend two opposite sides of the square to match that length. As you can see from the following diagram, AB = BC = 1, so by using the Pythagorean theorem, the length AC is equal to the square root of 2 (approximately 1.414). If AE = AC, we have a rectangle of "A" proportions. An A4 rectangle measures 8.27 inches × 11.69 inches (210mm × 297mm), but by using the following methods, you can make your paper the correct proportions.

Creating an A4 from a shorter rectangle:

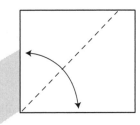

1. Fold a short edge to a long edge, crease, and unfold.

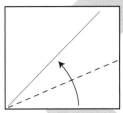

2. Fold the lower edge to the recent crease.

3. Fold the upper edge so it just touches the inside corner, crease, and unfold. (Turn the paper over if it helps.)

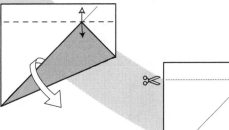

4. Remove the strip from the top.

Creating an A4 from a longer rectangle:

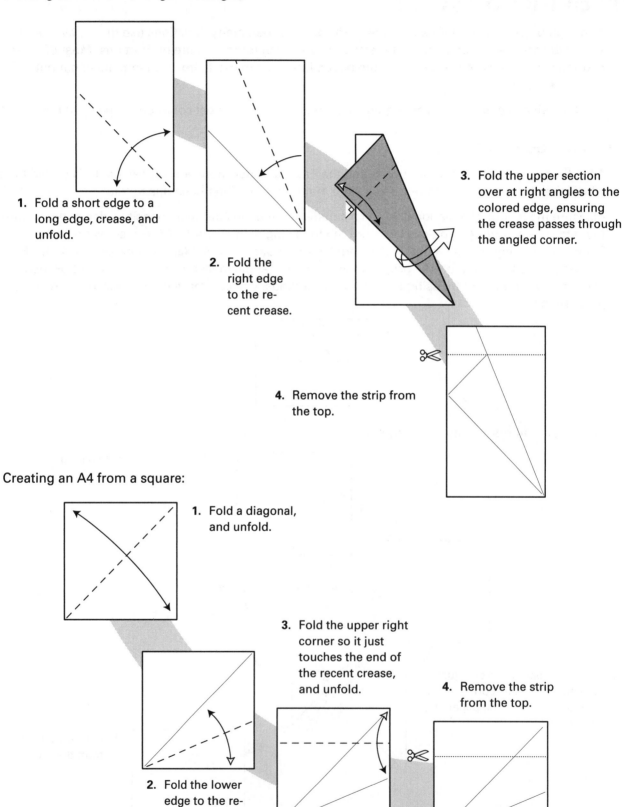

1. Fold a short edge to a long edge, crease, and unfold.

2. Fold the right edge to the recent crease.

3. Fold the upper section over at right angles to the colored edge, ensuring the crease passes through the angled corner.

4. Remove the strip from the top.

Creating an A4 from a square:

1. Fold a diagonal, and unfold.

2. Fold the lower edge to the recent crease.

3. Fold the upper right corner so it just touches the end of the recent crease, and unfold.

4. Remove the strip from the top.

Creating Hexagons

Hexagons are useful for many kinds of dishes, bowls, and flowers, such as the Desert Flower in Chapter 4. Several methods exist for folding a hexagon. Here is a common one:

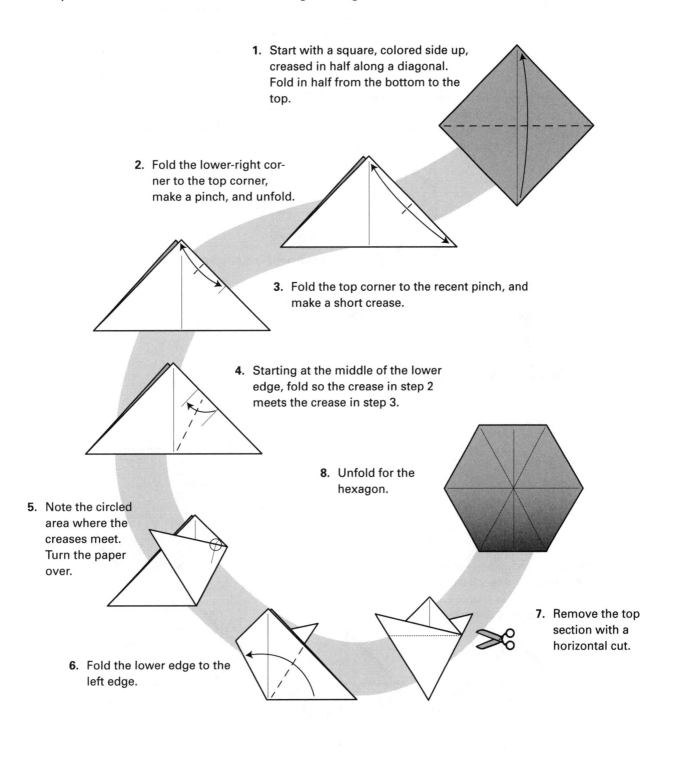

1. Start with a square, colored side up, creased in half along a diagonal. Fold in half from the bottom to the top.

2. Fold the lower-right corner to the top corner, make a pinch, and unfold.

3. Fold the top corner to the recent pinch, and make a short crease.

4. Starting at the middle of the lower edge, fold so the crease in step 2 meets the crease in step 3.

5. Note the circled area where the creases meet. Turn the paper over.

6. Fold the lower edge to the left edge.

7. Remove the top section with a horizontal cut.

8. Unfold for the hexagon.

Creating Triangles and Octagons

These shapes are used less often, but you never know when you'll need them!

To make a triangle:

1. Fold a square in half from left to right.

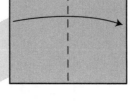

2. Starting the crease at the bottom right corner, fold the top right corner over to touch the left vertical edge.

3. Cut along the inside edge.

4. Unfold for the triangle.

To make an octagon:

4. Unfold for the octagon.

1. Start with a preliminary base (see "The Preliminary Base" section later in this chapter). Take a folded edge to the vertical center.

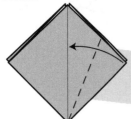

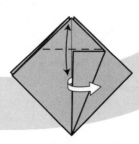

3. Cut along the recent crease.

2. Fold the upper flap over the edge, crease, and unfold.

Creating Pentagons

Another great way to design dishes, flowers, and containers is to take a design that uses a square, and fold it into a pentagon. You'll have to invent new folding methods, but that's half the fun!

1. Fold a square in half from the bottom to the top.

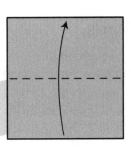

3. Starting the crease at the lower middle, fold the pinch on the right so it just touches the upper-left edge.

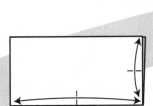

2. Fold in half both ways, making a tiny pinch on the right and the bottom.

4. Fold the inner folded edge to the right edge.

9. Unfold for the pentagon.

5. Fold the lower edge to the inner folded edge.

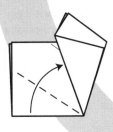

8. Cut along the recent crease.

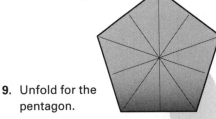

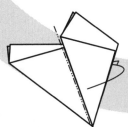

6. Fold the right half of the paper underneath.

7. Make a crease at right angles to the lower-left edge.

Creating Divisions

Many designs use divisions of 4, 8, 16, and so on, but you'll also need to know how to divide paper into thirds and possibly fifths. To have a "clean" division, use a spare sheet to make the following templates and then slide in the clean sheet and transfer the distance across.

Folding Thirds

Robert Lang invented this method using the amazing *ReferenceFinder* software he created. (You can download this for free from langorigami.com.)

1. Start with a square that has a diagonal crease. Fold the lower edge to the diagonal, crease, and unfold.

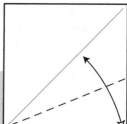

2. Fold the left edge to the recent crease.

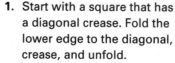

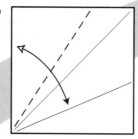

3. Where the last crease meets the top edge is the one-third mark.

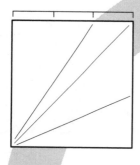

4. Fold the top left corner to the nearest crease.

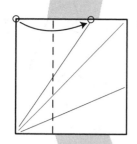

5. You've now made the template. Slide a clean square under the colored flap. It doesn't need to be vertically level.

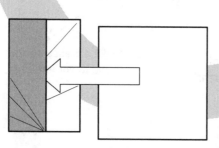

6. Fold the right edge of the clean sheet to the colored edge, crease, and unfold.

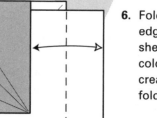

7. You now have a one-third crease.

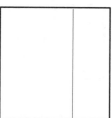

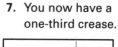

Folding Fifths

Dividing a square into fifths is a little unusual, but several designs require it, so it's best to learn it. The process takes a little concentration.

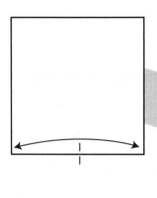

1. Fold a square in half, but only pinch the edge of the paper. Unfold.

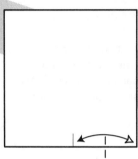

2. Fold the right corner to the first pinch, making another pinch.

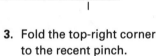

3. Fold the top-right corner to the recent pinch.

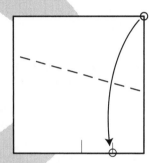

4. Fold the lower-left corner to the colored edge, where it meets the white edge. Make a short crease, and unfold back into a square. This marks one fifth.

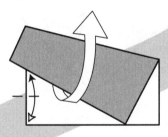

5. Fold over, extending the crease you made in step 4.

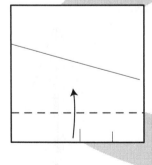

6. You've now made the template. Insert a clean sheet as you did with the previous thirds division.

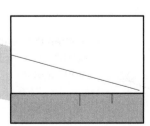

Techniques

Origami may seem complicated, but the more you fold, the more you recognize the same moves in many different designs. Recognizing these key techniques allows you to break down a sequence into stages, giving you more confidence in your folds. The following sections outline the key techniques you should know.

The Rabbit's Ear

This technique is usually applied to a triangular flap of paper, producing a smaller triangle, hinged at the center, showing the opposite side/color of the paper.

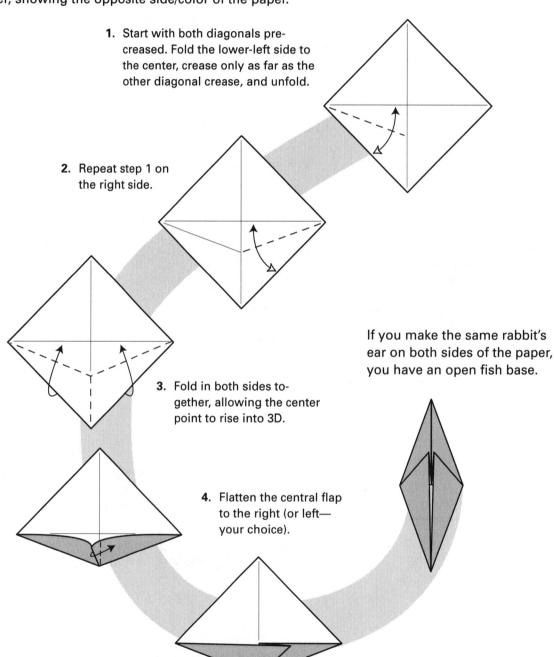

1. Start with both diagonals pre-creased. Fold the lower-left side to the center, crease only as far as the other diagonal crease, and unfold.

2. Repeat step 1 on the right side.

3. Fold in both sides together, allowing the center point to rise into 3D.

4. Flatten the central flap to the right (or left—your choice).

If you make the same rabbit's ear on both sides of the paper, you have an open fish base.

Making Reverse Folds

As the name implies, the direction of the fold is in some way reversed with this technique. It's most easily made by precreasing, as shown here, but more experienced folders can make them directly. When you make a precrease, one of the shorter creases always is correct to make the reverse, and the other needs changing from valley to mountain, or vice versa. The long crease always needs reversing. Fold and unfold your examples until you understand exactly what's happening with this.

The examples here are drawn for clarity—in reality, the inside of a narrow point would be the same color as the outside.

To make an outside reverse:

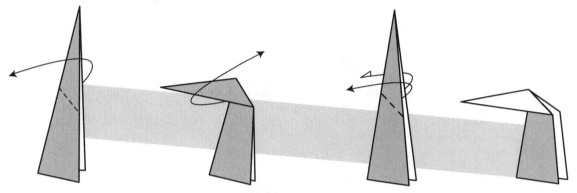

1. Fold the end of a flap over, away from the "open" side.

2. Crease firmly, and unfold.

3. Wrap the paper around the outside—the valley crease shown is the same on the underside.

To make an inside reverse:

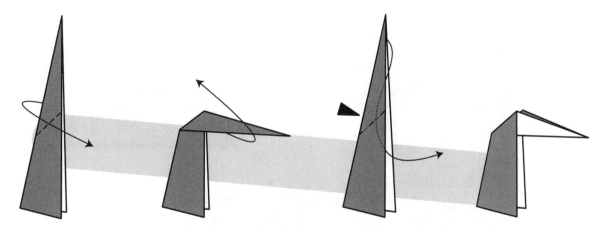

1. Fold the end of a flap over, toward the "open" side.

2. Crease firmly, and unfold.

3. Push the upper half of the paper inside—the mountain crease shown is the same on the underside.

Making a Sink

When you make a sink, you push in a corner that has no open edges, such as in the center of a square. If you can unfold the paper to make the sink, it's known as an "open" sink. On more complex folds, you may come across sinks that cannot be opened this way. These awkward beasts are called "closed" sinks—and are best avoided!

1. Start with a waterbomb base. Fold the top corner to the center of the lower edge, crease, and unfold.

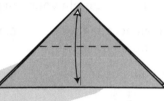

2. Open the paper out from underneath to a white square.

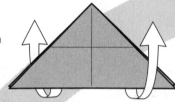

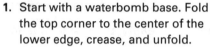

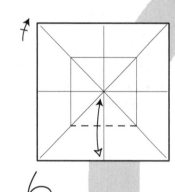

3. Fold each edge to the center, making sure the halfway crease is a mountain. (Two will already be so. The other two need to be changed.) Turn the paper over.

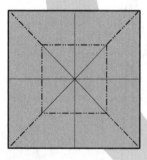

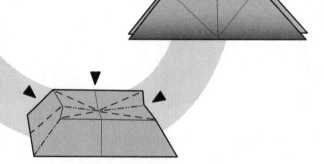

4. Emphasize the creases, pinching the model into 3D with a flat central section like a tabletop.

5. Press in the sides and the top, gently forming the creases shown in the diagram. Keep pressing together until the paper is flat again. This is a sunken point.

Creating Bases

Many designs start off with identical folding sequences, so these sequences have been given names and are generally described as "bases," as in a base from which to make different models. This allows a set of instructions to commence with, for example, "Fold a bird base." The following sections offer several bases you need to know.

The Preliminary Base

This is one of the first bases you learn in origami, hence the name. This base is the first of two configurations for the Union Jack crease pattern, where the paper is divided in half, side to opposite side, and then corner to corner, in both directions. It's the starting point for the bird base.

1. Start with the colored side up. Crease corner to opposite corner, and unfold. Repeat in the other direction. Turn the paper over.

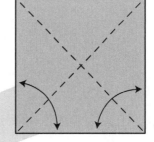

2. Fold side to opposite side, crease, and unfold in both directions.

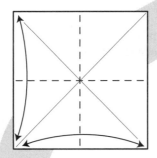

3. Rotate the paper 45 degrees. Fold both ends of the horizontal mountain crease down to the lower corner. The upper corner swings down with them.

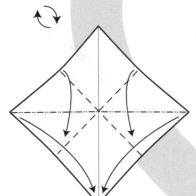

4. Complete.

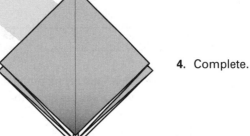

Here's an alternative way to fold the preliminary base:

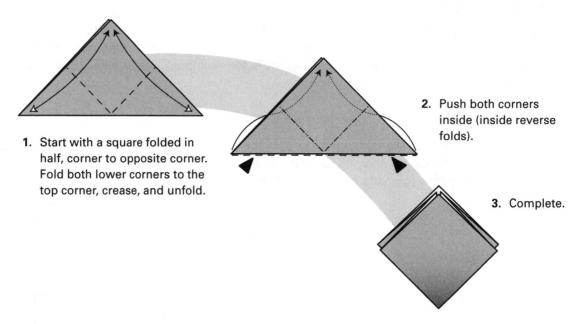

1. Start with a square folded in half, corner to opposite corner. Fold both lower corners to the top corner, crease, and unfold.

2. Push both corners inside (inside reverse folds).

3. Complete.

Here's another way:

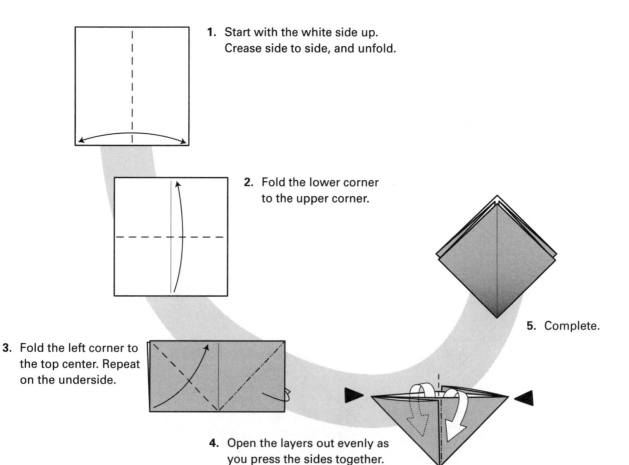

1. Start with the white side up. Crease side to side, and unfold.

2. Fold the lower corner to the upper corner.

3. Fold the left corner to the top center. Repeat on the underside.

4. Open the layers out evenly as you press the sides together.

5. Complete.

The Waterbomb Base

This base is the second of two configurations for the Union Jack crease pattern, the first being the preliminary base. You can transform one into the other simply by turning it inside out.

The base itself consists of a right-angled triangle with two points on either side. Other ways to form a waterbomb base include reverse-folding and opening/squashing.

1. Start with the colored side up. Fold side to opposite side, crease and unfold, in both directions. Turn the paper over.

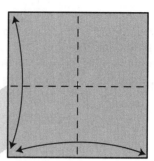

2. Crease and unfold both diagonals.

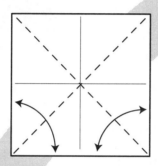

3. Fold the ends of the mountain crease forward and down to the center of the lower edge.

Or turn a preliminary base inside out:

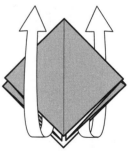

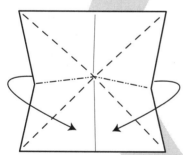

4. Complete.

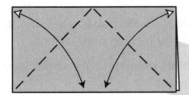

1. Start with a square folded in half. Fold each upper corner to the center of the lower edge, crease firmly, and unfold.

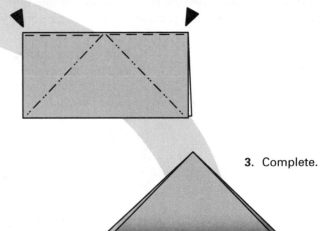

2. The creases you've made are mountain (underneath) and valley (on top). Change the valley to a mountain crease, pushing in (inside reverse) both corners using existing creases.

3. Complete.

Here's an alternative way to fold the waterbomb base:

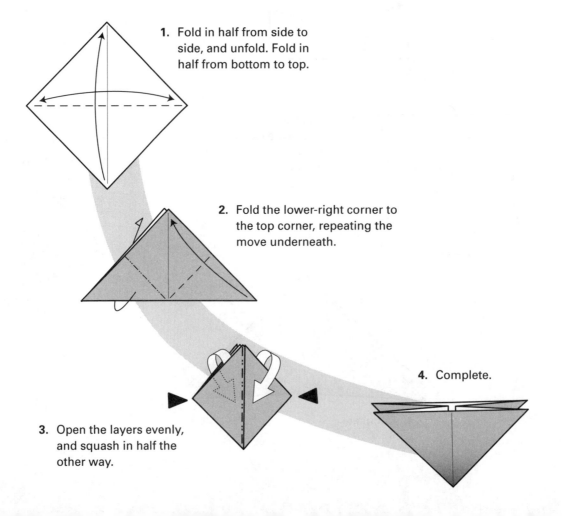

1. Fold in half from side to side, and unfold. Fold in half from bottom to top.

2. Fold the lower-right corner to the top corner, repeating the move underneath.

3. Open the layers evenly, and squash in half the other way.

4. Complete.

The Kite/Fish Base

With just three creases, the kite base is the simplest of all the bases. However, it's still the basis for many simple designs such as the Pecking Bird (see Chapter 2). It's also the basis for many more complex designs. The fish base is a development of the kite base. More experienced folders only fold the vertical diagonal of step 1, forming the mountain creases in steps 6 and 7 on the fly.

To make the kite base:

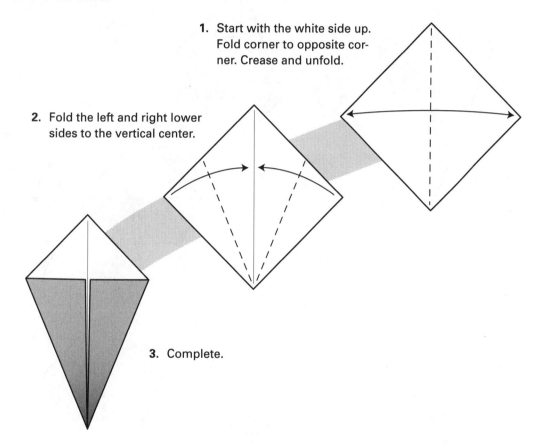

1. Start with the white side up. Fold corner to opposite corner. Crease and unfold.

2. Fold the left and right lower sides to the vertical center.

3. Complete.

To make the fish base:

1. Start with the white side up. Fold corner to opposite corner, crease, and unfold. Repeat in the other direction.

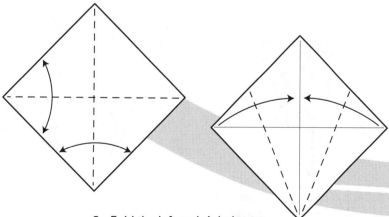

2. Fold the left and right lower sides to the vertical center.

continues

continued

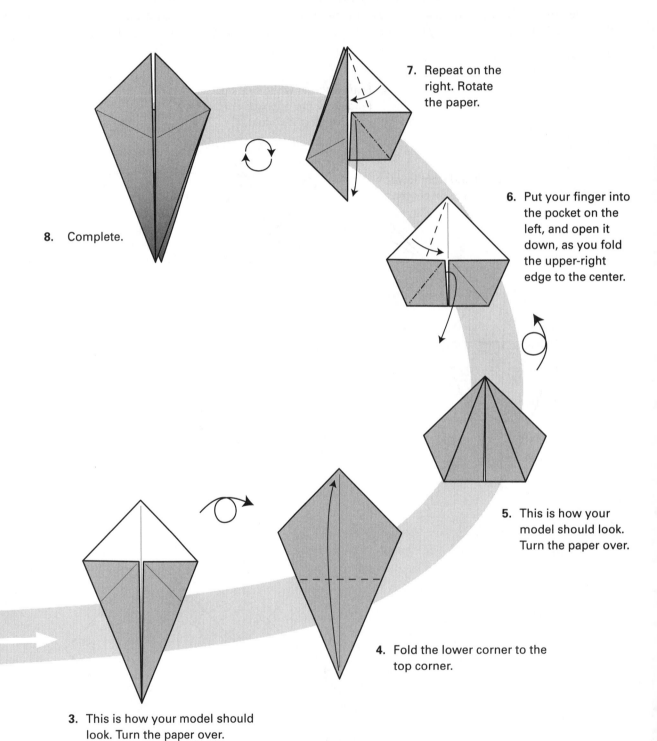

8. Complete.

7. Repeat on the right. Rotate the paper.

6. Put your finger into the pocket on the left, and open it down, as you fold the upper-right edge to the center.

5. This is how your model should look. Turn the paper over.

4. Fold the lower corner to the top corner.

3. This is how your model should look. Turn the paper over.

The Blintz Base

This base takes its name from a type of Jewish pastry whose corners are folded to the center. In folding terms, there are easy ways to find the center of a square, including folding corner to opposite corner both ways, or side to opposite side both ways, or any combination of the two!

1. Start with the white side up. Crease both diagonals and unfold.

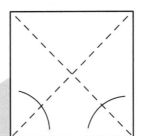

2. Fold a corner to the center.

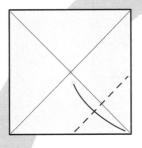

3. Repeat with the other three corners.

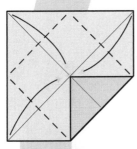

4. Complete.

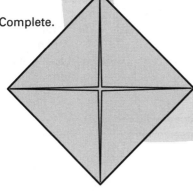

Here's an alternate method:

1. Start with a white square creased in half vertically. Fold in half from top to bottom.

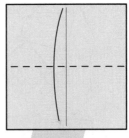

2. Fold both lower corners to the upper middle. Repeat underneath.

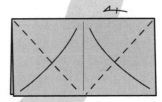

3. Unfold the lower layers to complete.

The Multiform Base

Also known as a "windmill" base, this classical form is hundreds of years old. With a highly logical crease pattern (each quarter of the square has creases from a preliminary base), this base is extremely flexible, capable of producing, boxes, frogs, birds, and butterflies.

1. Start with an unfolded preliminary base, colored side up. Fold each corner to the center, crease, and unfold.

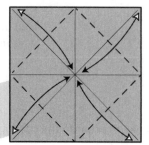

2. Add quarter creases all the way around.

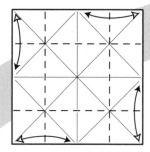

3. Fold the midpoint of each edge in to the center, encouraging the creases shown.

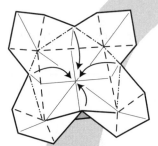

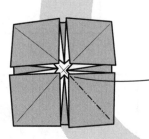

4. This is the "closed" form of the multiform. Open the lower-right corner out and to the right.

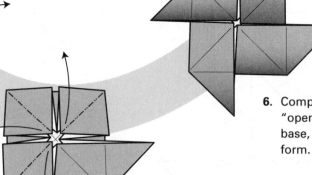

5. Repeat with the other three corners.

6. Complete. This is the "open" form of the base, in its windmill form.

The Bird Base

This is used as the basis for many birds, but it's also used to create a huge variety of models, from fish, to dragons, to stars. It's well worth practicing this until you can do it in your sleep because you'll find it useful in so many ways. You can judge your folding by the sharpness of the lower points!

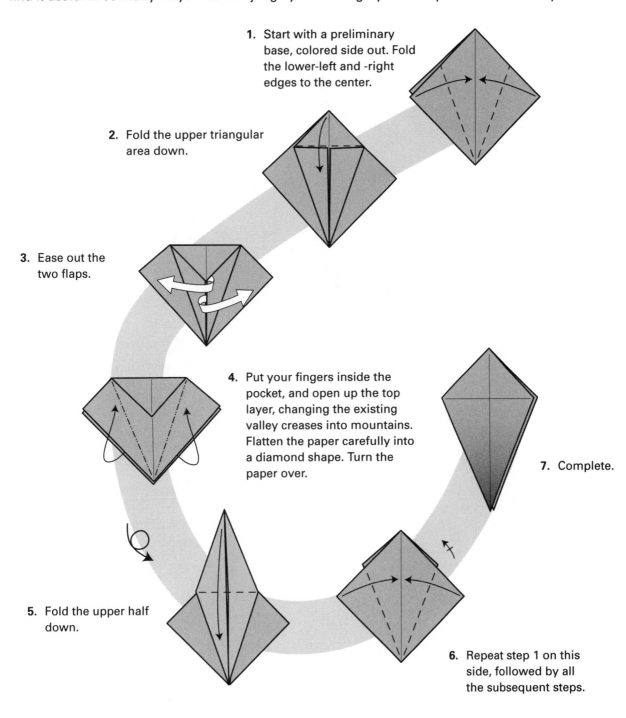

1. Start with a preliminary base, colored side out. Fold the lower-left and -right edges to the center.

2. Fold the upper triangular area down.

3. Ease out the two flaps.

4. Put your fingers inside the pocket, and open up the top layer, changing the existing valley creases into mountains. Flatten the paper carefully into a diamond shape. Turn the paper over.

5. Fold the upper half down.

6. Repeat step 1 on this side, followed by all the subsequent steps.

7. Complete.

Chapter 2
Birds

Birds are a very popular subject for origami creators because several of the traditional bases offer enough points and flaps to create a bird. For example, the bird base has four points, enough for a head, tail, and two wings. Folding a "nesting" bird means you don't need legs, so an even simpler folding solution is possible.

A bird is also a remarkably flexible shape, so you can adapt existing designs almost endlessly. Try altering the size and angle of the wings or the length of the tail and beak. Eventually you may make enough changes that the model becomes original—compare the traditional swan with the extraordinary version by Eric Joisel, for example.

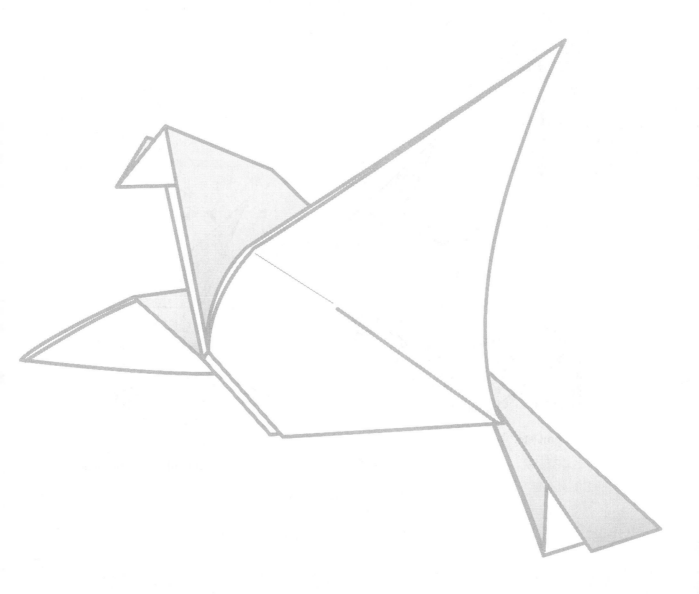

Pecking Bird   Difficulty level: 1

Traditional design

This model is useful for practicing making a reverse fold. Try altering the angle and distance in step 4 to see how it affects the final model. To make the bird peck, gently tap the tail where the double arrow is shown when you place the finished model on the table!

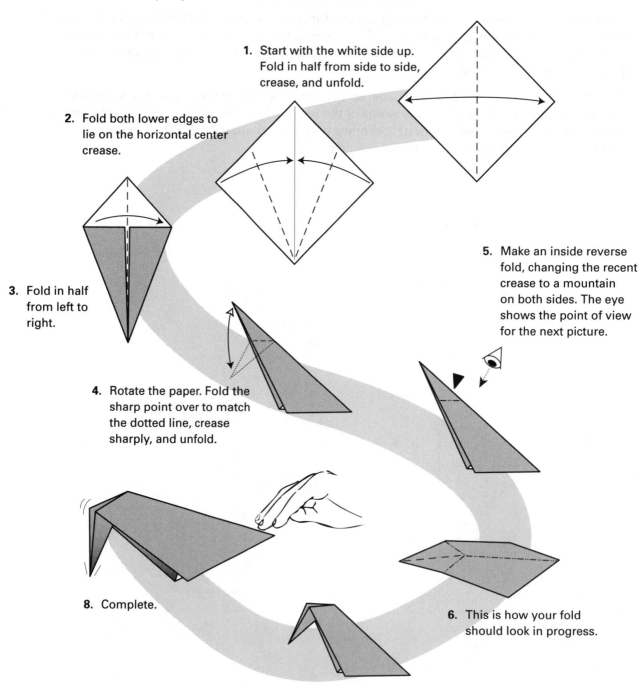

1. Start with the white side up. Fold in half from side to side, crease, and unfold.

2. Fold both lower edges to lie on the horizontal center crease.

3. Fold in half from left to right.

4. Rotate the paper. Fold the sharp point over to match the dotted line, crease sharply, and unfold.

5. Make an inside reverse fold, changing the recent crease to a mountain on both sides. The eye shows the point of view for the next picture.

6. This is how your fold should look in progress.

7. The reverse fold is complete.

8. Complete.

Swan Difficulty level: 1

Traditional design

This is a great model for teaching because the folding sequence is very straightforward. The only judgment fold is the length of the beak.

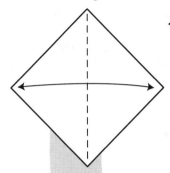

1. Start with the white side up, with a corner toward you. Crease in half from side to side, and unfold.

2. Fold both lower edges to meet the vertical center crease.

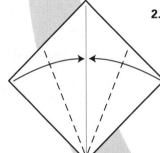

3. This is how your model should look. Turn the paper over.

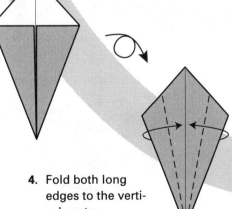

4. Fold both long edges to the vertical center.

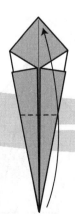

5. Fold the sharp corner to meet the opposite corner. It may help to put a finger inside this fold to help flatten the paper.

continues

continued

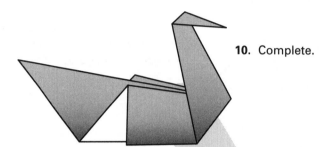

10. Complete.

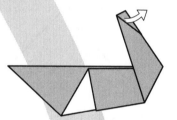

9. Lift up the beak, and once again, squash at the back to hold in position.

8. Hold the paper where circled, and ease the neck away from the body. When it's in the right position (sloping slightly back), squeeze the paper at the base of the neck to hold it in position.

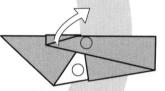

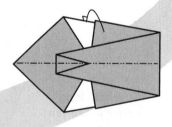

7. Rotate the paper. Fold the upper half of the paper behind using a mountain fold.

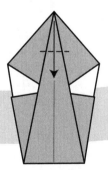

6. Fold down a small part of the narrow flap to form the beak.

Peacock   Difficulty level: 2

Traditional design

This design uses two sheets of square paper to create the look of many tail feathers. This could be achieved with a single square, but it would be much more complicated to fold.

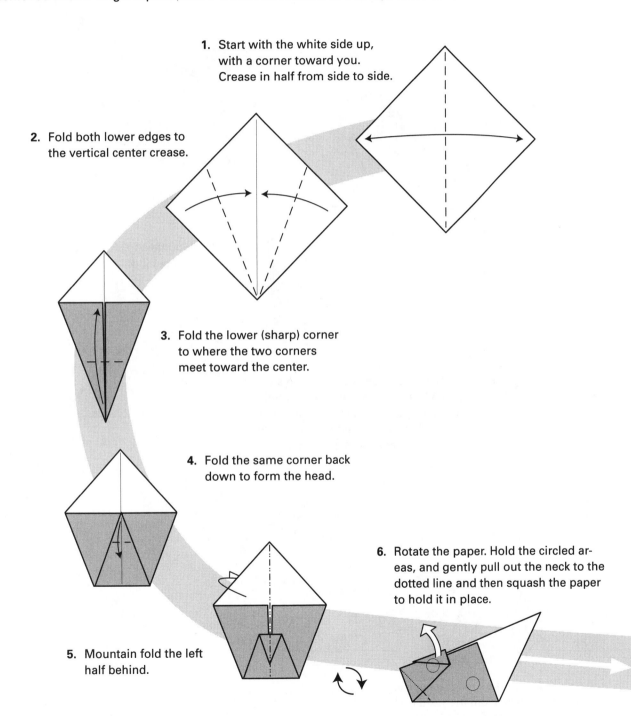

1. Start with the white side up, with a corner toward you. Crease in half from side to side.

2. Fold both lower edges to the vertical center crease.

3. Fold the lower (sharp) corner to where the two corners meet toward the center.

4. Fold the same corner back down to form the head.

5. Mountain fold the left half behind.

6. Rotate the paper. Hold the circled areas, and gently pull out the neck to the dotted line and then squash the paper to hold it in place.

continues

continued

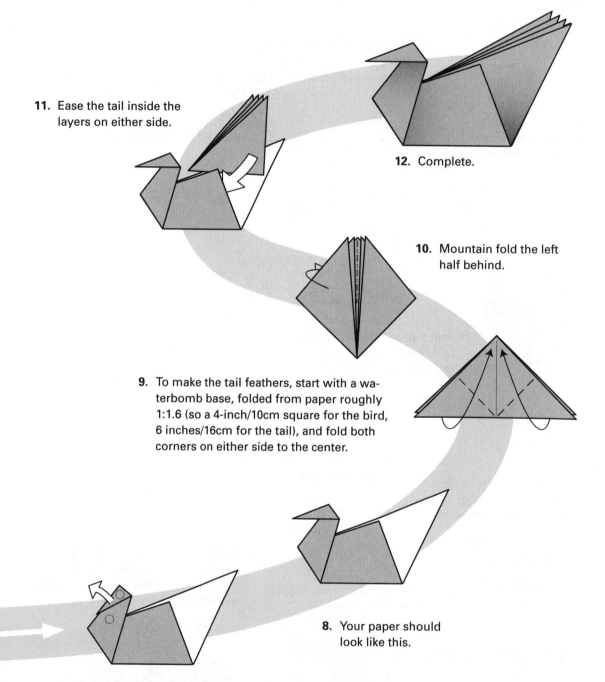

11. Ease the tail inside the layers on either side.

12. Complete.

10. Mountain fold the left half behind.

9. To make the tail feathers, start with a waterbomb base, folded from paper roughly 1:1.6 (so a 4-inch/10cm square for the bird, 6 inches/16cm for the tail), and fold both corners on either side to the center.

8. Your paper should look like this.

7. Make a similar maneuver, easing out the head and flattening it into place.

Hungry Chick Difficulty level: 2

by Javier Caboblanco

Javier is a designer who discovers simple and unusual ways to create his models. This beautiful 3D bird not only looks wonderful, but if you put two fingers inside the body, you can make it peck in a very realistic way!

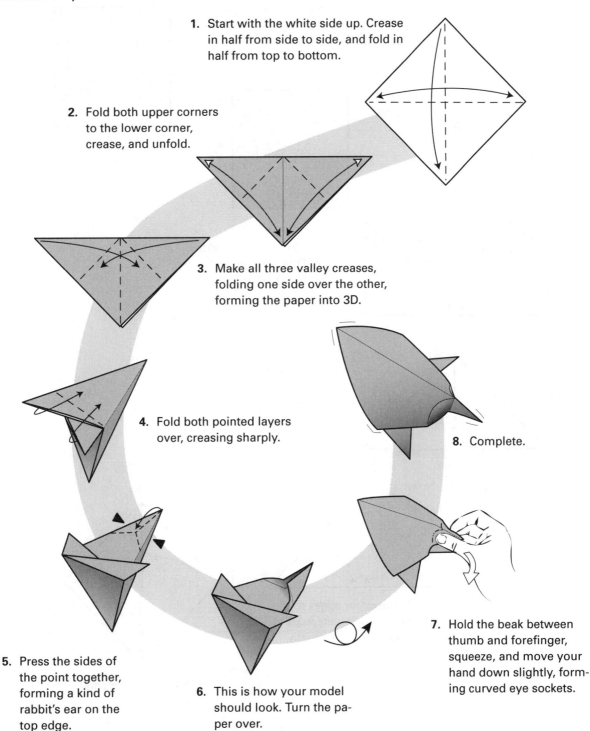

1. Start with the white side up. Crease in half from side to side, and fold in half from top to bottom.

2. Fold both upper corners to the lower corner, crease, and unfold.

3. Make all three valley creases, folding one side over the other, forming the paper into 3D.

4. Fold both pointed layers over, creasing sharply.

5. Press the sides of the point together, forming a kind of rabbit's ear on the top edge.

6. This is how your model should look. Turn the paper over.

7. Hold the beak between thumb and forefinger, squeeze, and move your hand down slightly, forming curved eye sockets.

8. Complete.

Perched Owl Difficulty level: 2

by Robert Neale

Owls are a favorite subject for origami designers due to their simple profile. This allows for many different outcomes for the same the subject. This owl starts from a 2×1 rectangle.

1. Start with a square.
Crease in half both ways.

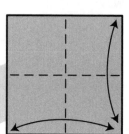

2. Cut in half to make a pair of 2×1 rectangles (so you can fold the owl twice).

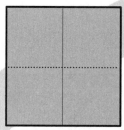

3. Turn to the colored side. Fold the sides down to the lower edge.

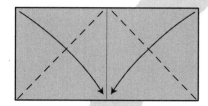

4. This is how your model should look. Turn the paper over.

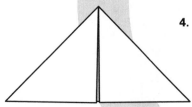

5. Fold the upper edges to the center, allowing the flaps to flip out from underneath.

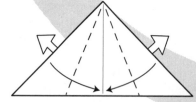

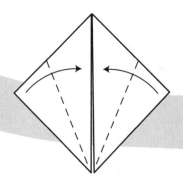

6. Fold the lower edges to the center.

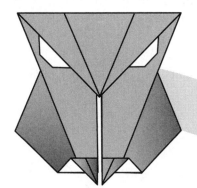

12. Complete.

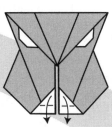

11. Leave a gap, and fold the points back down.

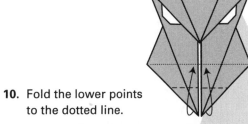

10. Fold the lower points to the dotted line.

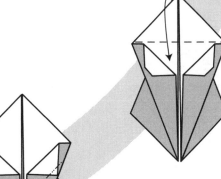

9. Fold the upper triangle down.

8. Fold the tips of the white corners behind.

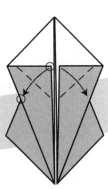

7. Fold both inner corners out to touch the inside angle change.

Songbird   Difficulty level: 3

by Kunihiko Kasahara

Kasahara is a designer who adds his own personality to his designs, and he is rightly regarded as a hugely influential and gifted origami master. He has been creating since the mid-1960s and still produces elegant and charming new work. This bird is unusual in that the fold that opens the wings creates a sense of 3D, which is often lacking in simple origami.

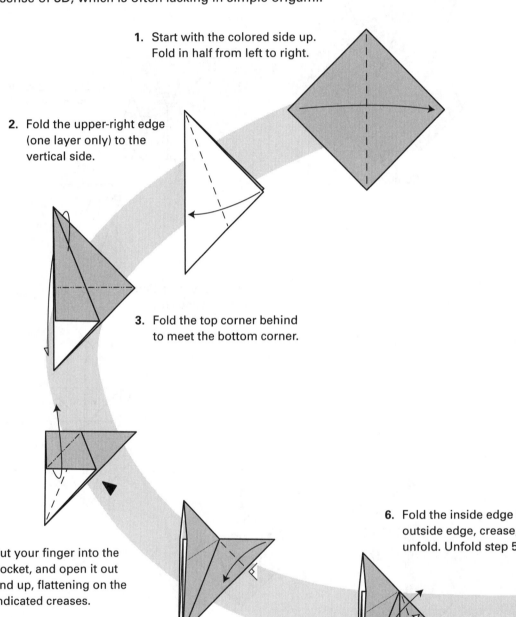

1. Start with the colored side up. Fold in half from left to right.

2. Fold the upper-right edge (one layer only) to the vertical side.

3. Fold the top corner behind to meet the bottom corner.

4. Put your finger into the pocket, and open it out and up, flattening on the indicated creases.

5. Fold the corner down at right angles to the lower-right edge.

6. Fold the inside edge to the outside edge, crease, and unfold. Unfold step 5 as well.

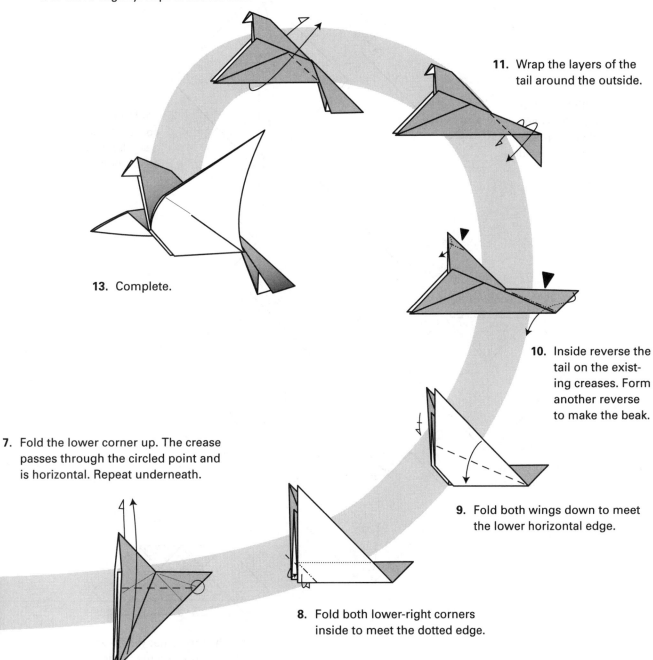

12. Partially open a wing using the crease shown. Don't worry if it won't lie flat, but do encourage it to curve slightly. Repeat underneath.

11. Wrap the layers of the tail around the outside.

13. Complete.

10. Inside reverse the tail on the existing creases. Form another reverse to make the beak.

7. Fold the lower corner up. The crease passes through the circled point and is horizontal. Repeat underneath.

9. Fold both wings down to meet the lower horizontal edge.

8. Fold both lower-right corners inside to meet the dotted edge.

Great-Horned Owl   Difficulty level: 3

by Giovanni Maltagliati

Here's another owl so you can see how two different origami designers interpret the same subject.

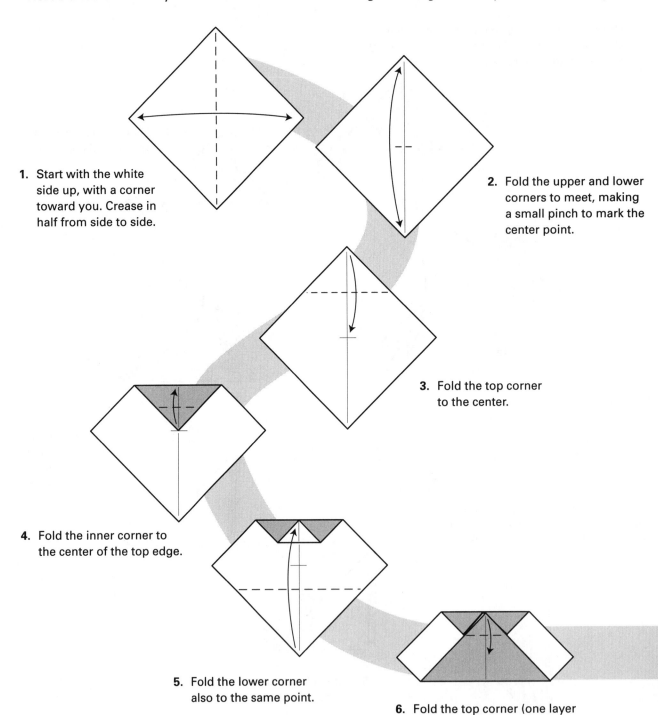

1. Start with the white side up, with a corner toward you. Crease in half from side to side.

2. Fold the upper and lower corners to meet, making a small pinch to mark the center point.

3. Fold the top corner to the center.

4. Fold the inner corner to the center of the top edge.

5. Fold the lower corner also to the same point.

6. Fold the top corner (one layer only) down along the hidden horizontal edge.

13. Fold the upper edge to each of the most recent creases. Don't extend the creases past the center.

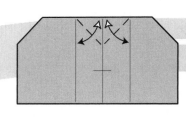

12. Make mountain creases that pass through the outer corners of the beak area. Turn the paper over.

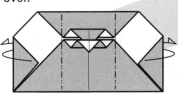

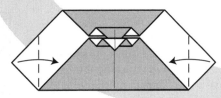

11. Fold the white corners in on either side.

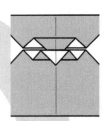

10. This is how your model should look.

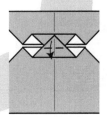

9. Fold the colored triangle down to a point just below the lower edge.

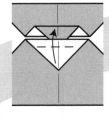

8. Fold the white corner to the top of the colored triangle.

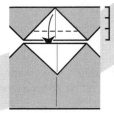

7. Fold the top corner down on a crease just below the one-third point. Tuck this corner under the lower flap.

continues

continued

14. Add creases that match the inner creases on the outsides of the outer vertical creases.

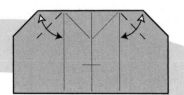

15. Fold the left side in using an existing crease.

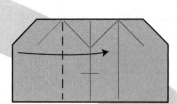

16. Fold the right side in as well, tucking it into a pocket on the left side.

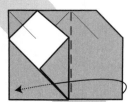

17. Gently squash the paper open into a cylinder.

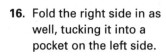

18. Using two existing creases, gently press in the center.

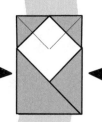

20. Complete.

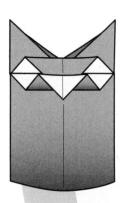

19. Turn the paper over, and repeat step 18 on this side.

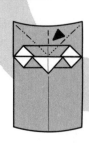

Mother and Baby Penguin   Difficulty level: 3

by Nick Robinson

Here's an example of how two creatures can be created from a single sheet of paper. Steps 8 through 11 show a different way to create outside reverse folds—see if you can use this technique elsewhere.

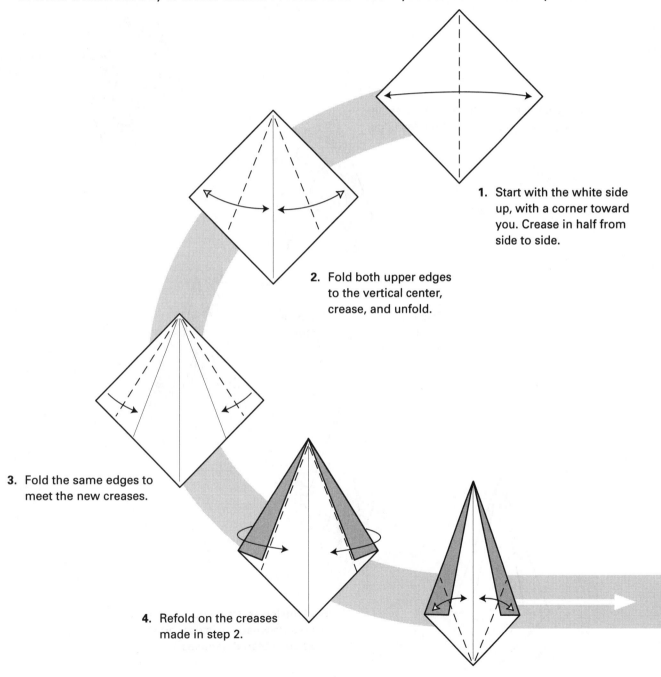

1. Start with the white side up, with a corner toward you. Crease in half from side to side.

2. Fold both upper edges to the vertical center, crease, and unfold.

3. Fold the same edges to meet the new creases.

4. Refold on the creases made in step 2.

5. Fold the lower edges to the center, crease, and unfold.

continues

continued

10. Mountain fold the right half behind.

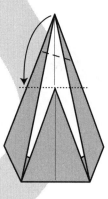

9. Fold the inner colored flap the same way, to meet an almost hidden edge.

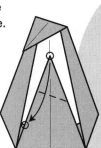

8. Fold the upper corner to lie on the upper-left edge, meeting the dotted line.

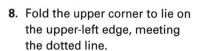

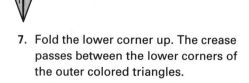

7. Fold the lower corner up. The crease passes between the lower corners of the outer colored triangles.

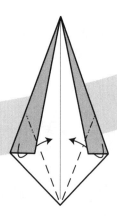

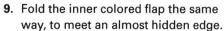

6. Refold step 5, but inside reverse the paper though the colored layers.

11. Pull the paper forward, and
flatten to form two beaks.

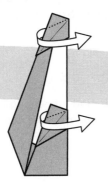

12. Ease out the paper to enlarge the
upper beak, and make a double reverse fold to form the lower beak.

13. Form the upper beak in the same way. Push
in a small triangle at the lower-right corner.

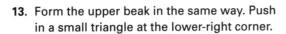

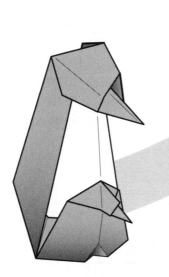

14. Gently press the sides to
form the paper into 3D.

15. Complete.

Fat Bird   Difficulty level: 3

by Gareth Louis

This is an alternative to the traditional flapping bird, which uses a completely different folding method. You make a number of inside reverse folds here, so please be sure you've read the techniques section on reversing. Make the creases in steps 10 through 12 firm and crisp so step 13 is as easy as possible.

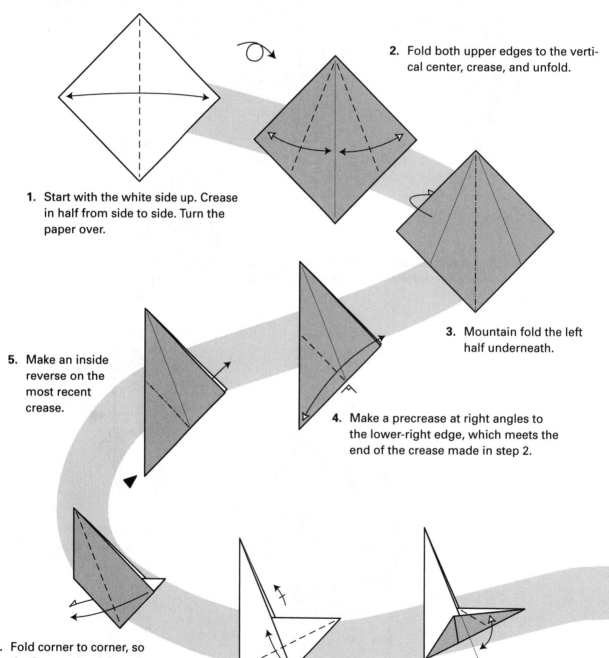

1. Start with the white side up. Crease in half from side to side. Turn the paper over.

2. Fold both upper edges to the vertical center, crease, and unfold.

3. Mountain fold the left half underneath.

4. Make a precrease at right angles to the lower-right edge, which meets the end of the crease made in step 2.

5. Make an inside reverse on the most recent crease.

6. Fold corner to corner, so the flap on the right swings to the left, using the crease made in step 2. Repeat the step underneath.

7. Fold two flaps up, corner to corner.

8. Fold the horizontal edge down to line up with the dotted line. Crease and unfold.

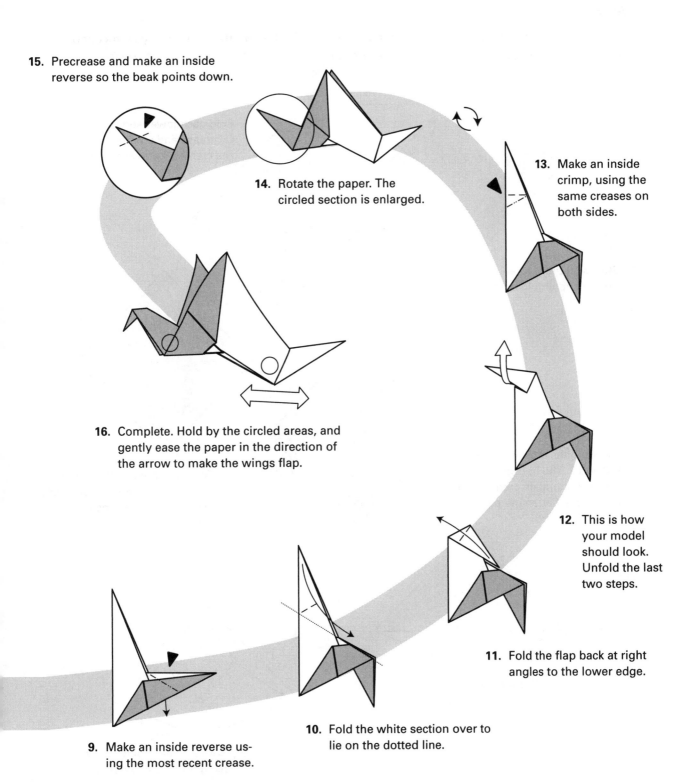

15. Precrease and make an inside reverse so the beak points down.

14. Rotate the paper. The circled section is enlarged.

13. Make an inside crimp, using the same creases on both sides.

16. Complete. Hold by the circled areas, and gently ease the paper in the direction of the arrow to make the wings flap.

12. This is how your model should look. Unfold the last two steps.

11. Fold the flap back at right angles to the lower edge.

10. Fold the white section over to lie on the dotted line.

9. Make an inside reverse using the most recent crease.

Bowing Bird   Difficulty level: 4

by Jeff Beynon

This design combines half a frog base with half a bird base. It also offers you many chances to practice your reverse folds. Remember, the key to this technique is sharp, accurate precreasing.

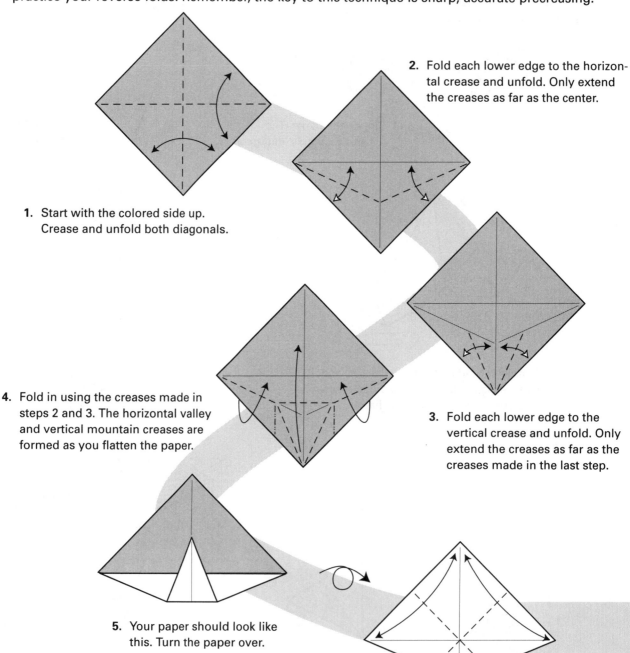

1. Start with the colored side up. Crease and unfold both diagonals.

2. Fold each lower edge to the horizontal crease and unfold. Only extend the creases as far as the center.

3. Fold each lower edge to the vertical crease and unfold. Only extend the creases as far as the creases made in the last step.

4. Fold in using the creases made in steps 2 and 3. The horizontal valley and vertical mountain creases are formed as you flatten the paper.

5. Your paper should look like this. Turn the paper over.

6. Fold the top corner to each of the outer corners, creasing firmly and unfolding.

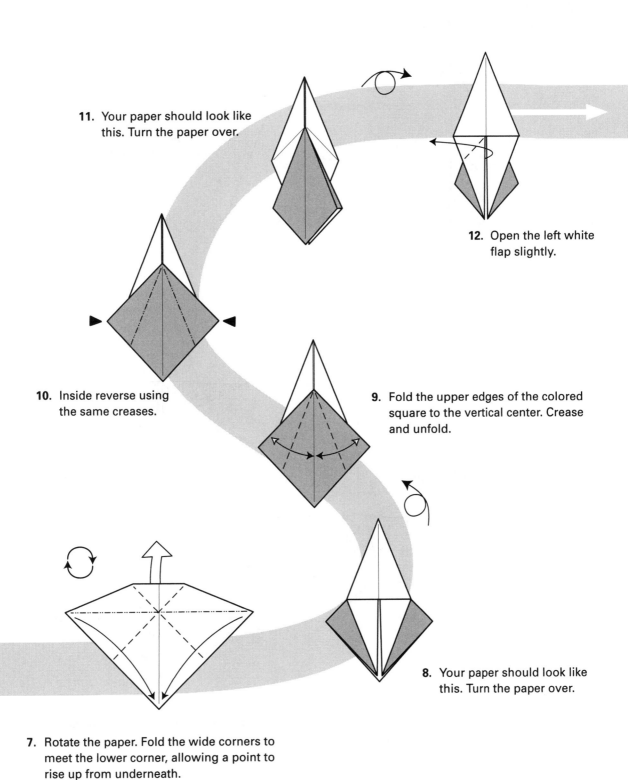

11. Your paper should look like this. Turn the paper over.

12. Open the left white flap slightly.

10. Inside reverse using the same creases.

9. Fold the upper edges of the colored square to the vertical center. Crease and unfold.

8. Your paper should look like this. Turn the paper over.

7. Rotate the paper. Fold the wide corners to meet the lower corner, allowing a point to rise up from underneath.

continues

continued

13. Fold the thin white flap in half,
forming a squash at the base.

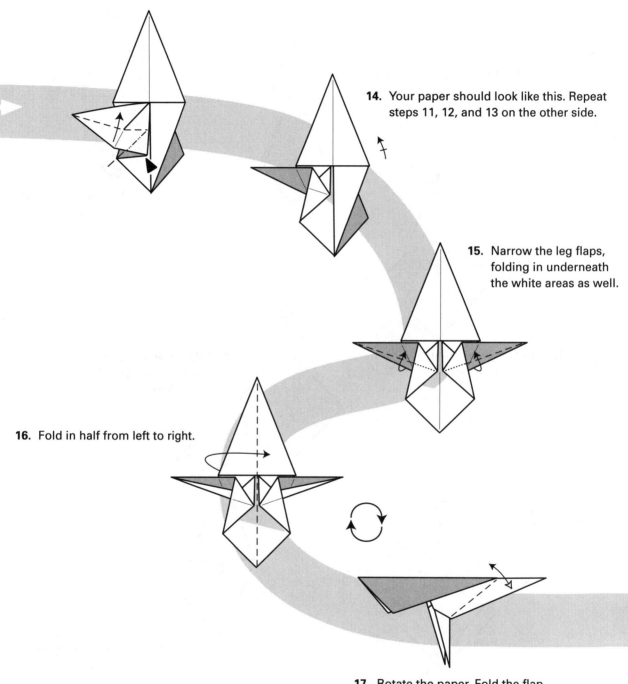

14. Your paper should look like this. Repeat
steps 11, 12, and 13 on the other side.

15. Narrow the leg flaps,
folding in underneath
the white areas as well.

16. Fold in half from left to right.

17. Rotate the paper. Fold the flap
over, crease firmly, and unfold.

22. Complete.

21. Tuck in at the tail, and form a beak with a double reverse fold.

20. Turn the precreases into reverse folds on the head, tail, and both feet.

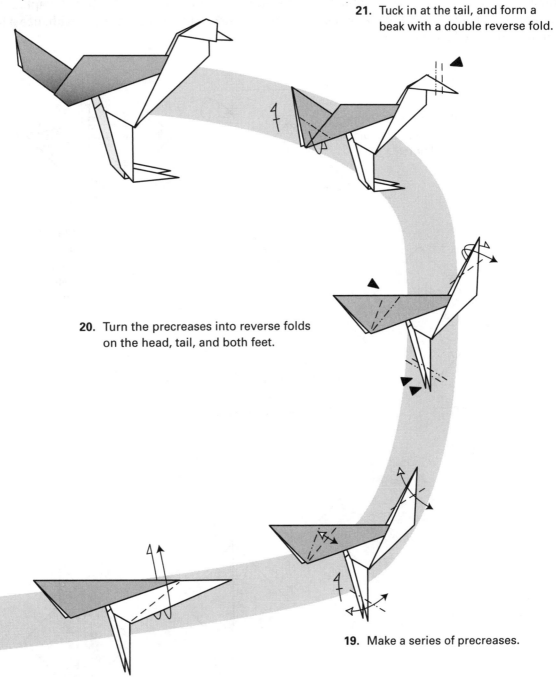

19. Make a series of precreases.

18. Outside reverse fold the neck.

Fancy Swan   Difficulty level: 5

by Eric Joisel

This is probably the most challenging model in the whole book. Finishing the model is your first goal; then you can focus on making it graceful and beautiful. The diagrams here (adapted from the creator's originals) show the method but not the artwork of the piece. To begin with, use a large square, at least 12 inches across.

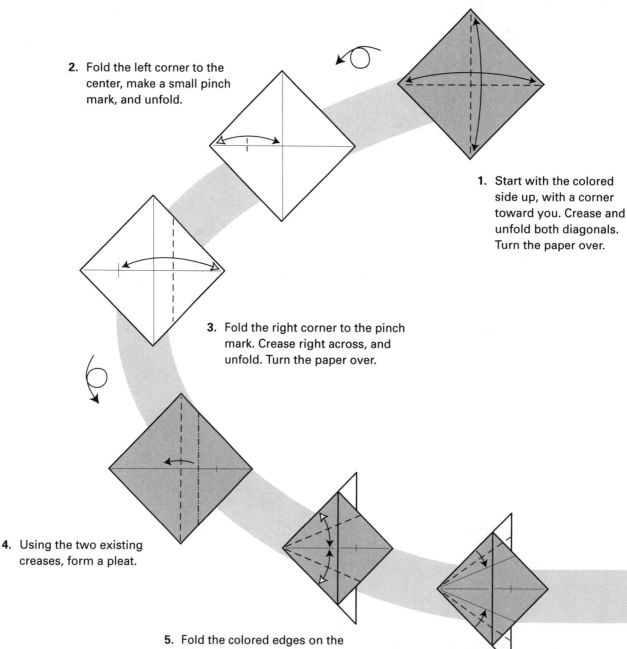

2. Fold the left corner to the center, make a small pinch mark, and unfold.

1. Start with the colored side up, with a corner toward you. Crease and unfold both diagonals. Turn the paper over.

3. Fold the right corner to the pinch mark. Crease right across, and unfold. Turn the paper over.

4. Using the two existing creases, form a pleat.

5. Fold the colored edges on the left to lay on the horizontal center, crease, and unfold.

6. Fold the same edges to meet the most recent creases.

12. Reverse the neck up as far as it will go.

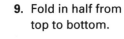

11. Fold the sides of the neck in half, tucking a small flap underneath at the top, so the paper lies flat. Repeat behind.

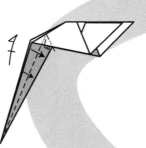

10. Precrease and inside reverse the long narrow flap.

9. Fold in half from top to bottom.

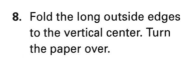

8. Fold the long outside edges to the vertical center. Turn the paper over.

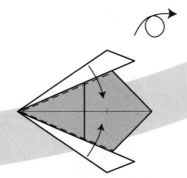

7. Fold in again using existing creases. Turn the paper over.

continues

continued

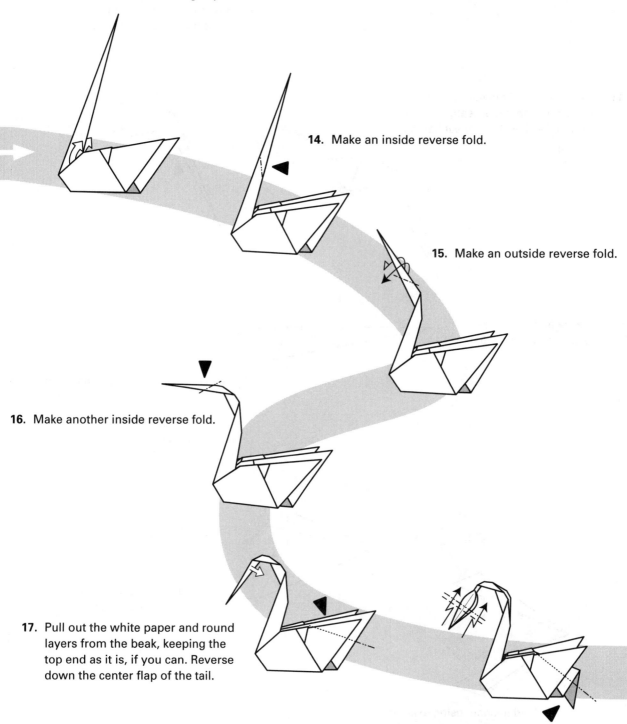

13. Separate the layers at the base of the neck to release the wing flaps.

14. Make an inside reverse fold.

15. Make an outside reverse fold.

16. Make another inside reverse fold.

17. Pull out the white paper and round layers from the beak, keeping the top end as it is, if you can. Reverse down the center flap of the tail.

18. Form the beak with a double reverse fold. Reverse the tail back up slightly.

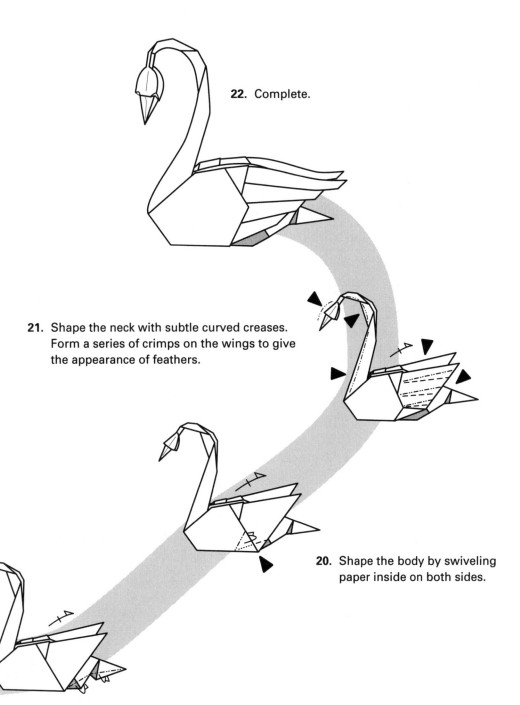

22. Complete.

21. Shape the neck with subtle curved creases. Form a series of crimps on the wings to give the appearance of feathers.

20. Shape the body by swiveling paper inside on both sides.

19. Wrap the inside edges to shape the tail.

Chapter 3
Animals

Animals present a wide variety of challenges to the origami creator. Some animals, such as dogs, mice, and elephants, are easy to fold and you'll find many different variations on these models. Others, such as cats and koalas, are more difficult and so you'll find only a few to choose from.

Another design problem is creating enough points in the paper to represent the animal. A cow, for example, needs four legs, two horns, a head, and a tail, so you have to produce eight individual points. A snake, by contrast, only needs two points. A general rule of thumb is that the more points you need, the more complicated the folding sequence is likely to be.

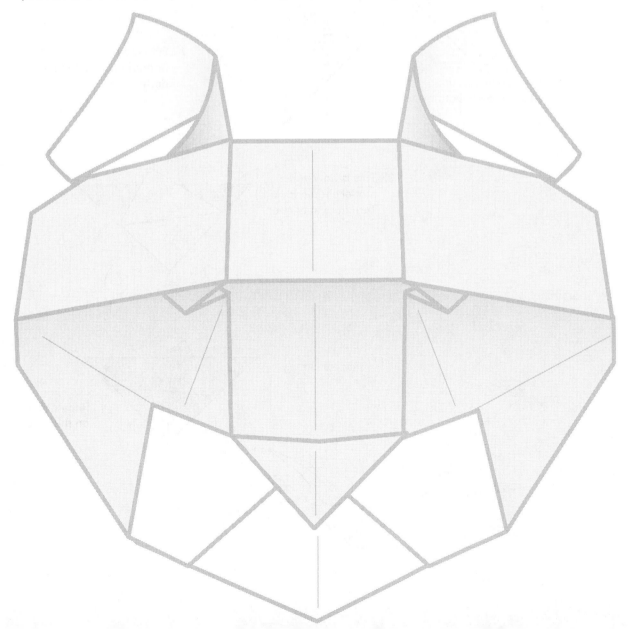

Cricket   Difficulty level: 1

Traditional design

Origami doesn't get much simpler than this ancient Japanese design. It's a great example of how you need to see simple origami more as a cartoon than a photograph. Most children are perfectly happy to see this as a cricket, but some less-imaginative adults may have difficulty! You can make the cricket hop by tapping down on one side.

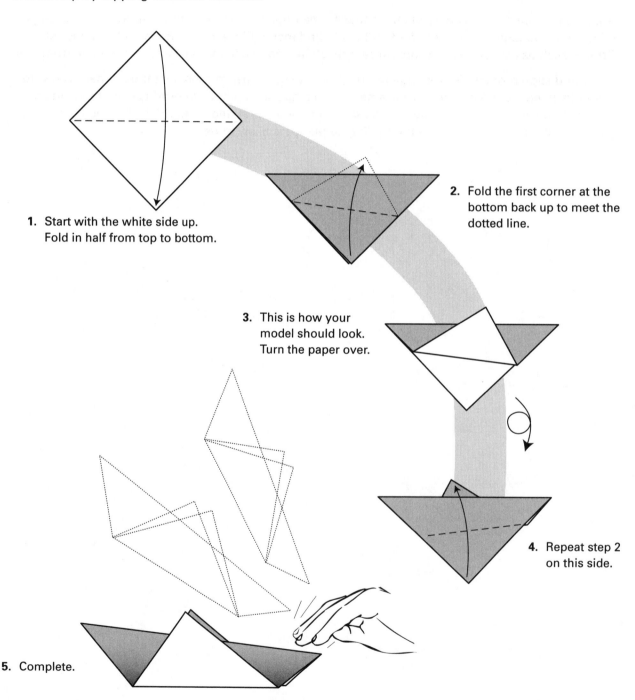

1. Start with the white side up. Fold in half from top to bottom.

2. Fold the first corner at the bottom back up to meet the dotted line.

3. This is how your model should look. Turn the paper over.

4. Repeat step 2 on this side.

5. Complete.

Pig Difficulty level: 1

by Nick Robinson

You can make a pig using a single sheet, but with three sheets, it's much easier—and it's fun to then assemble the pieces!

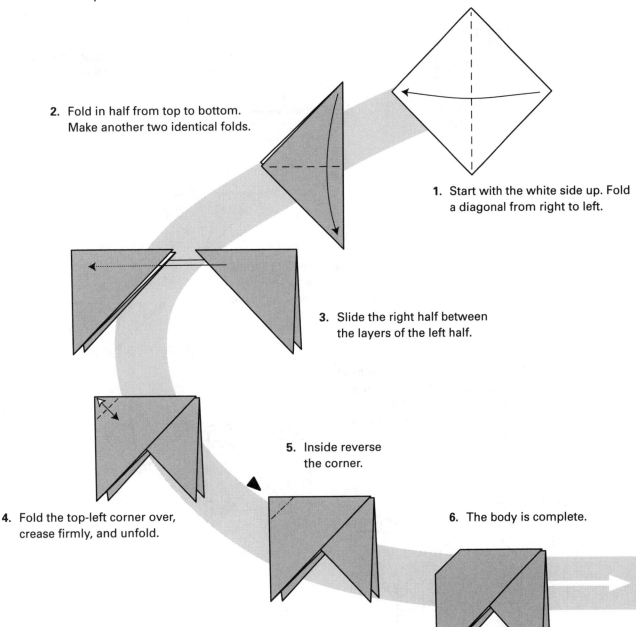

1. Start with the white side up. Fold a diagonal from right to left.

2. Fold in half from top to bottom. Make another two identical folds.

3. Slide the right half between the layers of the left half.

4. Fold the top-left corner over, crease firmly, and unfold.

5. Inside reverse the corner.

6. The body is complete.

continues

continued

7. Start with a new sheet, folded to step 2. Fold the lower corner to the top right, repeating behind.

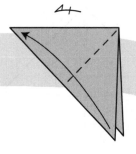

8. Fold the top-left corner over to the dotted line to form an ear. Repeat underneath.

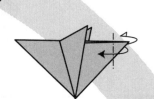

9. Wrap the end of the right corner around the outside to form the nose. The head is now complete.

10. Slide the inner layer of the head between the layers of the body. At the same time, slide/wrap the outer layer of the head around the top of the body.

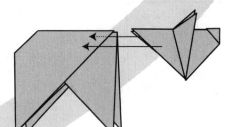

11. Complete.

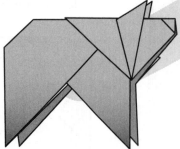

Cat's Head   Difficulty level: 2

by Evi Binzinger

Like the Cricket earlier in this chapter, this simple, stylized design shows that origami doesn't have to be like a photograph. We can also look for the basic features and exaggerate them slightly. The distance in step 3 isn't critical. Try altering it, and see what happens.

1. Start with the white side up. Fold corner to opposite corner, both ways.

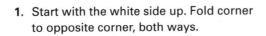

2. Fold the left and right corners to the center.

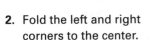

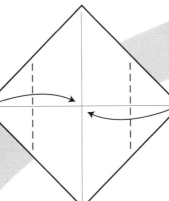

3. Fold the top corner down to somewhere near the small cross on the vertical center crease.

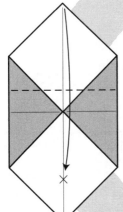

4. Fold the lower corner up to the dotted line.

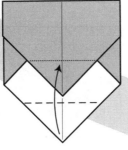

5. Fold the same corner down where the colored edges meet.

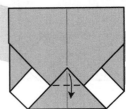

continues

10. Complete. Reinforce the vertical crease, and leave at a slight angle so the model will stand.

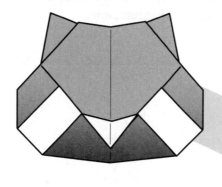

9. Fold the small triangular flap over at the top. Turn the paper over.

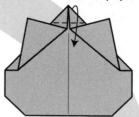

8. Fold the two corners back out to match the dotted lines.

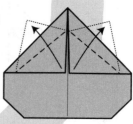

7. Fold each half of the upper edge to meet the vertical center crease.

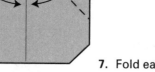

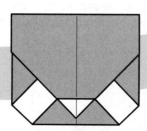

6. This is how your model should look. Turn the paper over.

Frog's Head Difficulty level: 2

by Edwin Corrie

As you've seen, origami designs don't have to represent a whole creature. They can, instead, just focus on the head. This model produces a frog's head—with a mouth you can make talk!

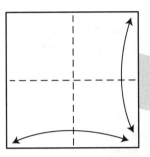

1. Start with the white side up. Crease and unfold in half both ways.

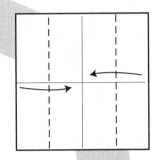

2. Fold the left and right edges to the center.

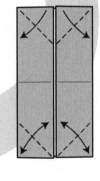

3. Fold back two single layers at the top. At the bottom, pre-crease through all the layers.

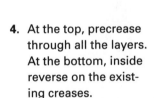
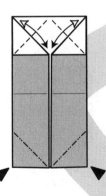

4. At the top, precrease through all the layers. At the bottom, inside reverse on the existing creases.

5. Fold the top edge to the center, crease, and unfold.

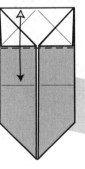

6. Make two more precreases at the bottom.

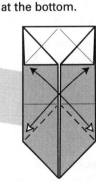

continues

continued

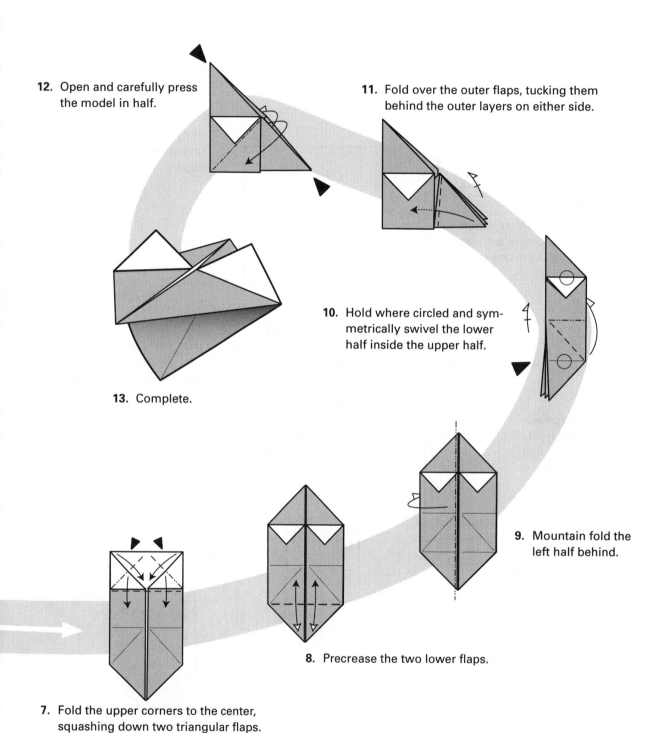

12. Open and carefully press the model in half.

11. Fold over the outer flaps, tucking them behind the outer layers on either side.

10. Hold where circled and symmetrically swivel the lower half inside the upper half.

13. Complete.

9. Mountain fold the left half behind.

8. Precrease the two lower flaps.

7. Fold the upper corners to the center, squashing down two triangular flaps.

Whale's Tail   Difficulty level: 2

by Mick Guy

This model is a brilliant example of how a creative mind can capture an unusual aspect of a chosen subject. A very familiar folding technique results in something completely new!

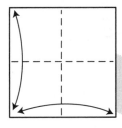

1. Start with the white side up. Crease in half from side to side, both ways.

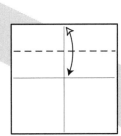

2. Fold the top edge to the center, crease, and unfold.

3. Fold left and right sides to the center, crease up as far as the top quarter crease, and unfold.

4. Refold the top edge to the center. Turn the paper over.

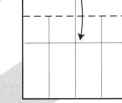

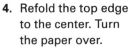

5. Fold the upper corners to the horizontal crease. Turn back over.

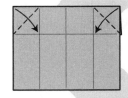

7. Fold the top section behind.

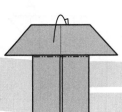

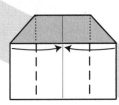

6. Fold the left and right edges to the vertical center, leaving the colored paper where it is.

continues

continued

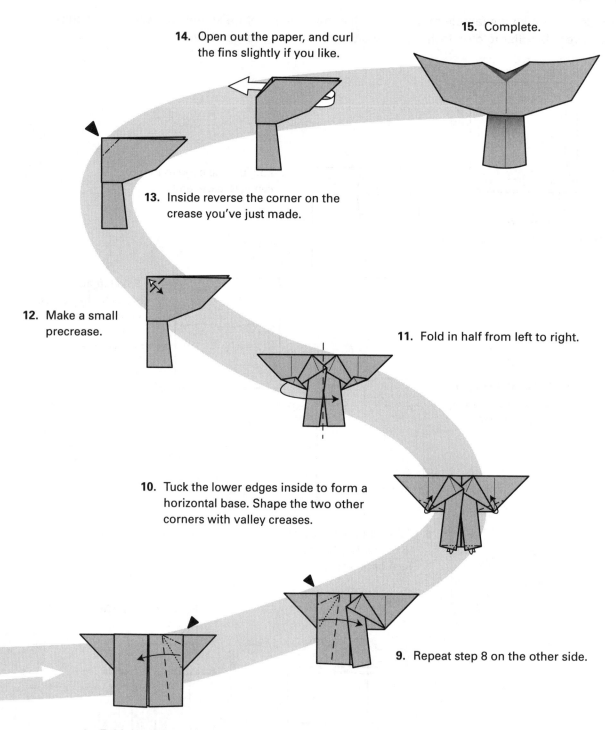

14. Open out the paper, and curl the fins slightly if you like.

15. Complete.

13. Inside reverse the corner on the crease you've just made.

12. Make a small precrease.

11. Fold in half from left to right.

10. Tuck the lower edges inside to form a horizontal base. Shape the two other corners with valley creases.

9. Repeat step 8 on the other side.

8. Fold the right edge in at a slight angle, squashing the paper at the top.

Fantail Goldfish Difficulty level: 3

Traditional design

This model shows that you can create quite a complex shape with a few simple folds. If you open the fins of the final model, you can make a bird with a moving beak!

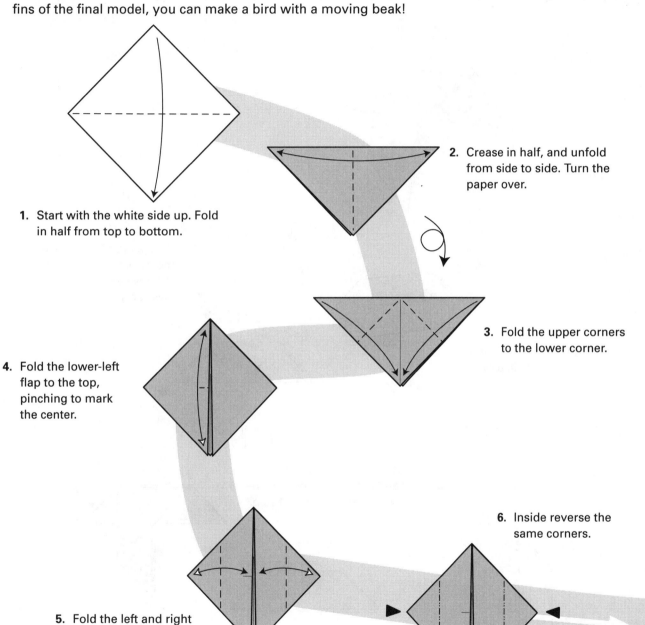

1. Start with the white side up. Fold in half from top to bottom.

2. Crease in half, and unfold from side to side. Turn the paper over.

3. Fold the upper corners to the lower corner.

4. Fold the lower-left flap to the top, pinching to mark the center.

5. Fold the left and right corners to the center, crease, and unfold.

6. Inside reverse the same corners.

continues

continued

12. Complete.

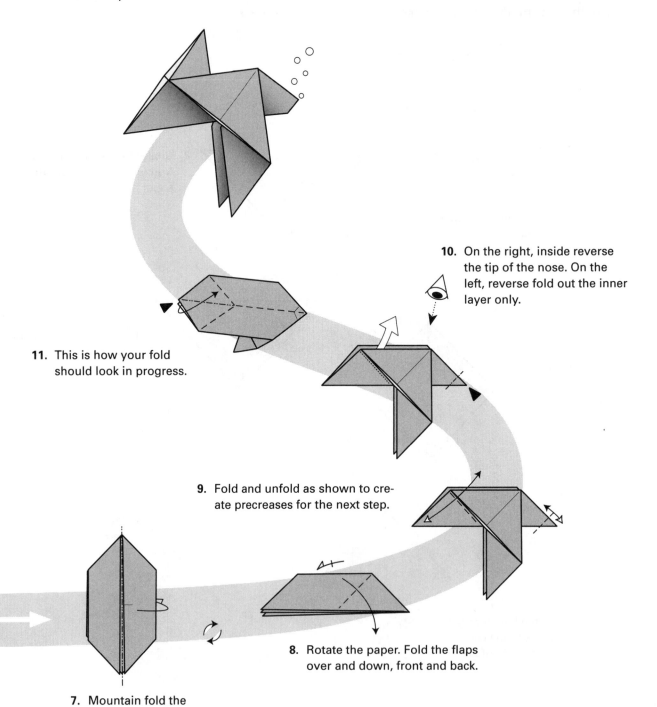

10. On the right, inside reverse the tip of the nose. On the left, reverse fold out the inner layer only.

11. This is how your fold should look in progress.

9. Fold and unfold as shown to create precreases for the next step.

8. Rotate the paper. Fold the flaps over and down, front and back.

7. Mountain fold the right half behind.

Horse   Difficulty level: 3

Traditional design

This design, a variation of the Spanish *pajarita*, or "little bird," has been found in German educational books dating from the end of the nineteenth century.

2. Fold all the corners to the center of the square.

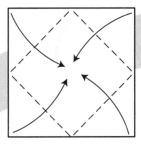

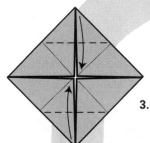

1. Start with the white side up. Crease and unfold both diagonals.

3. Fold the upper and lower corners to the center.

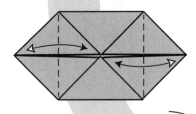

4. Fold the left and right corners to the center, crease, and unfold. Turn the paper over.

6. Form a rabbit's ear on the left, with the point facing down.

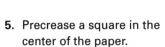

5. Precrease a square in the center of the paper.

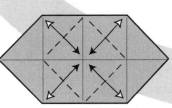

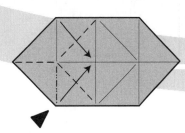

continues

continued

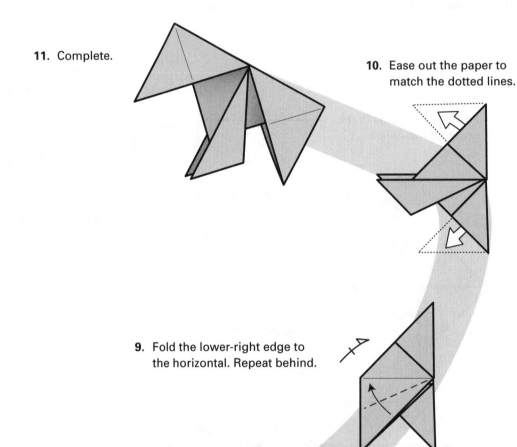

11. Complete.

10. Ease out the paper to match the dotted lines.

9. Fold the lower-right edge to the horizontal. Repeat behind.

8. Mountain fold the right half behind.

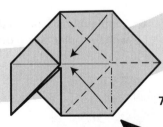

7. Repeat on the right.

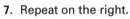

Mad March Hare Difficulty level: 3

by Nick Robinson

This is another stylized representation of the subject. Hold the sides of the head and flex in and out to waggle the ears and make the hare talk!

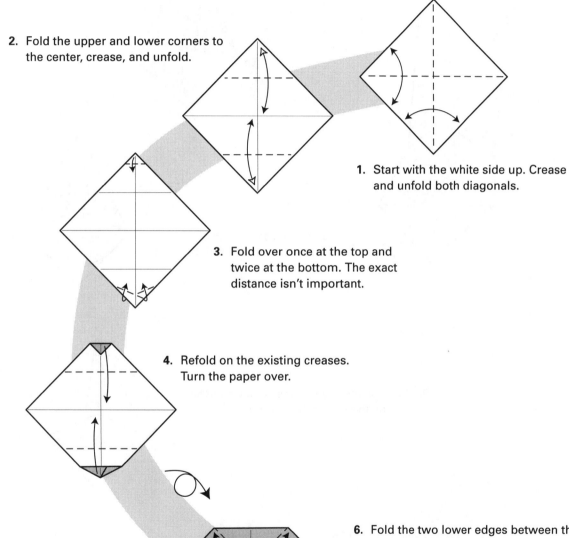

2. Fold the upper and lower corners to the center, crease, and unfold.

1. Start with the white side up. Crease and unfold both diagonals.

3. Fold over once at the top and twice at the bottom. The exact distance isn't important.

4. Refold on the existing creases. Turn the paper over.

5. Make two valley creases, corner to corner.

6. Fold the two lower edges between the outer corners and the lower center.

continues

continued

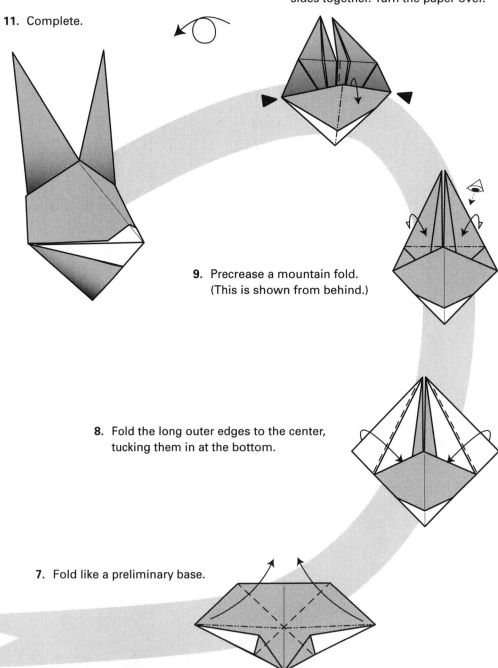

11. Complete.

10. Open out from the inside, pressing the
sides together. Turn the paper over.

9. Precrease a mountain fold.
(This is shown from behind.)

8. Fold the long outer edges to the center,
tucking them in at the bottom.

7. Fold like a preliminary base.

Dolphin   Difficulty level: 4

by Nick Robinson

Several techniques are used in this model, and you can adapt them to form your own original aquatic origami. Don't forget to rotate the tail fins to the horizontal. Otherwise, it would look like a shark!

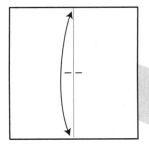

1. Start with a square, creased in half, white side up. Fold in half vertically, making a small pinch to mark the center.

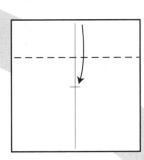

2. Fold the upper edge to the center pinch.

3. Fold the left and right sides to the vertical center.

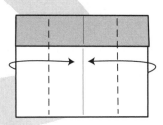

4. Fold the two upper corners out to the edges.

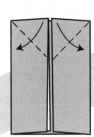

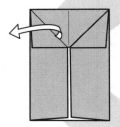

5. Ease out the left triangular point.

7. Repeat steps 5 and 6 on the top-right corner. Crease and unfold the lower corners to the vertical center crease.

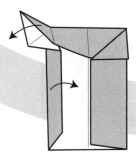

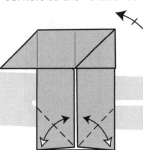

6. This is how the move should look in progress.

continues

continued

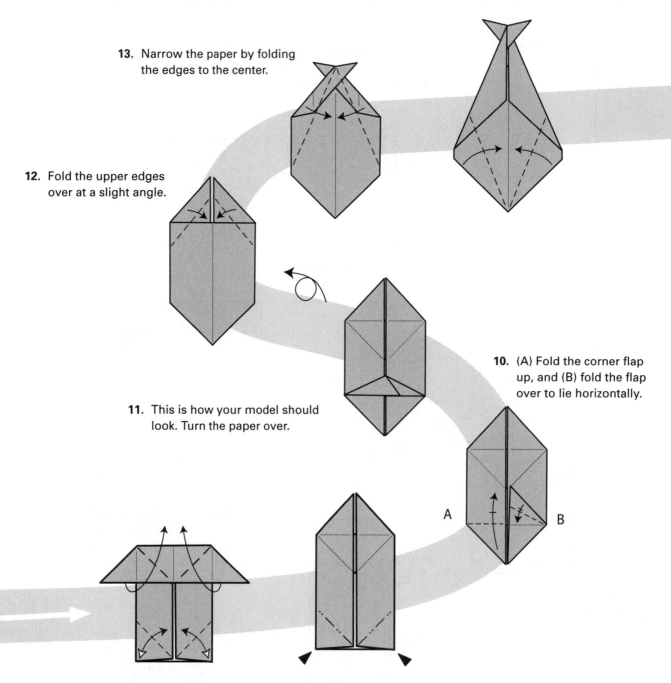

14. Narrow the bottom in the same way.

13. Narrow the paper by folding the edges to the center.

12. Fold the upper edges over at a slight angle.

10. (A) Fold the corner flap up, and (B) fold the flap over to lie horizontally.

11. This is how your model should look. Turn the paper over.

A   B

8. Fold the two flaps to point up.

9. Inside reverse the two lower corners.

15. Fold the model in half downward.

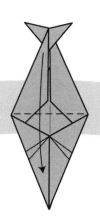

16. Leave a small gap, and fold the flap back up.

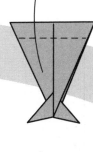

21. Complete.

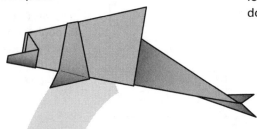

17. Make a pleat on the lower flap to form the dolphin's nose.

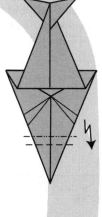

20. Twist the tail sideways, and open out the fins.

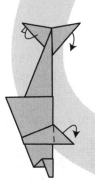

19. Fold in half, tucking the right flap behind the pleat to hold it in place.

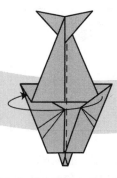

18. Fold over the tip of the nose. Ease out the paper on the right so it's above the pleat you made in step 17.

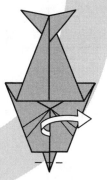

Frog on a Window   Difficulty level: 4

by Kunihiko Kasahara

Based on Neil Elias's "figure base," this quirky design by Japanese master Kasahara will test your folding skills. It helps if you make your initial creases as accurate as you can.

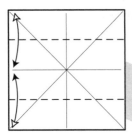

1. Start with an unfolded preliminary base, white side up. Fold the upper and lower edges to the center, crease, and unfold.

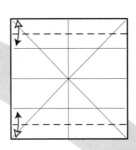

2. Add the outer one-eighth creases.

1-3

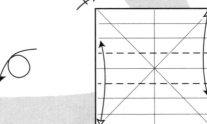

3. Add the inner three-eighth creases. Repeat steps 1 through 3 on the other axis. Turn the paper over.

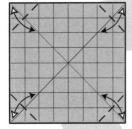

4. Fold each corner to the nearest one-quarter crease, and unfold. Turn the paper over.

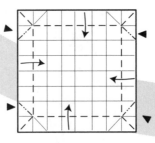

5. Use the creases shown to collapse the outer edges into an extended windmill base.

6. Form a central "box."

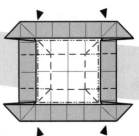

11. And the lower legs. The eye
shows the next point of view.

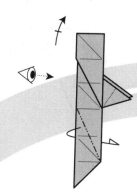

10. Wrap the upper legs
inside themselves.

9. Fold in half from left to
right, opening up two
pockets as you do so.

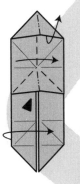

8. This is how your model should
look. Turn the paper over.

7. Fold all four legs in and down. The
sides should meet in the center.

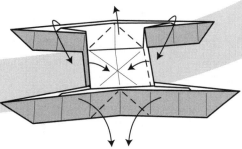

continues

continued

12. Open and squash the end of a leg.

13. Fold back the inner corner to reveal the white side. Repeat steps 12 and 13 on the other three legs.

12-13

14. Carefully squash open the center flaps, and form into a circle. Turn the paper over.

15. Complete.

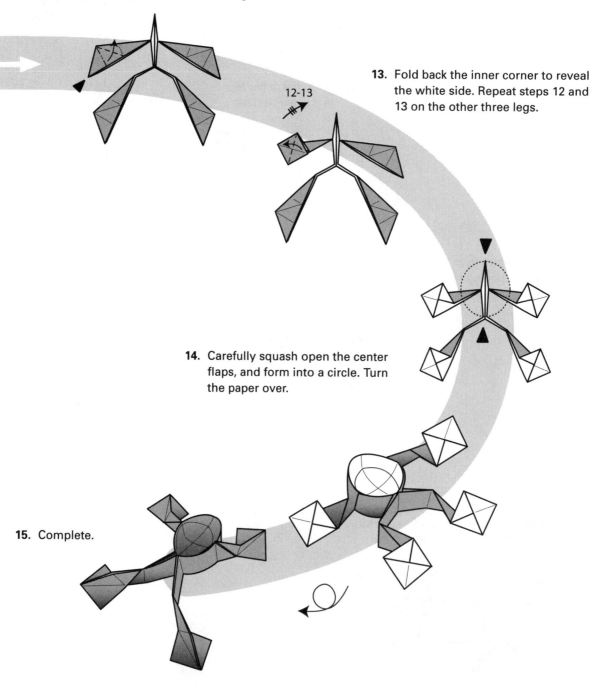

Howling at the Moon Difficulty level: 4

by Chris Alexander

In this model, some traditional techniques are combined to form a very unusual result. It might seem like this has a lot of steps, but this model could be classified as "intermediate" compared to some modern designs!

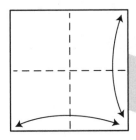

1. Start with the white side up. Crease and unfold in half both ways.

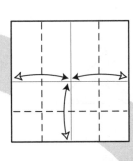

2. Crease the left, right, and lower edges to the center, and unfold. Turn the paper over.

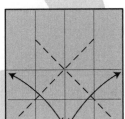

3. Crease the two diagonals, but leave the upper corners clear. Turn the paper over.

4. Fold the upper edge to the lower.

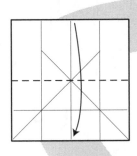

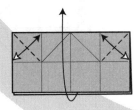

5. Crease the small diagonals on the upper layer only, and unfold.

6. Using the creases shown, collapse the paper.

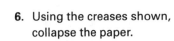
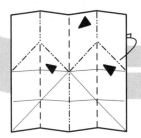

continues

continued

12. Squash open using the creases you've just made.

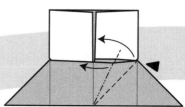

11. Fold the recent crease to the vertical, adding a new crease, and unfold.

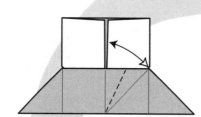

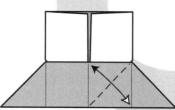

10. Precrease a small diagonal.

9. Rotate the paper. Fold down on the dotted line, opening the corners to form points.

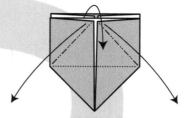

7. Precrease and inside reverse the lower-right edge.

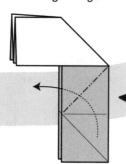

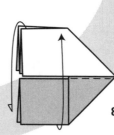

8. Swing the lower layer up. Repeat behind. This move is known as "flipping your flaps"!

13. Open and squash the triangular flap.

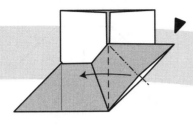

14. Fold the lower edges to the vertical, crease, and unfold.

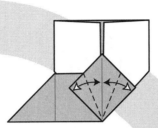

15. Inside reverse on the same creases.

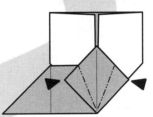

16. Fold the flap on the left over to the right.

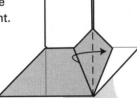

17. Fold the flap on the left down.

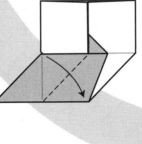

18. Fold the same flap underneath to point up.

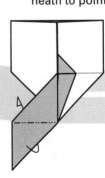

continues

continued

25. Narrow the sides of the moon.

26. Complete.

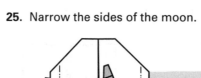

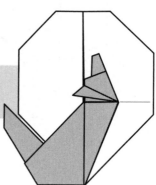

24. Fold three corners behind.

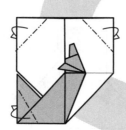

23. This is what your model should look like.

22. Making suitable precreases first, inside reverse the top corner, and make a pleat lower down.

20. Precrease and outside reverse the point to just above the horizontal.

21. Reverse the hidden point up.

19. This is how your model should look. Focus on the circled area.

Elephant   Difficulty level: 4

by Ann LaVin

Ann is a good friend who invented this elephant while at an origami convention in Japan. It's her first-ever creation, and she's very proud of it! You may need to make a few examples to get the proportions just right, but stick with it.

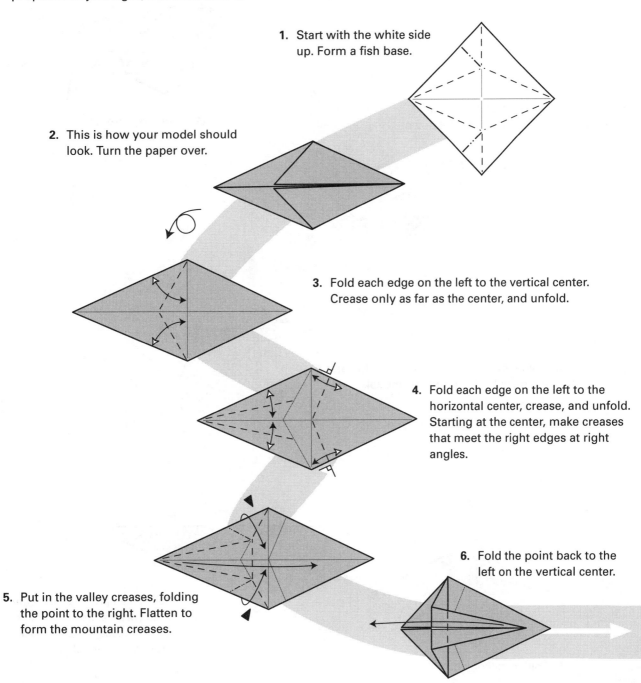

1. Start with the white side up. Form a fish base.

2. This is how your model should look. Turn the paper over.

3. Fold each edge on the left to the vertical center. Crease only as far as the center, and unfold.

4. Fold each edge on the left to the horizontal center, crease, and unfold. Starting at the center, make creases that meet the right edges at right angles.

5. Put in the valley creases, folding the point to the right. Flatten to form the mountain creases.

6. Fold the point back to the left on the vertical center.

continues

continued

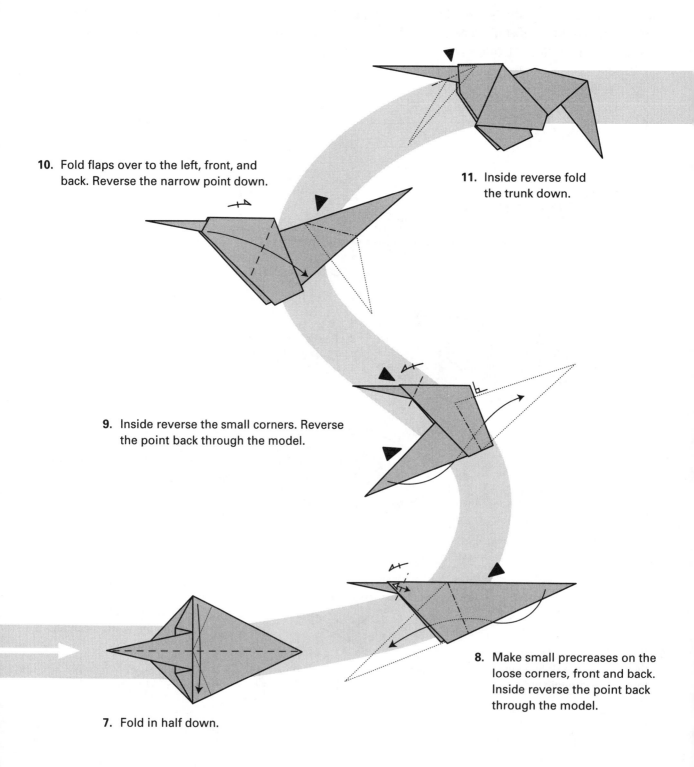

10. Fold flaps over to the left, front, and back. Reverse the narrow point down.

11. Inside reverse fold the trunk down.

9. Inside reverse the small corners. Reverse the point back through the model.

7. Fold in half down.

8. Make small precreases on the loose corners, front and back. Inside reverse the point back through the model.

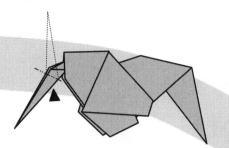

12. Inside reverse the trunk up.

13. Inside reverse the trunk forward. Reverse the rear point up.

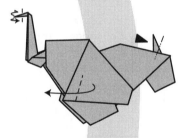

14. Outside reverse the trunk, and inside reverse the tail. Make a partial fold on the ear, curling it forward.

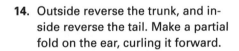

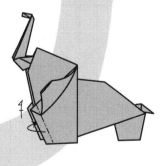

15. Fold in the front legs to hold the ear creases in place. Repeat on the other side.

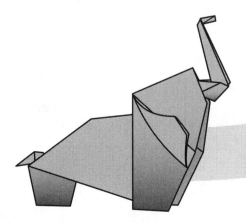

16. Complete. Well done if you got this far!

Puma's Head   Difficulty level: 5

by Róman Díaz

Although this is perhaps the most complex model in this chapter, stick with it because the end result is well worth the effort. You need to fold this a few times to understand the sequence, but it's a truly elegant design.

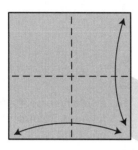

1. Start with a square, colored side up. Crease and unfold in half both ways. Turn the paper over.

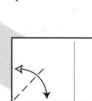

2. Fold both upper corners to the center, but only crease where shown. Turn the paper over.

4. Fold the lower-right edge to the horizontal center, make a pinch mark in the center, and unfold.

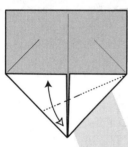

3. Fold both lower corners to the center.

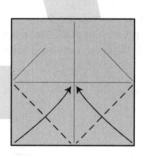

6. Ease out the white paper on both sides.

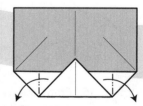

5. Make a valley fold that passes through the pinch mark.

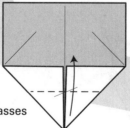

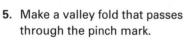

12. Make two valley creases using the most recent creases as a guide.

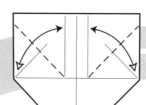

11. Fold the left edge to the right, using the dotted edges as a guide, and unfold. Repeat on the right.

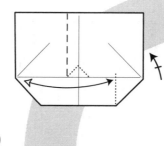

10. Fold the two inner corners out to lie on the horizontal crease. Turn the paper over.

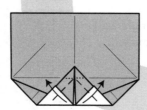

9. Fold the two lower corners up on horizontal creases.

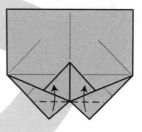

7. Refold on the existing creases.

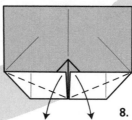

8. Fold the white flaps down as far as possible.

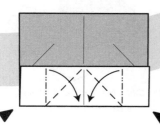

continues

continued

13. Fold the two lower corners up between the lower middle and the outer corners. Turn the paper over.

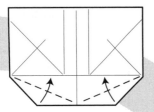

14. Fold down the small triangular flap.

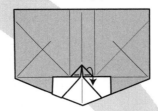

15. Bisect the 45-degree angle with a valley, and repeat on the left.

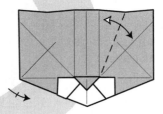

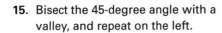

16. Form into 3D with these creases.

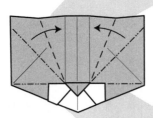

17. Extend the existing crease across the model as a mountain crease.

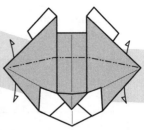

22. Complete.

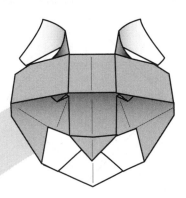

21. Make more shaping creases, and
fold the ears forward slightly.

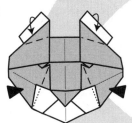

20. Make some gentle shaping creases.

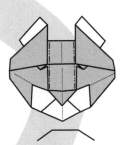

19. Fold the outer ends behind. If you can,
ease the paper out to form the eyes.

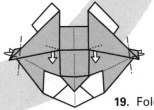

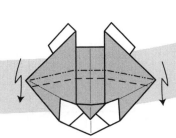

18. Make a narrow pleat forming a valley
crease. (It looks harder than it is!)

Squarosaurus   Difficulty level: 5

by Nick Robinson

This is what a baby diplodocus might have looked like if made from a square sheet of paper. You can do many extra shaping folds at the end if you want it to be more curved.

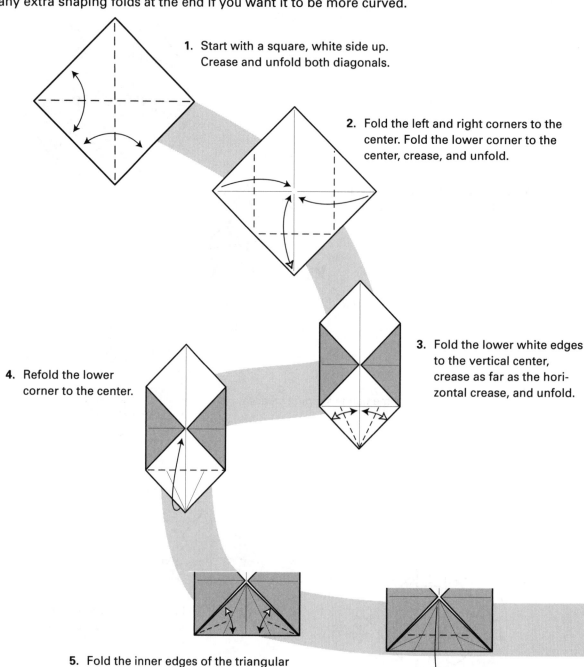

1. Start with a square, white side up. Crease and unfold both diagonals.

2. Fold the left and right corners to the center. Fold the lower corner to the center, crease, and unfold.

3. Fold the lower white edges to the vertical center, crease as far as the horizontal crease, and unfold.

4. Refold the lower corner to the center.

5. Fold the inner edges of the triangular flap to the lower edges, creasing only as far as the first crease, and unfold.

6. Fold the corner down, making the (valley) crease pass through the intersections of the existing creases.

12. Put in the long mountain crease along the back. At the same time, wrap the far end around using the valley creases. Continue until the paper folds flat.

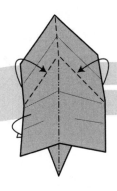

11. Fold the lower edge underneath to meet the horizontal center crease, but only pinch in the creases as far as the dotted lines. Turn the paper over.

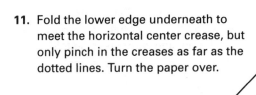

10. Fold the upper white edges to the creases you just made, crease, and unfold.

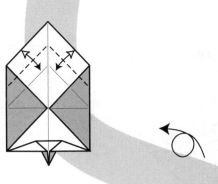

9. Fold the upper half of each vertical edge to meet the horizontal center, crease, and unfold. Turn the paper over.

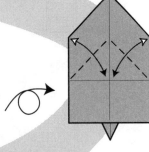

8. This is how your model should look. Turn the paper over.

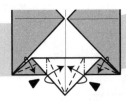

7. Fold the white edges to the center, allowing the creases you made in step 6 to fold in place. As you flatten the paper, the small mountain creases are formed.

continues

continued

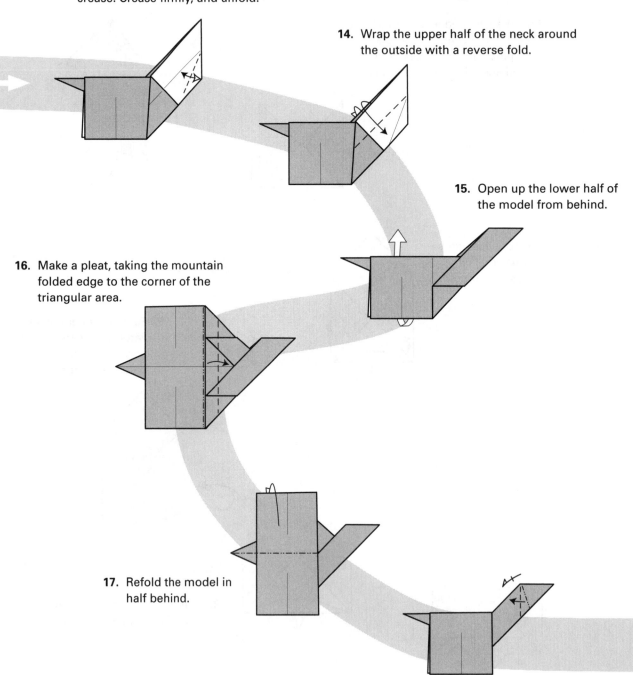

13. Fold the lower half of the vertical white edge to meet the nearest crease. Crease firmly, and unfold.

14. Wrap the upper half of the neck around the outside with a reverse fold.

15. Open up the lower half of the model from behind.

16. Make a pleat, taking the mountain folded edge to the corner of the triangular area.

17. Refold the model in half behind.

18. Precrease, and fold each side of the head back.

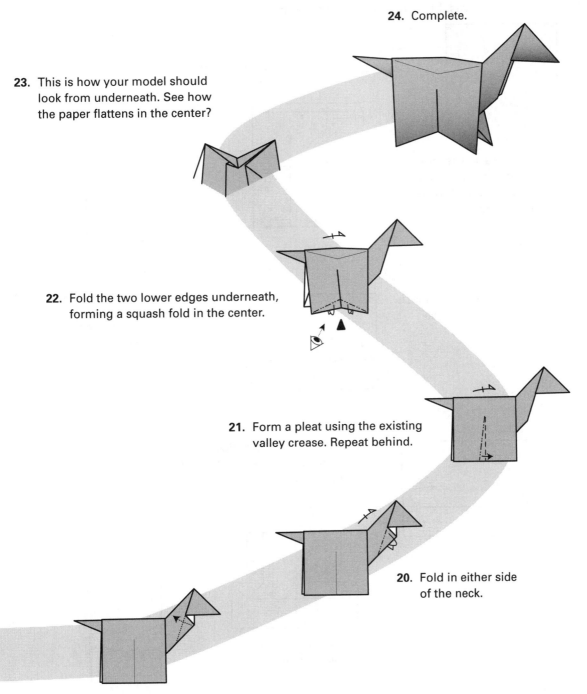

24. Complete.

23. This is how your model should look from underneath. See how the paper flattens in the center?

22. Fold the two lower edges underneath, forming a squash fold in the center.

21. Form a pleat using the existing valley crease. Repeat behind.

20. Fold in either side of the neck.

19. Refold the small valley you made in step 13.

Koala   Difficulty level: 5

by Edwin Corrie

This animal has a wonderful 3D head and will impress everyone who sees it. The design involves several slightly tricky moves, but it gets easier with practice!

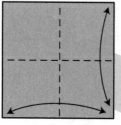

1. Start with a square, colored side up. Crease and unfold in half both ways. Turn the paper over.

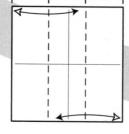

2. Divide into thirds horizontally.

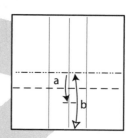

3. (a) Pinch the lower quarter point, and (b) pleat the halfway crease down to meet it.

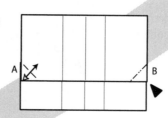

4. Precrease to meet the hidden edge, and inside reverse.

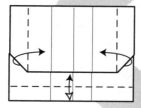

5. Fold the upper (side) edges in. Fold the lower edge to the folded edge, crease, and unfold.

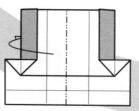

6. Mountain fold the left half behind.

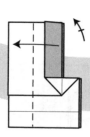

7. Fold the right side over on the one-third crease made in step 2. Repeat behind.

14. Make a small precrease on the left. Fold the top edge of the head to meet the vertical edge of the front leg.

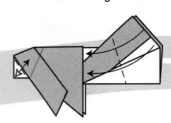

13. Make a precrease, bisecting the lower angle at the rear. Fold up both outer front flaps as far as they'll go.

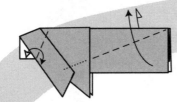

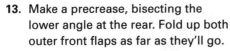

12. Fold flat again, and repeat steps 8 through 11 on the other side.

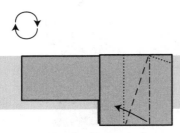

11. Ease out the white triangular flap from underneath (see step 10), and slip the colored flap underneath.

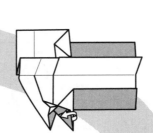

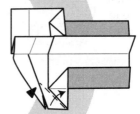

10. Rotate the paper to this position. Fold the lower edge to the right, forming a squash fold so the paper lies flat.

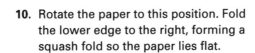

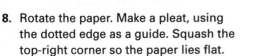

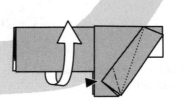

8. Rotate the paper. Make a pleat, using the dotted edge as a guide. Squash the top-right corner so the paper lies flat.

9. Precrease, and reverse the corner to meet the hidden edge. Open the paper out slightly.

continues

continued

15. Make a small vertical precrease on the right. Inside reverse the tail section. Open the head out.

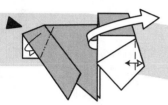

16. Wrap the head around on both sides, forming a small reverse at the bottom.

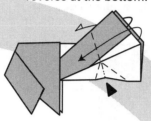

17. Fold both ears forward, squashing them at the top.

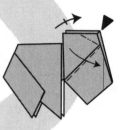

18. Shape the tail end with a small sink. Inside reverse the nose area.

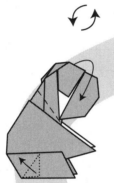

19. Rotate the paper. Lock the back end together by folding up the small interior triangle using the precrease from step 14. Fold the head to the left, opening it out into 3D.

20. Shape the head with small mountain creases.

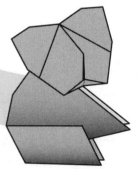

21. Complete.

Chapter 4
Flowers

Flowers are a popular subject in origami. Using art paper, you can make flowers that are very realistic, but take special care when folding the petals. You want them clean and unspoiled. If the completed design reveals both sides of the square, use paper that has suitable colors on both sides.

Origami flowers can be flat or 3D, and a square piece of paper is best suited for creating models with four petals. If you want more, you can use a pentagon or hexagon to create the extra petals.

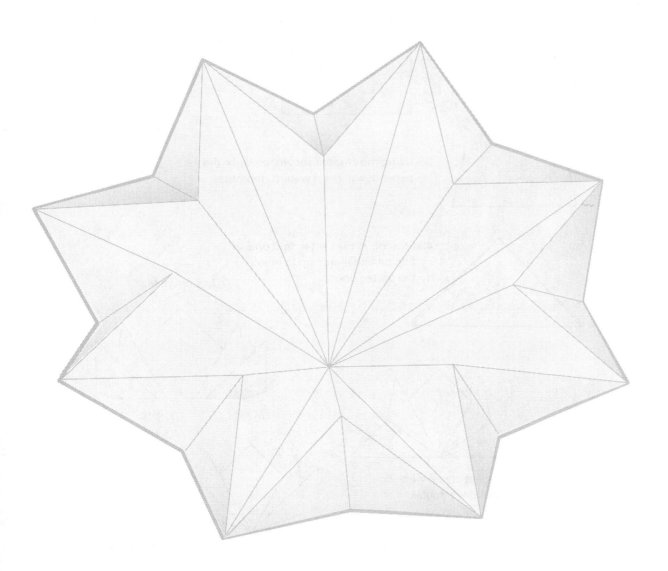

Water Lily   Difficulty level: 1

Traditional design

This is a simple and elegant representation of a water lily. You can vary the angles in steps 4 and 5 to create different stages of flowering.

1. Start with the white side up. Fold side to opposite side, crease, and unfold. Repeat in the other direction. Turn the paper over.

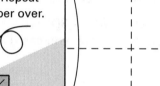

2. Crease and unfold both diagonals.

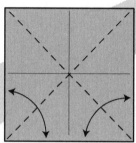

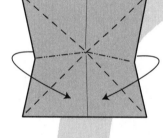

3. Using the creases shown, collapse the paper down into a waterbomb base.

4. Starting at the center, fold one flap on either side up to match the dotted lines.

7. Complete.

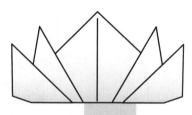

5. Repeat step 4 with slightly shallower angles.

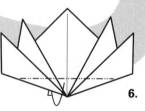

6. Fold the lower corner underneath.

Tulip and Stem Difficulty level: 1

by Zsuzanna Kricskovics

Zsuzanna works tirelessly in her native Hungary, making simple origami for children. You could make this tulip and stem from a single sheet of paper, but it's easier if you use two. And both tulip and stem can be placed inside a Cup (see Chapter 9) made from the same-size square. The tulip uses paper ¼ the size of the stem.

Tulip

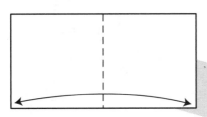

1. Start with a 2×1 rectangle (cut a square in half), the white side up. Fold in half from side to side.

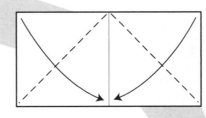

2. Fold the upper corners to the center of the lower edge.

4. This is how your model should look. Repeat step 3 on the left.

3. Leaving a slight gap at the center, fold up the right corner to match the dotted line.

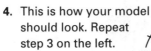

5. This is how your model should look. Turn the paper over.

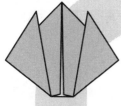

7. This is how your model should look. Turn the paper over.

8. Complete.

6. Fold the sides in to narrow the vertical points.

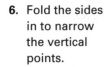
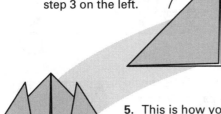
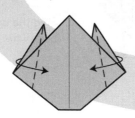

continues

continued

Stem

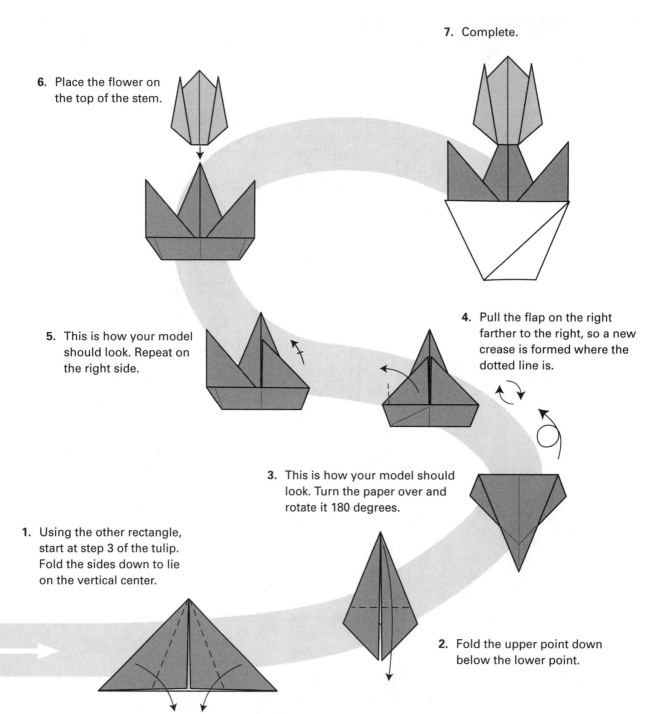

7. Complete.

6. Place the flower on the top of the stem.

5. This is how your model should look. Repeat on the right side.

4. Pull the flap on the right farther to the right, so a new crease is formed where the dotted line is.

3. This is how your model should look. Turn the paper over and rotate it 180 degrees.

1. Using the other rectangle, start at step 3 of the tulip. Fold the sides down to lie on the vertical center.

2. Fold the upper point down below the lower point.

Long-Stemmed Rose   Difficulty level: 1

by Nick Robinson

Here's another simple 2D flower with a stem. If you can find paper that's the same color both sides, use it for this model. The end result is much nicer. Feel free to experiment with this flower. You can alter almost every step to produce subtle variations.

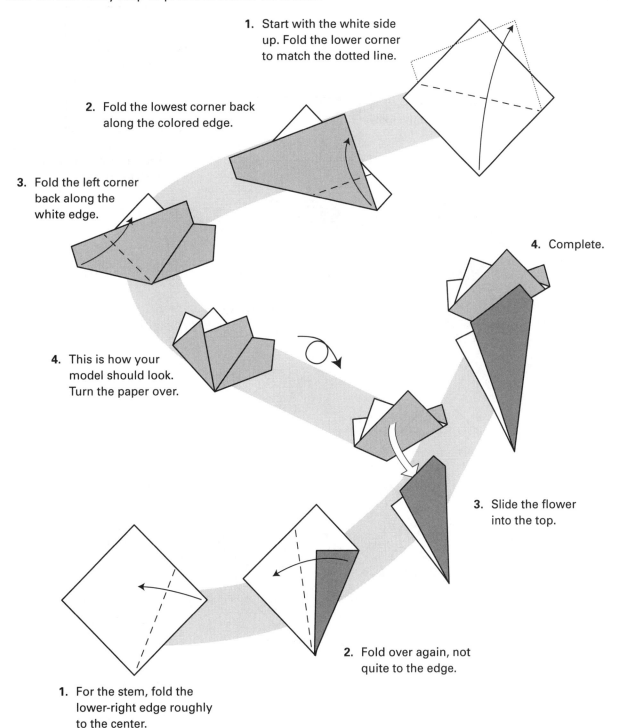

1. Start with the white side up. Fold the lower corner to match the dotted line.

2. Fold the lowest corner back along the colored edge.

3. Fold the left corner back along the white edge.

4. Complete.

4. This is how your model should look. Turn the paper over.

3. Slide the flower into the top.

2. Fold over again, not quite to the edge.

1. For the stem, fold the lower-right edge roughly to the center.

Boutonniere Blossom Difficulty level: 2

Traditional design

This model makes a perfect boutonniere for elegant parties. If you can find paper that's green on one side and, for example, red on the other, use it to create a very lifelike flower. In the final step, the petals open out at the same time.

1. Start with the white side up. Precrease both diagonals. Turn the paper over.

2. Fold edge to opposite edge, crease, and unfold in both directions.

3. Rotate the paper. Collapse into a preliminary base using the existing creases.

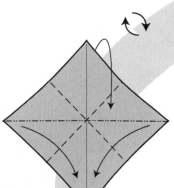

4. Fold the upper edges to the vertical center. Turn the paper over.

6. Fold the first layer on the right over to the left.

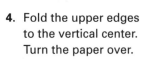

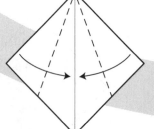

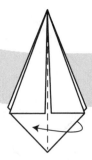

5. Repeat step 4.

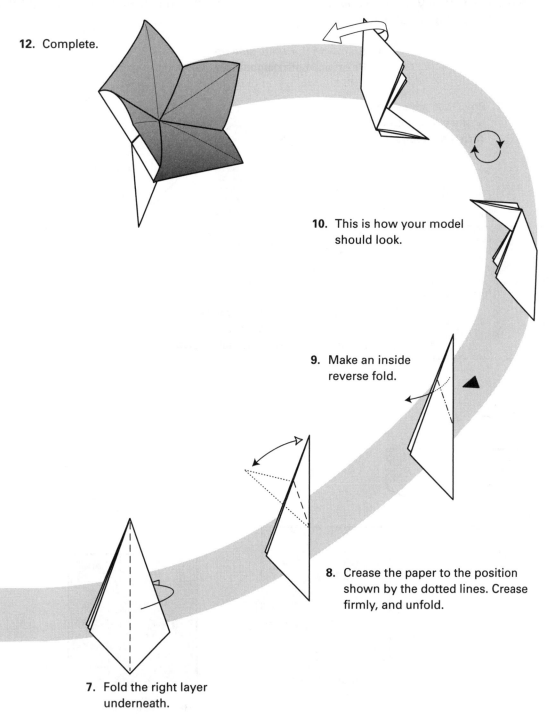

11. Rotate the paper. Holding the outer layer, peel it like a banana so it wraps around the outer edge.

12. Complete.

10. This is how your model should look.

9. Make an inside reverse fold.

8. Crease the paper to the position shown by the dotted lines. Crease firmly, and unfold.

7. Fold the right layer underneath.

Sunflower Difficulty level: 2

by Nick Robinson

This model is essentially an exercise in precreasing and requires no complicated moves or techniques. Nevertheless, take your time and aim to create as elegant a result as you can. Using thin, translucent paper makes a beautiful result.

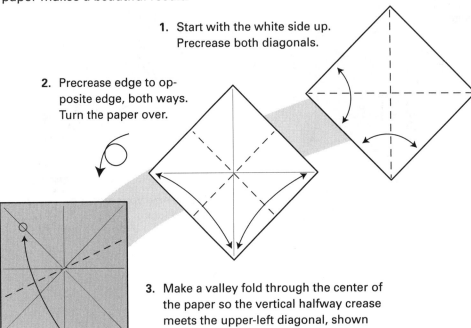

1. Start with the white side up. Precrease both diagonals.

2. Precrease edge to opposite edge, both ways. Turn the paper over.

3. Make a valley fold through the center of the paper so the vertical halfway crease meets the upper-left diagonal, shown with circles.

4. Unfold the paper.

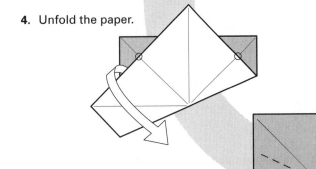

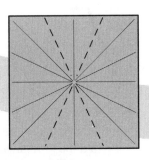

5. Repeat the move to the upper right.

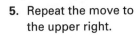

6. Repeat the move to add the "missing" creases.

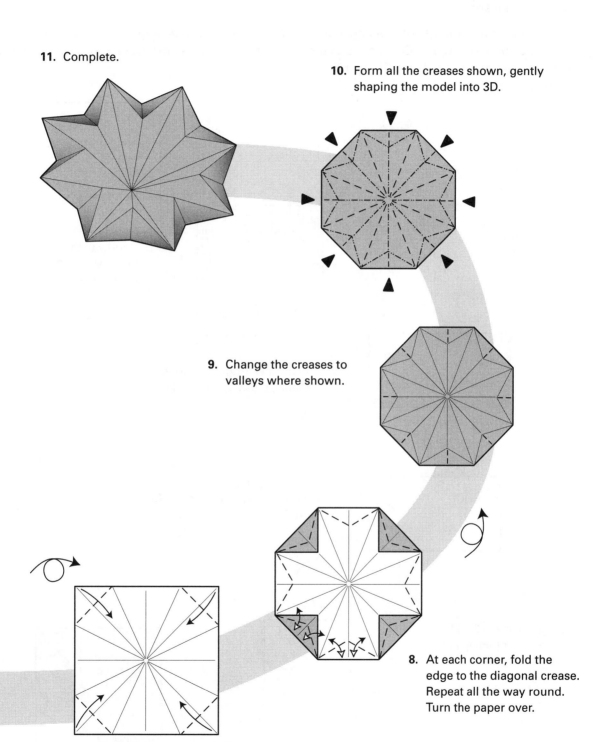

11. Complete.

10. Form all the creases shown, gently shaping the model into 3D.

9. Change the creases to valleys where shown.

8. At each corner, fold the edge to the diagonal crease. Repeat all the way round. Turn the paper over.

7. Turn the paper over. Fold each corner in between the creases on either edge of the diagonal.

Snowdrop Difficulty level: 2

by Nick Robinson

This design is an example of creating a 3D shape with minimal creasing. The tension in the paper holds the creases in place. Compare this method of producing the main creases with an alternative method used in the Bowl (see Chapter 6).

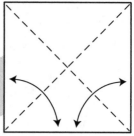

1. Start with the white side up. Precrease both diagonals. Turn the paper over.

2. Fold in half from bottom to top.

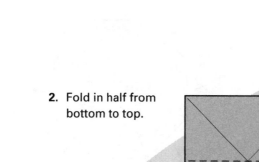

3. Fold the lower-right half to the diagonal, crease, and unfold.

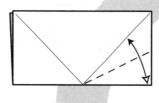

4. Fold the right edge to the recent crease, crease firmly, and unfold. Turn the paper over.

5. Repeat steps 3 and 4 before unfolding back to the square.

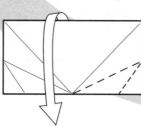

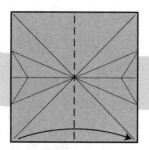

6. Fold in half from left to right.

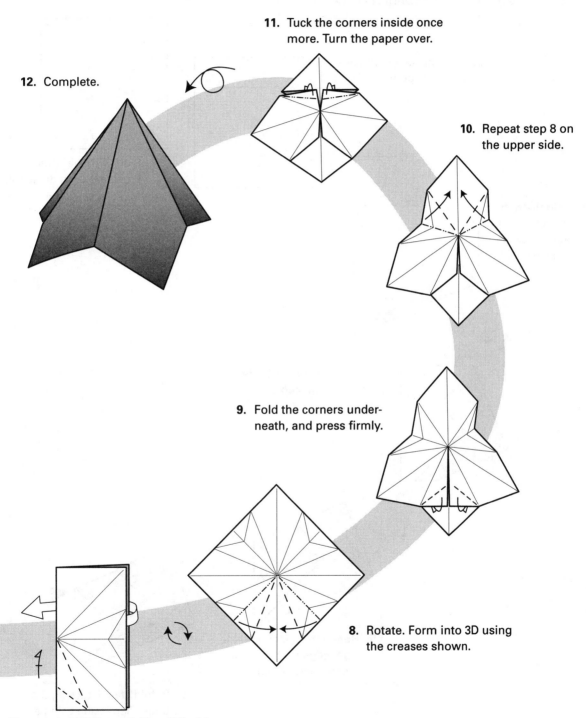

11. Tuck the corners inside once more. Turn the paper over.

12. Complete.

10. Repeat step 8 on the upper side.

9. Fold the corners underneath, and press firmly.

8. Rotate. Form into 3D using the creases shown.

7. Repeat steps 3 through 5 on this side before unfolding the lower side.

Camellia Difficulty level: 2

Traditional design

This model uses a perfectly symmetrical fold where each edge is folded in exactly the same way. The result is a very pleasing flowerlike shape.

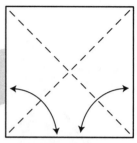

1. Start with the white edge up. Precrease both diagonals.

2. Fold the lower-left edge to the diagonal.

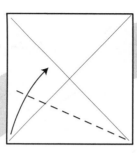

3. Fold the right edge to the diagonal, where the circled points meet.

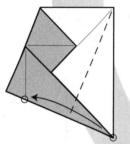

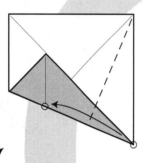

4. Rotate the paper 90 degrees, and repeat step 3.

5. Rotate the paper, fold the right edge to the center, crease, and unfold.

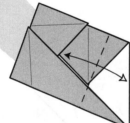

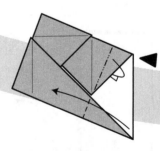

6. Refold step 5, tucking the upper flap inside using a reverse fold.

12. Tuck the final flap under a layer.

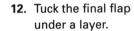

11. Fold and squash the corner in the same way as before.

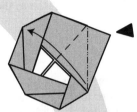

13. Complete.

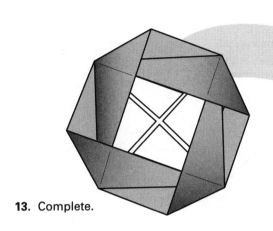

10. Pull out a layer so the loose flap is underneath it.

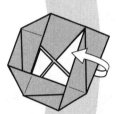

9. Tuck the last two flaps underneath the layers.

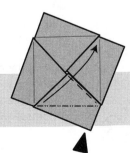

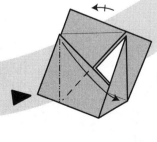

8. This is how your model should look. Repeat on the next (clockwise) flap. Repeat a second and third time.

7. Fold up the loose lower flap, flattening the lower corner.

Orchid   Difficulty level: 3

by Jonathon Shapcott

This design is the result of a doodle Jonathon came up with. He was just playing with a waterbomb base when the flower emerged. It shows how a little imagination can result in an elegant, curved form.

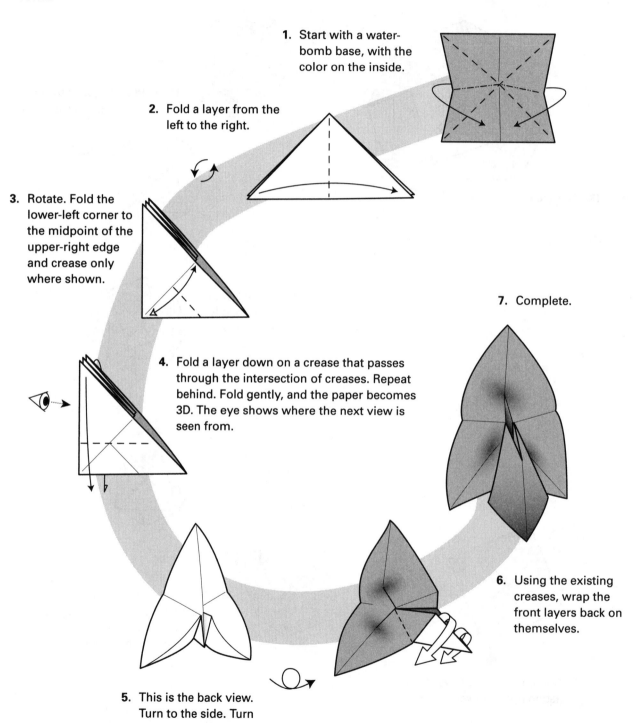

1. Start with a water-bomb base, with the color on the inside.

2. Fold a layer from the left to the right.

3. Rotate. Fold the lower-left corner to the midpoint of the upper-right edge and crease only where shown.

4. Fold a layer down on a crease that passes through the intersection of creases. Repeat behind. Fold gently, and the paper becomes 3D. The eye shows where the next view is seen from.

5. This is the back view. Turn to the side. Turn the paper over.

6. Using the existing creases, wrap the front layers back on themselves.

7. Complete.

Bluebell   Difficulty level: 3

by Adolfo Cerceda

Cerceda was an Argentinean magician and circus star who performed as Carlos Corda during the 1940s and 1950s. He also invented several hundred origami designs!

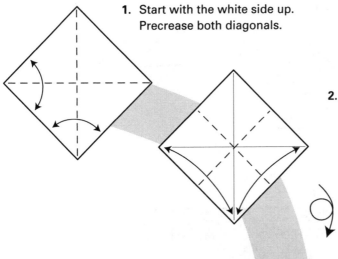

1. Start with the white side up. Precrease both diagonals.

2. Precrease edge to opposite edge, both ways. Turn the paper over.

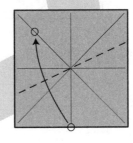

3. Make a valley fold through the center of the paper so the vertical halfway crease meets the upper-left diagonal, shown with circles.

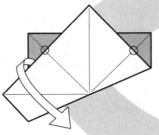

4. This is how your model should look. Note the circled areas where the creases meet. Unfold the paper.

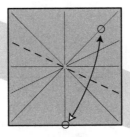

5. Repeat the last move to the upper right.

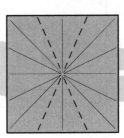

6. Repeat the last move twice more to add the "missing" creases.

continues

continued

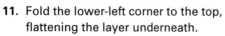

12. This is how your model should look. Repeat on the three other flaps.

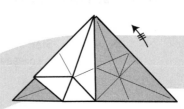

11. Fold the lower-left corner to the top, flattening the layer underneath.

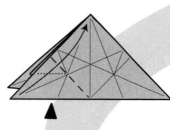

10. Make a double reverse fold using the creases shown on both edges of the paper. Repeat on the right.

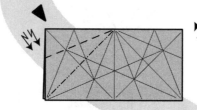

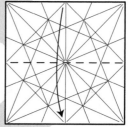

9. Fold in half from top to bottom.

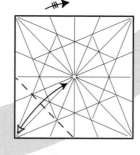

8. Fold each corner to the center, crease, and unfold.

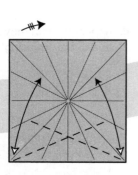

7. Fold each lower corner to the farthest diagonal, crease, and unfold. Repeat on each edge. Turn the paper over.

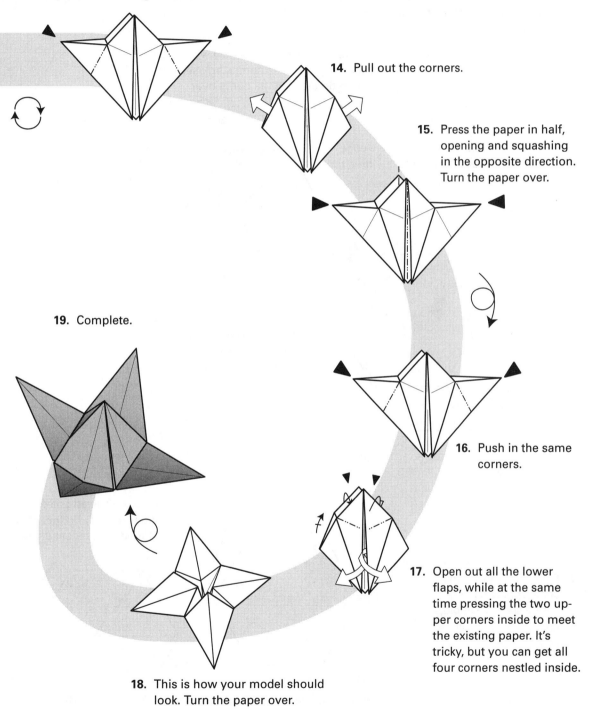

13. Rotate the paper. Push in the two corners on the existing creases.

14. Pull out the corners.

15. Press the paper in half, opening and squashing in the opposite direction. Turn the paper over.

16. Push in the same corners.

17. Open out all the lower flaps, while at the same time pressing the two upper corners inside to meet the existing paper. It's tricky, but you can get all four corners nestled inside.

18. This is how your model should look. Turn the paper over.

19. Complete.

Desert Flower   Difficulty level: 5

by Nick Robinson

You'll rarely see a six-edged sheet of paper called for in origami diagrams, but it's perfect if you're trying to create a flower such as this one. You must be methodical with this model, and perform the same folds on each of the six edges.

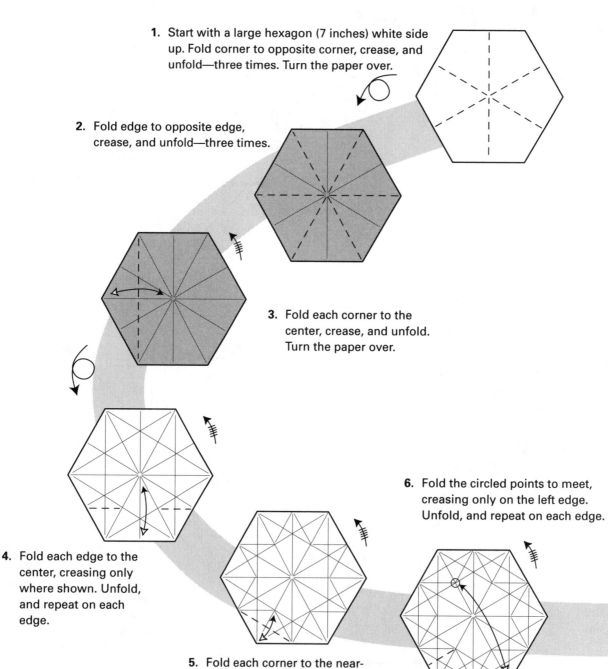

1. Start with a large hexagon (7 inches) white side up. Fold corner to opposite corner, crease, and unfold—three times. Turn the paper over.

2. Fold edge to opposite edge, crease, and unfold—three times.

3. Fold each corner to the center, crease, and unfold. Turn the paper over.

4. Fold each edge to the center, creasing only where shown. Unfold, and repeat on each edge.

5. Fold each corner to the nearest crease intersection. Unfold, and repeat on each edge.

6. Fold the circled points to meet, creasing only on the left edge. Unfold, and repeat on each edge.

12. On the final corner, fold the lower half of the point underneath with a mountain fold.

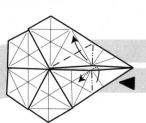

11. And repeat it again!

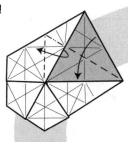

10. Repeat step 8 again.

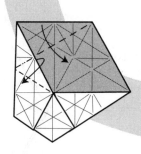

9. Moving clockwise, repeat step 8.

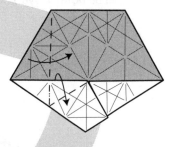

7. Turn the paper over. Fold a corner to the center.

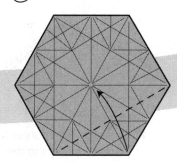

8. Fold part of the white side over, folding in the colored side at the same time.

continues

continued

13. Swing the flaps over at the top right and bottom left.

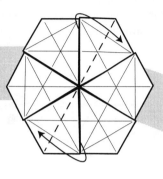

14. This is how your model should look. Turn the paper over.

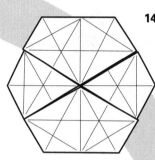

15. Form all the creases shown, collapsing the paper. The six upper edges should all be double layers with color inside.

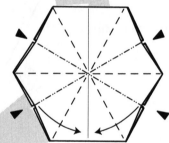

16. Fold the top corner to the right corner, folding also on the dotted valley crease.

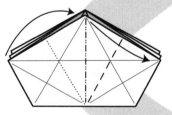

17. Fold the right corner to the bottom center, squashing the flap underneath on the dotted crease.

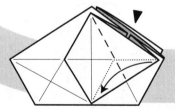

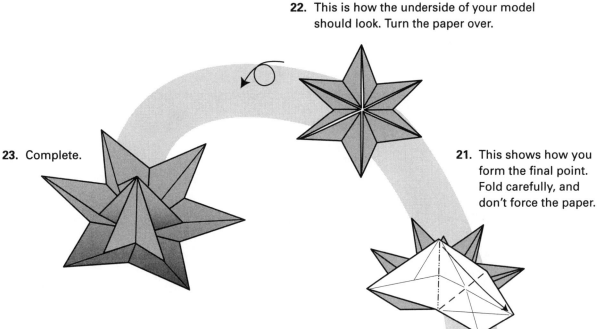

22. This is how the underside of your model should look. Turn the paper over.

23. Complete.

21. This shows how you form the final point. Fold carefully, and don't force the paper.

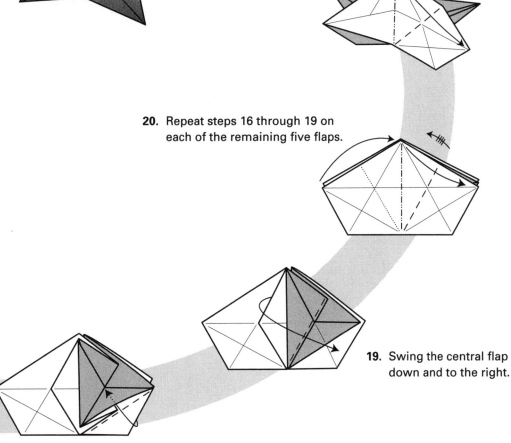

20. Repeat steps 16 through 19 on each of the remaining five flaps.

19. Swing the central flap down and to the right.

18. Tuck the white triangular flap into the pocket.

Chapter 5
People

It's actually quite difficult to create a well-proportioned human figure using origami; most have limbs that are just too short. For this reason, much of the simple origami is almost cartoonlike, capturing the basic elements of the subject. When folding people (or faces), this is especially true.

However, your goal is not to make the designs in this book especially realistic, just recognizable! Most of the faces can be interpreted very widely by altering angles and distances to create different emotions or facial types.

Girl's Head 1 <small>Difficulty level: 1</small>

by Eric Kenneway

The face is the part of the body we look at most often, and the image is hard-coded into our brains. This allows us to simplify it to an extraordinary degree and still have it be instantly recognizable. You can vary every step of this model to produce different proportions of the face and hair.

1. Start with the white side up. Crease and unfold a diagonal.

2. Fold side to side, pinching the center point on the lower side of the horizontal diagonal.

3. Fold the top corner to the center. If you can do this accurately without step 2, so much the better!

4. Fold down on the diagonal.

7. Complete.

5. Fold the upper corners down so the circled points meet.

6. Fold the three right-angled corners behind to round the face.

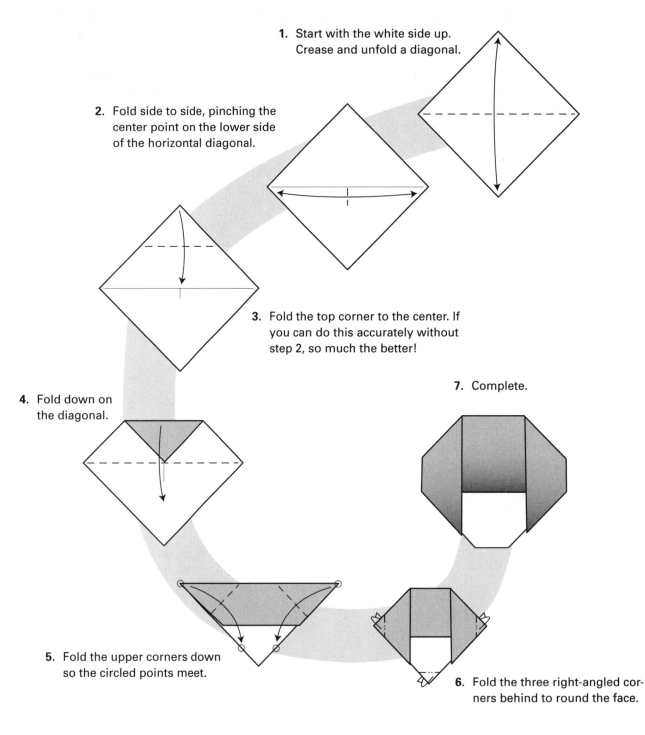

Girl's Head 2 Difficulty level: 2

by Eric Kenneway

This model uses a couple small pleats to shape the neck and hair. As with Girl's Head 1, this is a highly stylized representation of a face. You also can alter the proportions and experiment as much as you like.

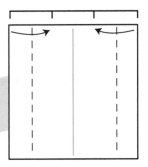

2. Fold the upper-left edge to meet the right inner vertical colored edge. Crease where shown and unfold. Repeat on the other side.

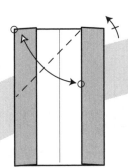

1. Start with the white side up. Fold in half from side to side. Fold the left and right sides in to (approximately) one third of the width.

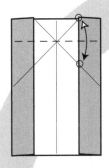

3. Fold the upper edge down to the crease so the circled points meet, crease, and unfold.

4. Fold the sides to the center, creasing where shown, and unfold. Turn the paper over.

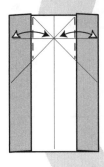

6. Using the creases shown, collapse the upper edge down.

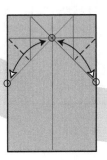

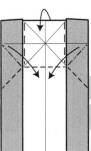

5. Fold the circled points to meet, creasing only where shown Turn the paper over.

continues

continued

12. Complete.

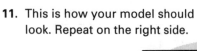

11. This is how your model should look. Repeat on the right side.

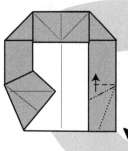

10. Make a pleat, forming a new mountain crease at the dotted line.

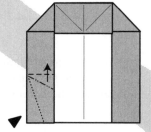

9. Starting at the outer end of the most recent crease, fold the lower corner to lie on the inner colored edge. Crease and unfold.

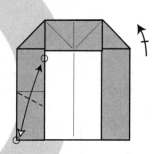

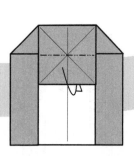

7. Tuck the flap underneath.

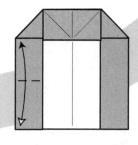

8. Fold the lower corner to the angle change above it, crease, and unfold.

Simple Santa   Difficulty level: 2

by Nick Robinson

Origami Santas come in all shapes and sizes and are usually recognizable by the red and white color combination. Here's a very simple Santa. He'll be happy sitting on your desk during the holidays.

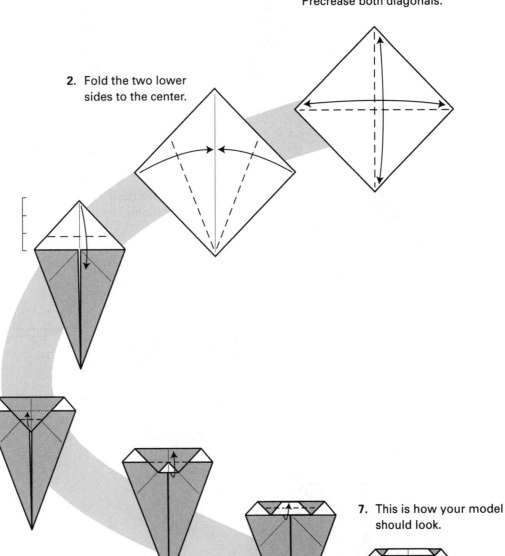

1. Start with the white side up. Precrease both diagonals.

2. Fold the two lower sides to the center.

3. Fold down about two thirds of the white flap.

4. Fold the inner corner back to the dotted line.

5. Fold the lower white edge to the upper edge.

6. Repeat step 5.

7. This is how your model should look.

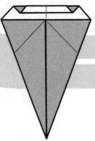

continues

continued

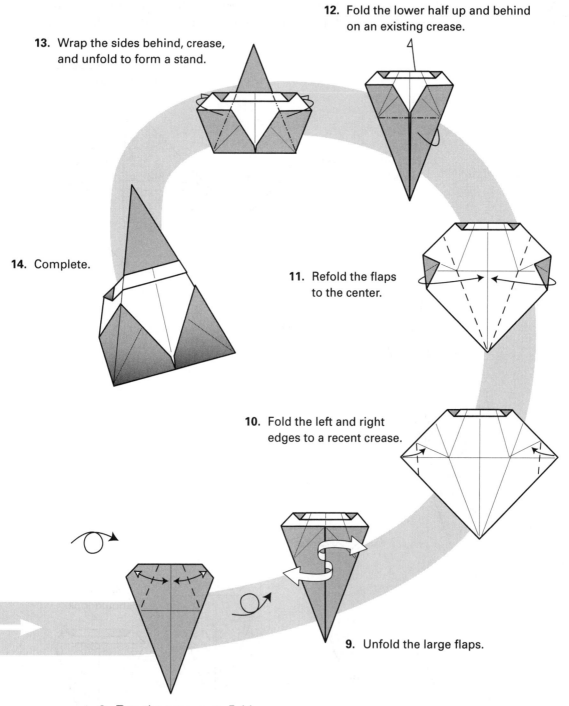

12. Fold the lower half up and behind on an existing crease.

13. Wrap the sides behind, crease, and unfold to form a stand.

14. Complete.

11. Refold the flaps to the center.

10. Fold the left and right edges to a recent crease.

9. Unfold the large flaps.

8. Turn the paper over. Fold the short upper edges to the center, crease, and unfold. Turn the paper over again.

Napoleon Difficulty level: 2

by Nick Robinson

This is another example of a doodle, inspired by the work of cartoonist Roger Price. Here, your goal is to create a visual joke or cartoon, using the paper almost as if you were drawing a sketch. (In case you don't get it, it's the *inside* of Napoleon's jacket!)

1. Start with the white side up. Crease in half both ways. Fold both right corners to the center.

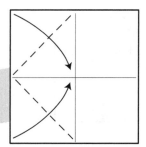

2. Fold the touching colored edges back to the outside.

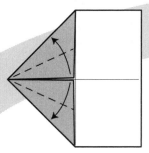

3. Fold the left half to the right.

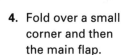

4. Fold over a small corner and then the main flap.

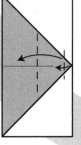

6. Fold the corners to the recent crease.

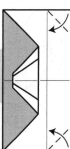

5. Fold the right side over, about one third of the way. Crease and unfold.

continues

continued

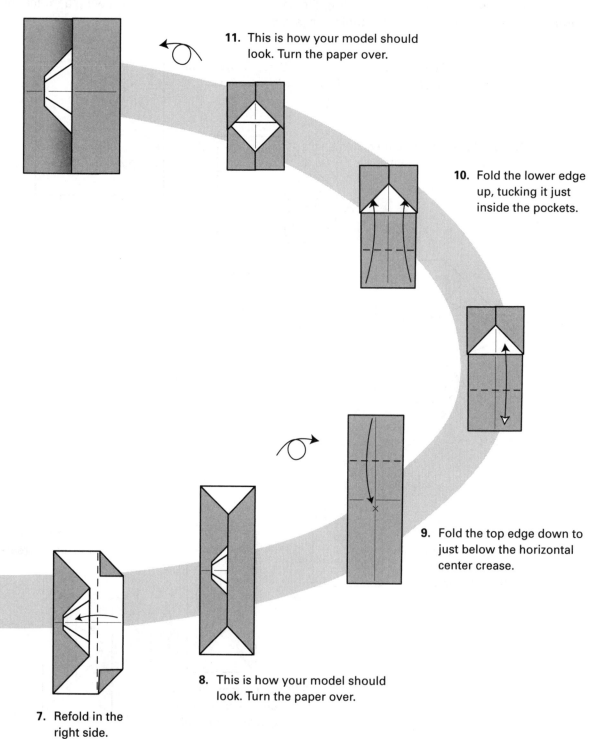

12. Complete.

11. This is how your model should
look. Turn the paper over.

10. Fold the lower edge
up, tucking it just
inside the pockets.

9. Fold the top edge down to
just below the horizontal
center crease.

8. This is how your model should
look. Turn the paper over.

7. Refold in the
right side.

Grumpy Alien Difficulty level: 2

by Nick Robinson

Here's a lighthearted design depicting the classic bug-eyed alien. As is often the case, you can alter distances and angles to produce a number of variations. Why not adapt it—using green paper—to make a frog?

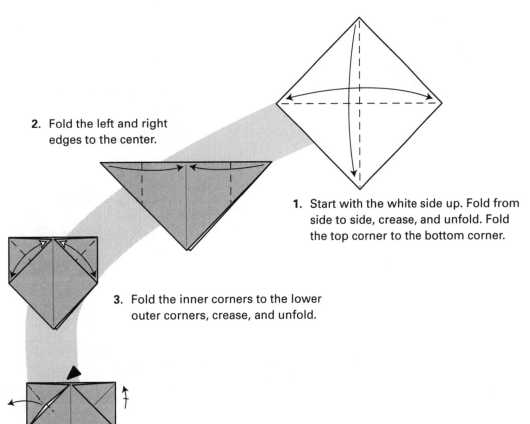

2. Fold the left and right edges to the center.

1. Start with the white side up. Fold from side to side, crease, and unfold. Fold the top corner to the bottom corner.

3. Fold the inner corners to the lower outer corners, crease, and unfold.

4. Open and squash the left flap. Repeat on the right.

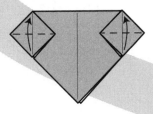

5. Fold up the corners on both sides to reveal the eyes.

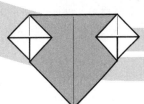

6. This is how your model should look.

continues

continued

12. Complete.

11. Fold the upper corners behind.

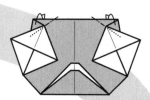

10. Fold in the sides at a slight angle, allowing the flaps to swing out to the sides.

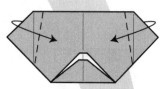

9. Fold a tiny corner over at the bottom and then fold up all the white section.

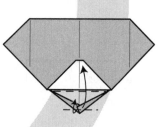

8. Fold part of the white triangle over, first on the left and then on the right.

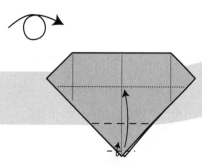

7. Turn the paper over. Fold over a small corner at the bottom, and fold up the whole flap to roughly where the dotted line lies.

Vampyra   Difficulty level: 3

by Paul Hanson

This elegant design is characteristic of Hanson's work. Some folders put so much of their own personality into a design that you can recognize their work after a while, and that's true of this model. The final shaping creases on the cowl should be soft folds, so put them in gently!

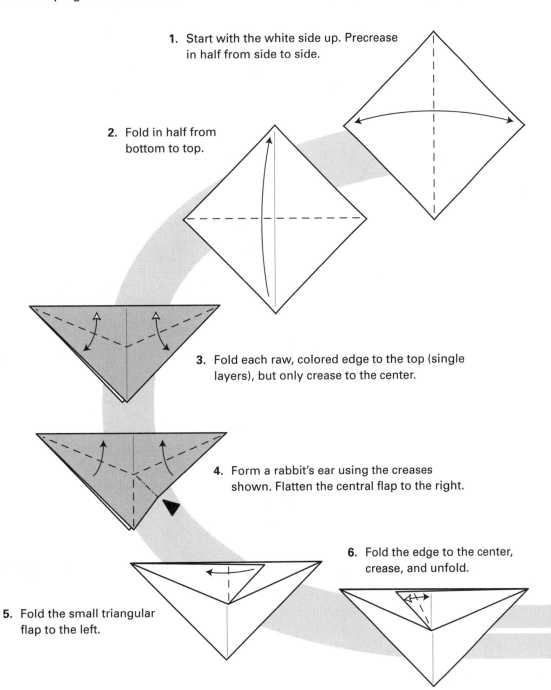

1. Start with the white side up. Precrease in half from side to side.

2. Fold in half from bottom to top.

3. Fold each raw, colored edge to the top (single layers), but only crease to the center.

4. Form a rabbit's ear using the creases shown. Flatten the central flap to the right.

5. Fold the small triangular flap to the left.

6. Fold the edge to the center, crease, and unfold.

continues

continued

12. This is how your model should look. Repeat steps 8 through 11 on the right side.

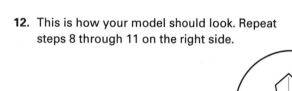

13. Fold down the top triangular flap.

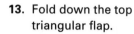

11. Fold all the upper layer to the left.

9. Fold the corner of the kite to the left.

10. Fold between the circled points to narrow the flap further.

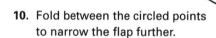

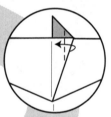

8. Fold the kite-shape flap in half to the right. Now focus on the circled area.

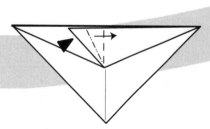

7. Squash the triangular flap.

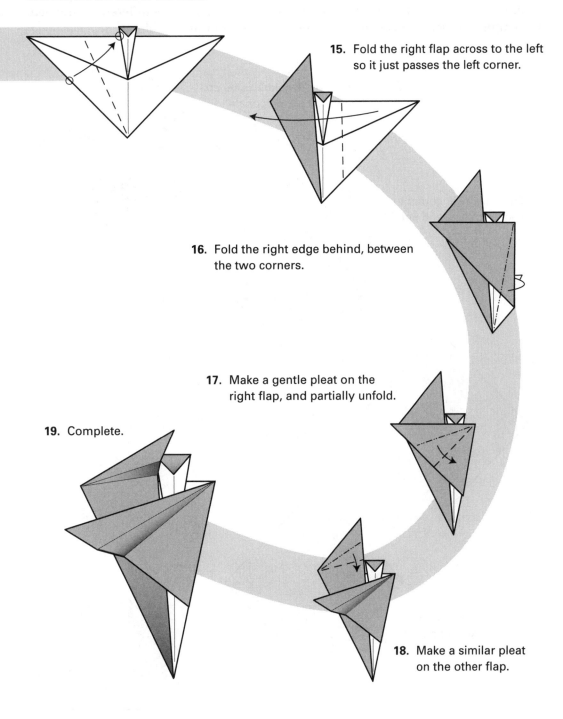

14. Fold the left side up so the edge just touches the left side of the head.

15. Fold the right flap across to the left so it just passes the left corner.

16. Fold the right edge behind, between the two corners.

17. Make a gentle pleat on the right flap, and partially unfold.

19. Complete.

18. Make a similar pleat on the other flap.

Crying Baby Difficulty level: 3

by Gilad Aharoni

Humor in origami is surprisingly rare, but it does exist, as shown in this quirky design of a baby with a single tooth in mid-cry. You can vary steps 13 through 15 to produce different-shape heads. Choose paper with high contrast between one side and the other for this model.

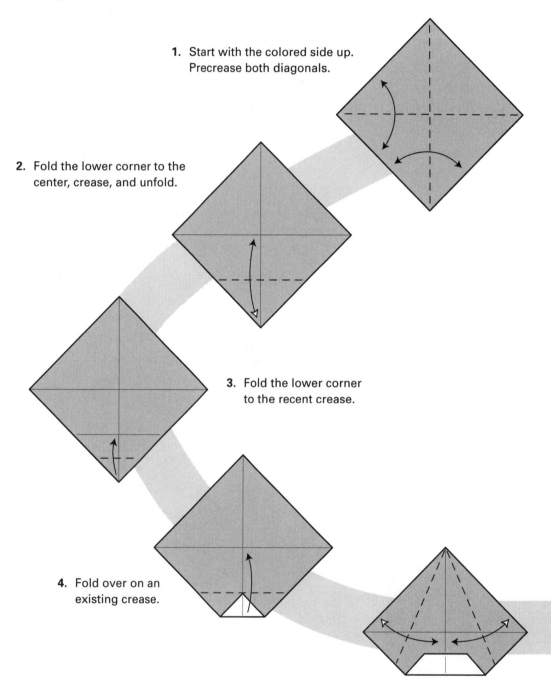

1. Start with the colored side up. Precrease both diagonals.

2. Fold the lower corner to the center, crease, and unfold.

3. Fold the lower corner to the recent crease.

4. Fold over on an existing crease.

5. Fold both upper edges to the center, crease, and unfold.

11. Fold the outer corners in at right angles to the edge.

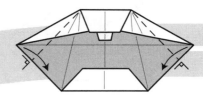

10. Fold the tip underneath. This makes the baby's single tooth.

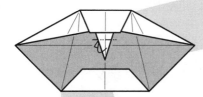

9. Form a pleat on the thin triangular flap.

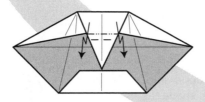

8. Fold the sides under using existing mountain creases. The short valleys form as you flatten the paper.

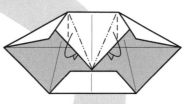

7. Fold the upper corners in between the circled points. The paper does not meet the horizontal center.

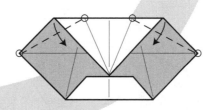

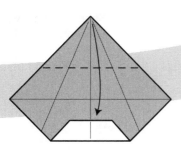

6. Fold the top corner to the center of the inner white edge.

continues

continued

12. Fold in the outer lower edges.

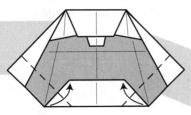

13. Form the ears with two pleats.

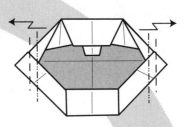

14. Fold the upper and lower edges behind to shape the face.

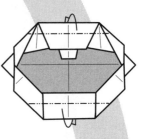

15. Shape the ears with short mountain folds.

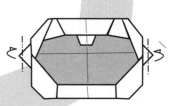

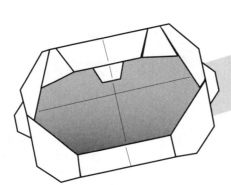

16. Complete.

Robot's Head   Difficulty level: 4

by Mike Thomas

This design starts in a familiar way but then it uses a series of "squash in half and open out the other way" moves to come up with a face full of character. To make the finished robot talk, gently press the white flap at the back of the head.

1. Start with the colored side up. Precrease in half both ways.

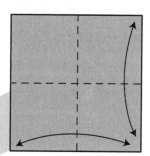

2. Fold the lower edge to the center, crease, and unfold.

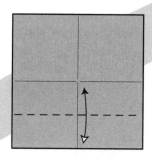

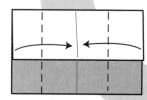

3. Fold the upper edge to the recent crease.

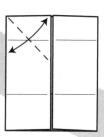

4. Fold the sides to the center.

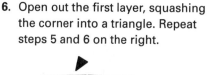

5. Fold the corner from the top center out to the left edge, crease, and unfold.

6. Open out the first layer, squashing the corner into a triangle. Repeat steps 5 and 6 on the right.

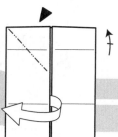

continues

continued

11. Fold the lower edge to the side, creasing where shown through both layers. Repeat on the other corner.

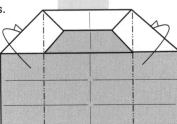

12. Pleat the upper section down.

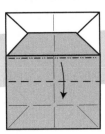

10. Fold the outer sides of the model underneath on vertical creases.

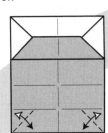

9. Fold up the lower edge to the nearest crease, and unfold.

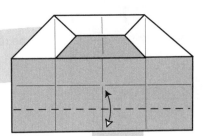

8. Fold up the smaller colored flap.

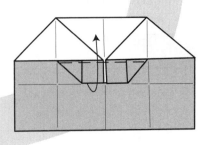

7. Fold up the inner colored corners to the white edge.

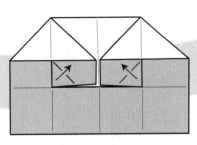

13. Turn the paper over. Press in the lower corners, and squash open symmetrically.

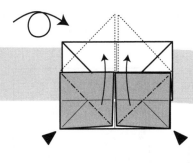

14. Fold the center points of the colored triangles out to their respective sides, pressing in at the top and bottom. This has to happen at the same time.

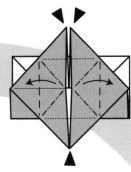

15. This is how your model should look. Turn the paper over.

16. Open the pocket slightly from underneath, and press in the center as you squeeze in the sides. Your goal is to flatten the model in half in the opposite direction.

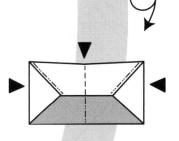

17. Fold down the white flap on either side.

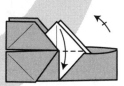

18. Open out the model from underneath, and open the eye flaps.

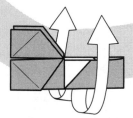

19. Complete.

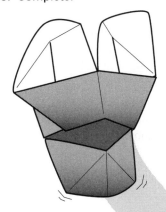

Human Face Difficulty level: 4

by Nick Robinson

When creating origami faces, the nose is usually the most important area in terms of technique. This design produces a 3D nose—and requires very careful folding to create it. Other features such as eyes, ears, and mouth are less critical, and you can experiment to create different looks.

1. Start with the colored side up. Crease in half from side to side. Fold both corners on the right to the vertical crease, and unfold.

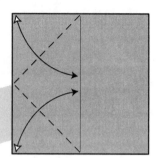

2. Fold in half from bottom to top.

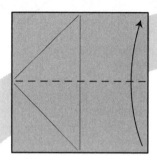

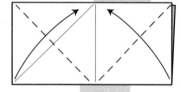

3. Fold the two lower corners to the top center.

4. Fold the lower corner underneath, about one quarter of the height.

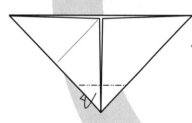

5. Fold the corners out so they lie along the lower horizontal edge.

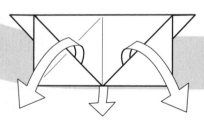

6. Unfold back to a square.

11. Fold the angled layer over as far as it will go, crease, and unfold. Repeat on the lower edge, but don't crease through the central triangle. Swing it out of the way before creasing.

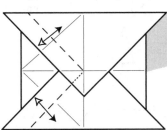

12. Crease the central triangle in half firmly, and unfold.

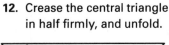

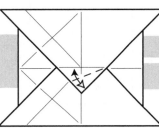

10. This is how your model should look. Turn the paper over.

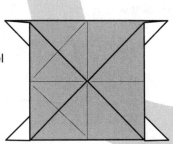

9. Open out, and fold down the upper layer of paper.

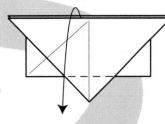

8. This is how your model should look. Repeat step 7 on the left.

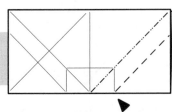

7. Make a double reverse fold on the right corner.

continues

continued

13. Fold open and flatten half of the nose, leaving the nose in 3D.

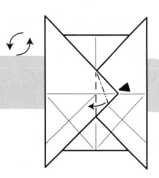

14. Open out the paper fully. Your goal is to reverse the dotted areas so they're inside the model.

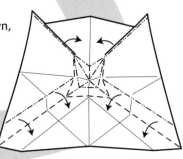

15. Now comes the fun! Arrange the paper as shown, and start to introduce the indicated creases. You're refolding much of the paper as it was in step 13, but the lower areas will be hidden.

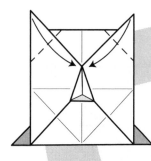

16. If your model doesn't look like this, compare it with step 14. It may help to look at step 13 from underneath. Fold the upper corners to touch the center.

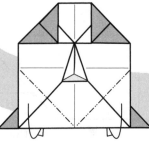

17. Fold the lower corners behind on existing creases.

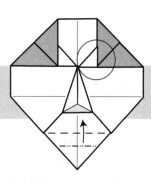

18. Form the mouth with a pleat. Note the circled area.

24. Tuck the loose triangular flaps underneath the layers. Round the corners of the chin. Turn the paper over.

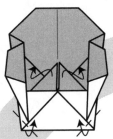

25. Complete.

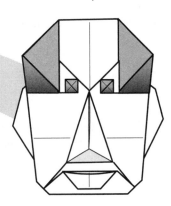

23. Fold out the ears—however big you want them!

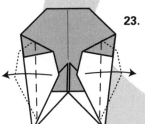

22. Fold the lower corner of the mouth underneath. Fold the right and left sides behind on a crease between the circled points. Turn the paper over.

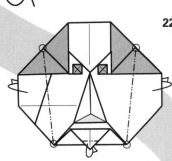

21. Fold over the lower-left corner to reveal the colored side.

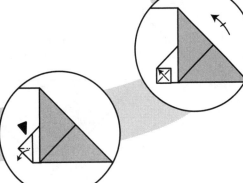

20. Squash open the triangular flap.

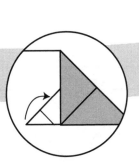

19. Fold the white corner over, just short of the colored edge.

Mr. Muppet Difficulty level: 5

by Gilad Aharoni

You need to concentrate when you work this model, but each step is relatively straightforward. I recommend you make the model two or three times, simply to learn the folding method. Then you can focus on achieving a really fantastic result!

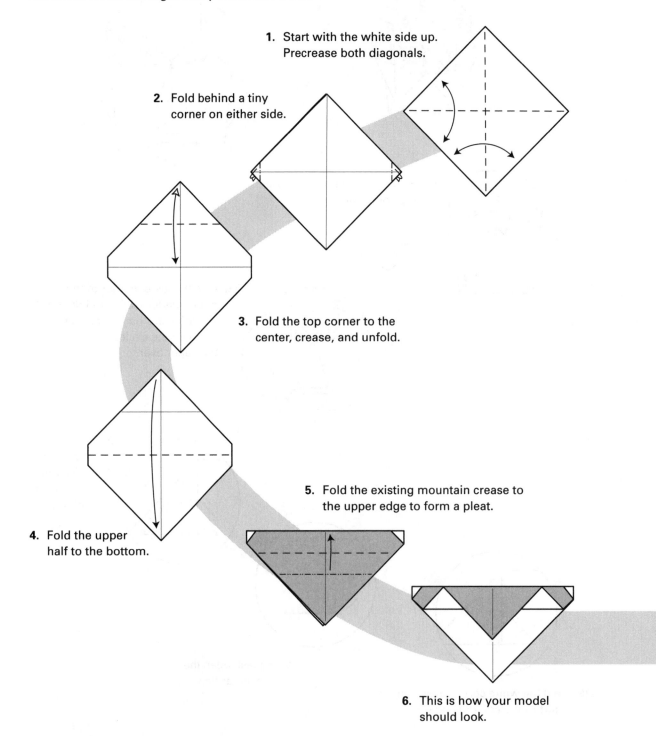

1. Start with the white side up. Precrease both diagonals.

2. Fold behind a tiny corner on either side.

3. Fold the top corner to the center, crease, and unfold.

4. Fold the upper half to the bottom.

5. Fold the existing mountain crease to the upper edge to form a pleat.

6. This is how your model should look.

12. Fold a flap down to the horizontal crease.

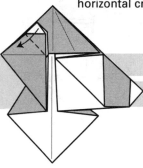

11. Fold up the flap on the left toward the top.

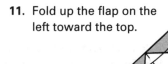

9. Fold the upper edges to the center, allowing paper to swing out from underneath.

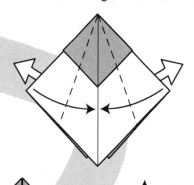

10. Pull out a hidden colored flap.

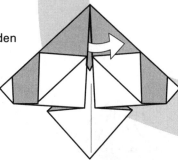

7. Turn the paper over. Fold each half of the upper edge to the vertical center.

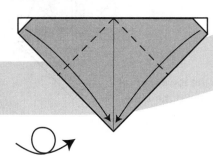

8. This is how your model should look. Turn the paper over.

continues

continued

13. Open and squash the
    white triangle.

14. Fold the triangular flap to the
    left. Repeat steps 11 through
    13 on the right side.

15. Squash the flap
    symmetrically.

16. Fold the sides of the
    nose underneath.

17. Fold the lower corner
    up to the dotted line.

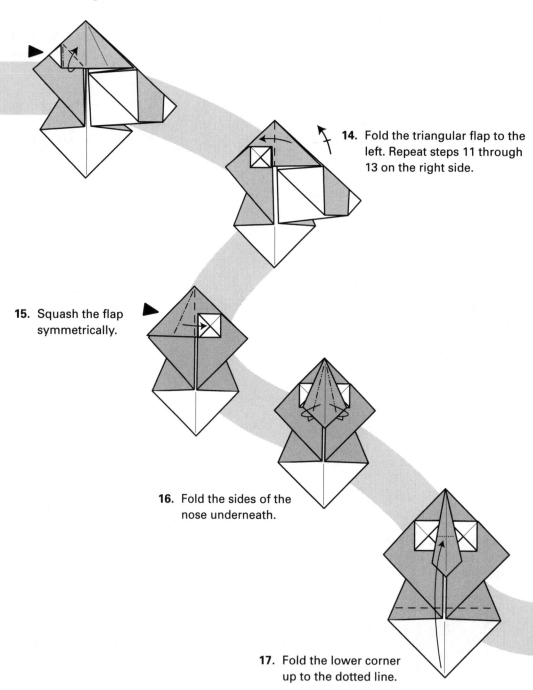

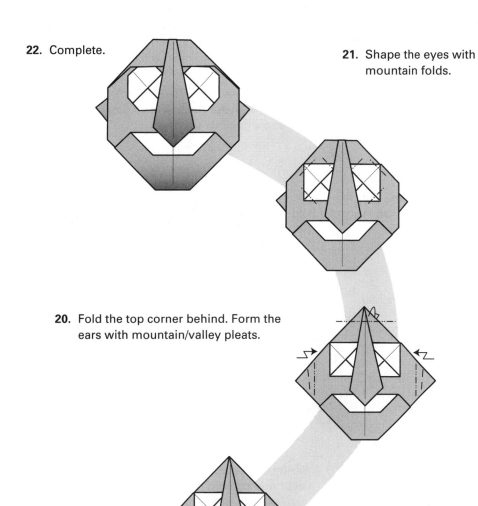

22. Complete.

21. Shape the eyes with mountain folds.

20. Fold the top corner behind. Form the ears with mountain/valley pleats.

19. Pull the nose above the mouth. Fold flaps behind and left and right.

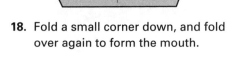

18. Fold a small corner down, and fold over again to form the mouth.

Angel Difficulty level: 5

by Neil Elias

This design dates from 1968 and shows no signs of aging. It will test your folding skills because it uses folding sequences you may not have come across elsewhere. Elias's original diagrams were minimal and only for his own benefit, so over the years, folders have had to guess at some of the moves. This is the interpretation I've been taught. Advanced folders can try adding small pleats to the wings to make them look like feathers.

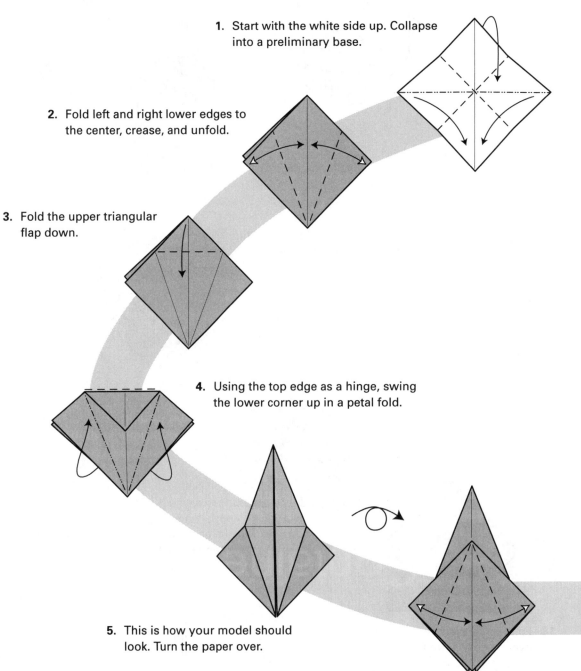

1. Start with the white side up. Collapse into a preliminary base.

2. Fold left and right lower edges to the center, crease, and unfold.

3. Fold the upper triangular flap down.

4. Using the top edge as a hinge, swing the lower corner up in a petal fold.

5. This is how your model should look. Turn the paper over.

6. Fold the upper edges of the square section to the center, crease, and unfold.

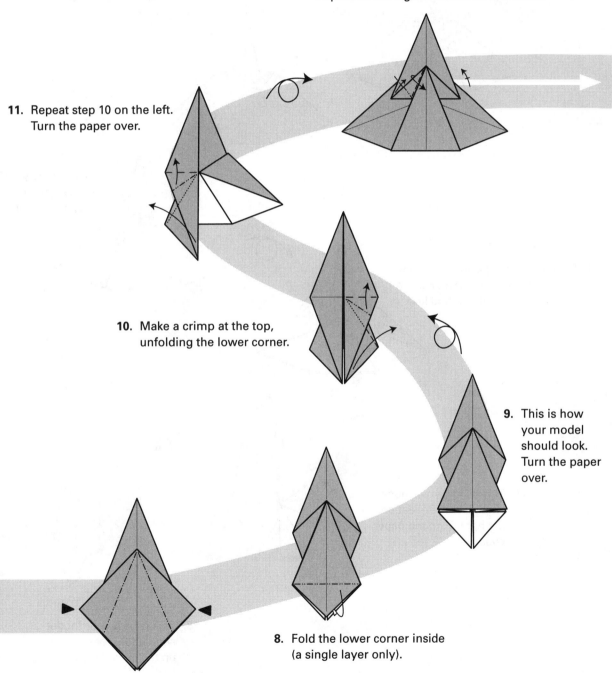

12. Fold an edge to the center, squashing the lower corner of the upper triangular section. Repeat on the right. This forms the hands.

11. Repeat step 10 on the left. Turn the paper over.

10. Make a crimp at the top, unfolding the lower corner.

9. This is how your model should look. Turn the paper over.

8. Fold the lower corner inside (a single layer only).

7. Inside reverse the sides on existing creases.

continues

continued

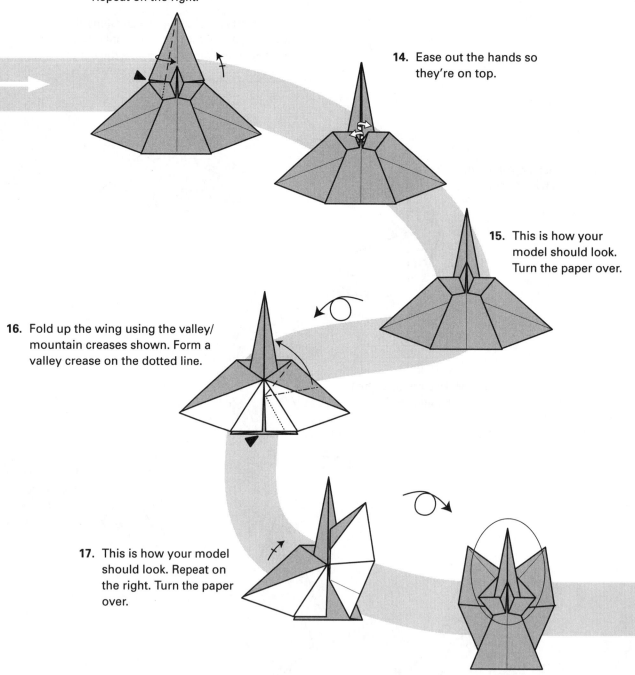

13. Fold the upper-left edge to the center, over the hands. Repeat on the right.

14. Ease out the hands so they're on top.

15. This is how your model should look. Turn the paper over.

16. Fold up the wing using the valley/mountain creases shown. Form a valley crease on the dotted line.

17. This is how your model should look. Repeat on the right. Turn the paper over.

18. This is how your model should look. Now focus on the circled area.

24. Wrap the point behind.

25. Fold the top behind firmly to hold things together.

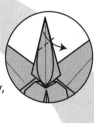

23. Form a gentle valley, keeping the head layers open.

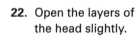

22. Open the layers of the head slightly.

26. Complete.

21. Make a small valley crease through all layers, bringing the point back up.

20. Form a small waterbomb base. Fold the top point behind.

19. Form the creases shown, pressing the sides together and down into 3D. This cleverly forms praying hands.

Chapter 6
Containers

You might think it rather dull to make a box or bowl from paper, but nothing could be further from the truth! Many paper-folders find endless fascination in discovering new ways to fold the sides of a square and "lock" them into place.

Because they're generally quite geometric in form, you should take special care to add the creases as accurately as you can. Any irregularity will be easily apparent on a symmetrical shape. Try to find paper that enhances the beauty of the paper form instead of distracting from it.

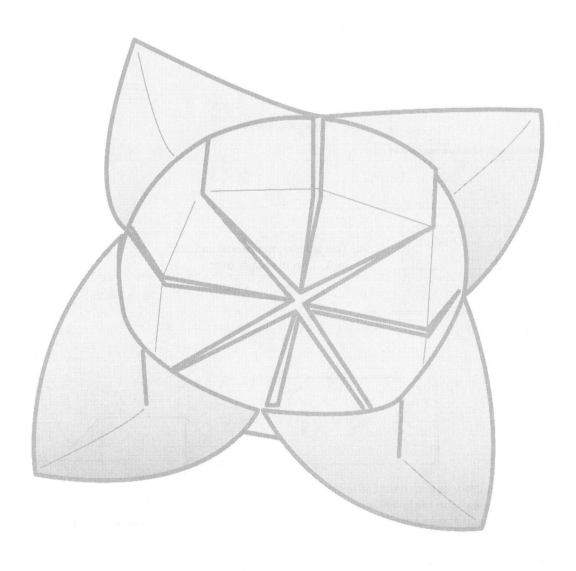

Simple Tray   Difficulty level: 1

Traditional design

This is an adaptation of a well-known simple boat model. By opening out the boat and forming two squashes on the base, it becomes a practical and attractive tray. You can vary the distance you fold in step 10, but the more you fold, the lower the sides of the tray become.

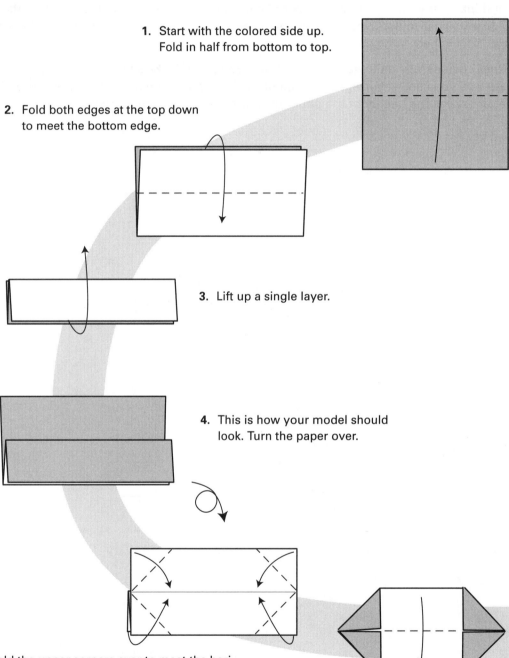

1. Start with the colored side up.
   Fold in half from bottom to top.

2. Fold both edges at the top down
   to meet the bottom edge.

3. Lift up a single layer.

4. This is how your model should
   look. Turn the paper over.

5. Fold the upper corners over to meet the horizontal center. Repeat with the lower corners,
   taking all layers over at the same time.

6. Fold in half from top to bottom.

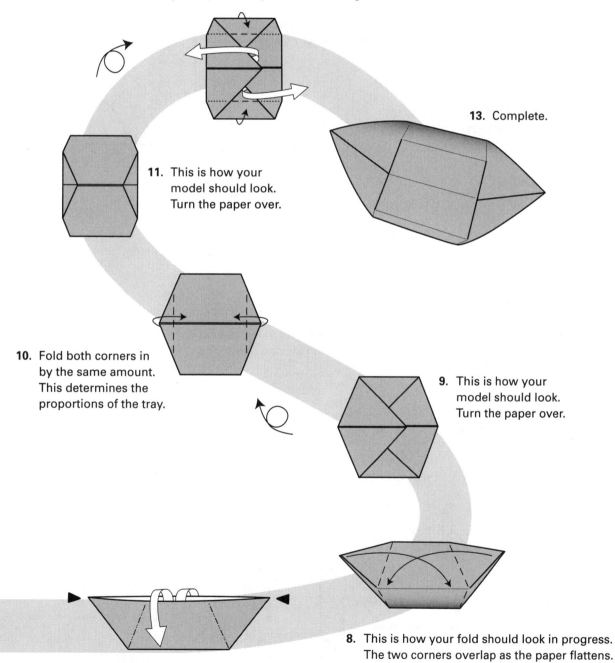

12. Open out the corners, raising the sides by forming valley creases parallel to the edges.

13. Complete.

11. This is how your model should look. Turn the paper over.

10. Fold both corners in by the same amount. This determines the proportions of the tray.

9. This is how your model should look. Turn the paper over.

8. This is how your fold should look in progress. The two corners overlap as the paper flattens.

7. Open both upper edges, and flatten them to either side. At the same time, press in the left and right corners.

Square Bowl Difficulty level: 2

Traditional design

This attractive and elegant bowl is an old, traditional design. The opening at the top matches the base, but it's rotated 45 degrees. By adjusting the final creases, you can form it into a more conventional box shape.

1. Start with the white side up. Precrease both diagonals.

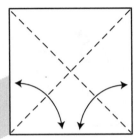

2. Fold each corner to the center, crease, and unfold.

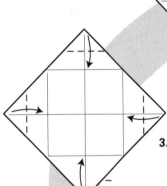

3. Fold each corner to the nearest intersection of creases.

4. Refold the flaps in on existing creases.

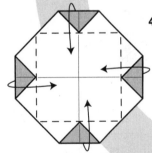

5. This is how your model should look. Turn the paper over.

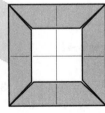

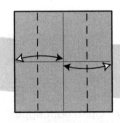

6. Fold the left and right sides to the center, crease, and unfold.

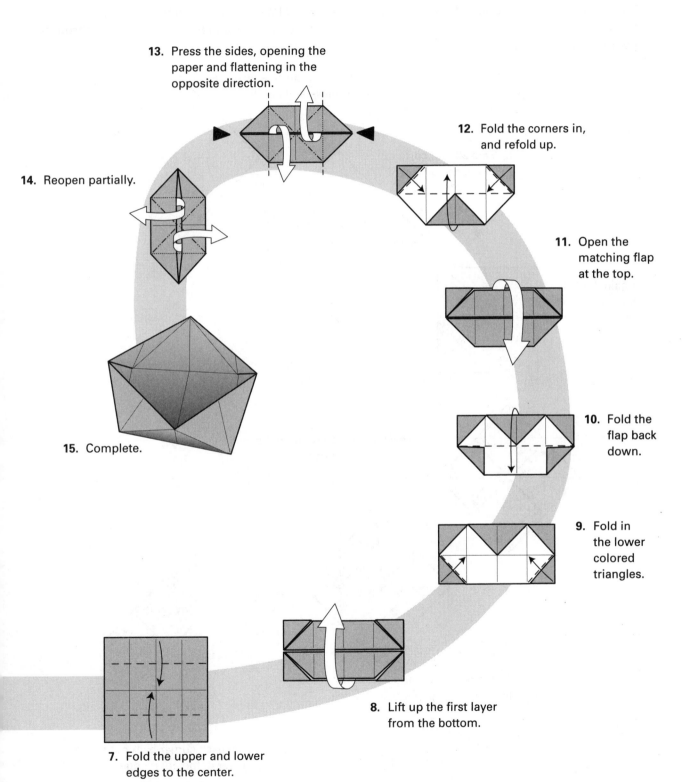

13. Press the sides, opening the paper and flattening in the opposite direction.

12. Fold the corners in, and refold up.

14. Reopen partially.

11. Open the matching flap at the top.

10. Fold the flap back down.

15. Complete.

9. Fold in the lower colored triangles.

8. Lift up the first layer from the bottom.

7. Fold the upper and lower edges to the center.

Spanish Box   Difficulty level: 2

Traditional design

This design has been around for a long time. For such a relatively simple folding sequence, the finished box looks remarkably complicated! You can make more, thinner pleats at steps 7 through 9 if your technique is up to it.

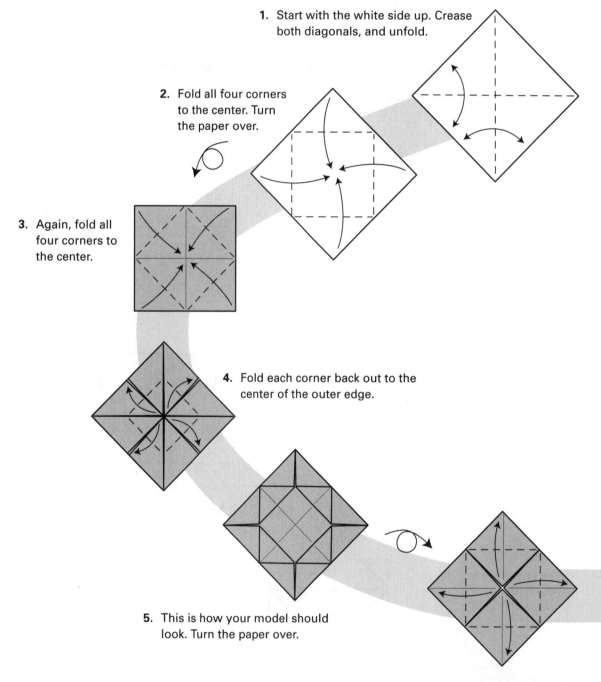

1. Start with the white side up. Crease both diagonals, and unfold.

2. Fold all four corners to the center. Turn the paper over.

3. Again, fold all four corners to the center.

4. Fold each corner back out to the center of the outer edge.

5. This is how your model should look. Turn the paper over.

6. Fold each corner back out to the center of the outer edge.

12. Complete.

11. Looking from underneath, reinforce these existing creases as you press the paper into 3D. Turn the paper over.

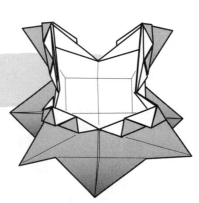

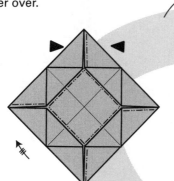

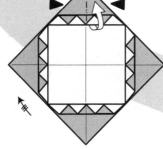

9. Make alternating mountain and valley folds to form a pleat. Repeat steps 7 through 9 on the remaining corners.

10. Lift up the center of each pleated section, and gently press the sides together into 3D. Repeat on the other three corners. Turn the paper over.

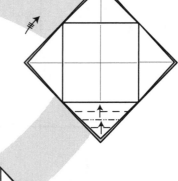

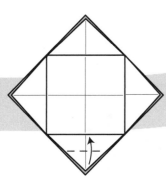

8. Fold the small colored triangular flap in half, crease, and unfold. Unfold the corner as well.

7. Fold a corner in to the center of the nearest folded edge.

Poppy Dish   Difficulty level: 3

by Nick Robinson

This dish has a beautiful central starlike crease pattern. Folded in red paper, it looks like the head of a poppy. Like all such designs, take time and care while making the initial creases. You'll be rewarded at the final stages.

1. Start with the colored side up. Add the Union Jack pattern using valley creases.

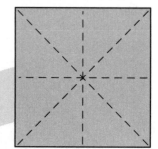

2. Fold each corner to the center, crease, and unfold. Turn the paper over.

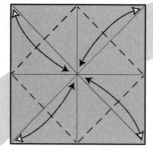

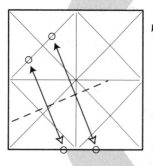

3. Fold the lower edge to the upper-left 45-degree crease, shown with circles. Crease only where shown and unfold. Repeat on the other three edges.

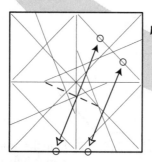

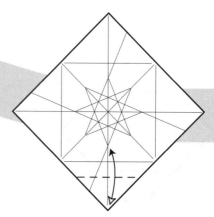

4. Make the same fold, but to the upper-right 45-degree crease. Crease only where shown and unfold. Repeat on the other three edges.

5. Fold the lower corner to the lower point of the "star" creases.

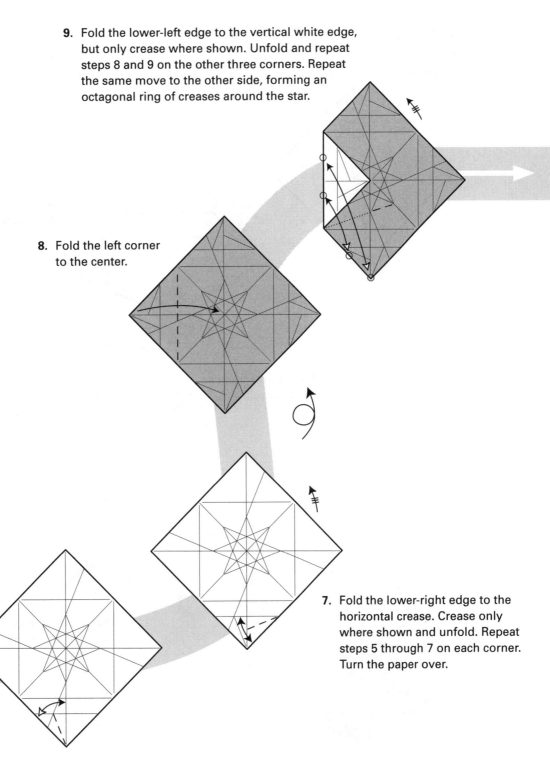

9. Fold the lower-left edge to the vertical white edge, but only crease where shown. Unfold and repeat steps 8 and 9 on the other three corners. Repeat the same move to the other side, forming an octagonal ring of creases around the star.

8. Fold the left corner to the center.

7. Fold the lower-right edge to the horizontal crease. Crease only where shown and unfold. Repeat steps 5 through 7 on each corner. Turn the paper over.

6. Fold the lower-left edge to the vertical center, creasing only as far as shown.

continues

continued

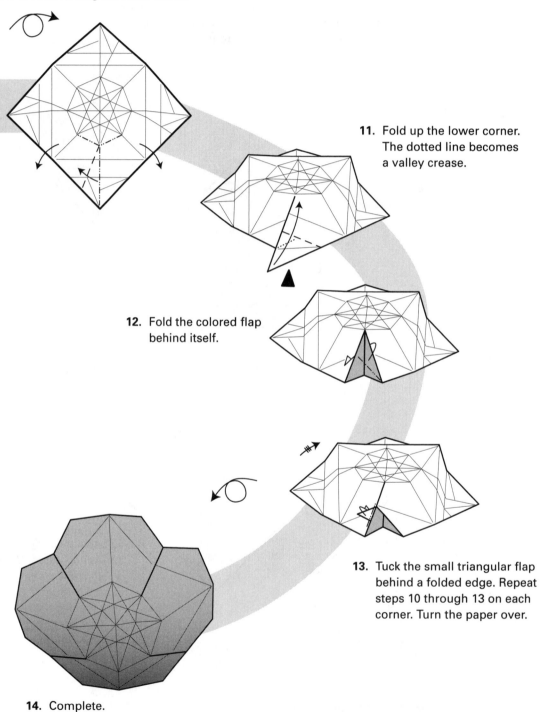

10. Turn the paper over. Form a pleat at the corner, folding the sides down.

11. Fold up the lower corner. The dotted line becomes a valley crease.

12. Fold the colored flap behind itself.

13. Tuck the small triangular flap behind a folded edge. Repeat steps 10 through 13 on each corner. Turn the paper over.

14. Complete.

Triangular Box Difficulty level: 3

by Assia Veli

You can re-create this box, designed by a creative Russian origami artist, with many variations, all of which form an attractive and practical box. Be very accurate when preparing your initial paper sizes.

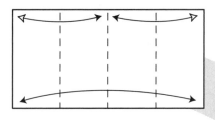

1. Start with a 2×1 rectangle, white side up. Fold in half from side to side, and add quarter creases before unfolding.

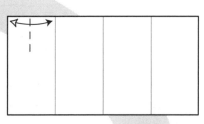

2. Fold the left edge to the quarter crease, making a light crease almost halfway down. Turn the paper over.

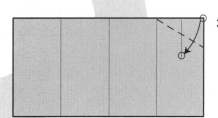

3. Starting the crease exactly at the top of the quarter crease, fold the corner down to touch the incomplete crease.

4. This is how your model should look. You have formed a 30-degree angle. Turn the paper over.

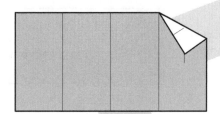

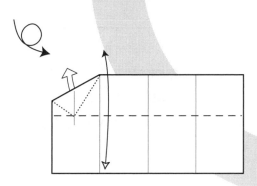

5. Make a horizontal center crease that passes through the lower corner of the hidden flap. Unfold the hidden flap.

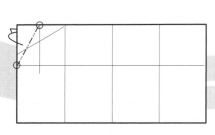

6. Fold the upper-left corner behind on a crease between the circled points.

continues

continued

12. You have formed a three-sided tube. Tighten up the paper so it fits snugly.

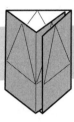

11. This is how your model should look (omitting an early location crease). Add the "missing" crease on the top right, and fold the left side around, tucking it into the pocket on the right.

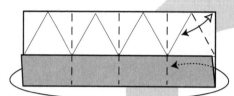

10. Unfold the paper. Using the creases you've made, repeat steps 8 through 10 on the remaining quarters.

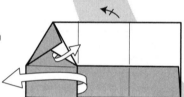

9. Fold the upper-left corner over the raw white edge.

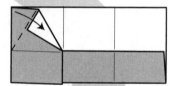

8. Fold the left side over on the quarter crease.

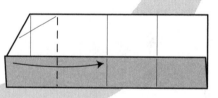

7. Fold the lower edge to meet the horizontal crease.

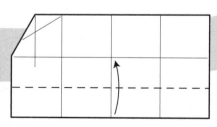

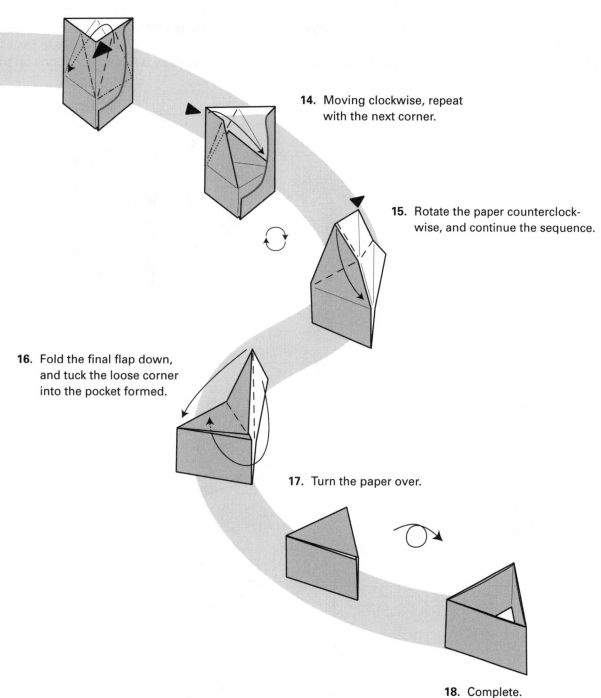

13. Ignoring the outer double layer (hidden here), press in the nearest vertical edge and partially flatten down inside.

14. Moving clockwise, repeat with the next corner.

15. Rotate the paper counterclockwise, and continue the sequence.

16. Fold the final flap down, and tuck the loose corner into the pocket formed.

17. Turn the paper over.

18. Complete.

Desk Tidy

All the elements of this desk tidy use the same folding principle as the Triangular Box, but with different heights and sizes of paper. For example, the crease pattern in diagram A shows that height H produces the basic triangular box described earlier. Doubling the distance H, as shown in diagram B, produces a box with the same profile but twice as high.

As you can see from the final diagram, the side of the base is twice as long as the side of a smaller box. Therefore, to produce the base, you need paper measuring 2×W, with a height equal to (or less than) H. Using this basic principle, you should be able to make many different variations on the theme.

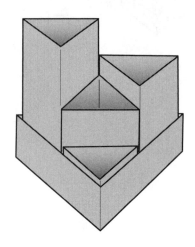

A

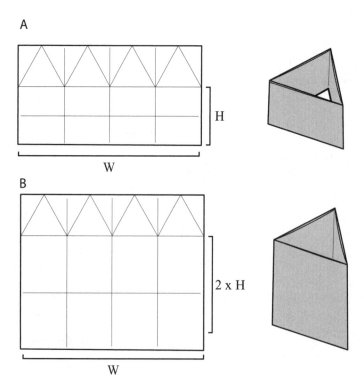

Fox Dish   Difficulty level: 3

by Nick Robinson

This dish has a square central section, but it still appears circular in form. The move in step 12 isn't obvious, but once you see it, it should prove no problem for you. The shapes at each corner are intended to represent fox heads. For your first attempt, use slightly larger paper.

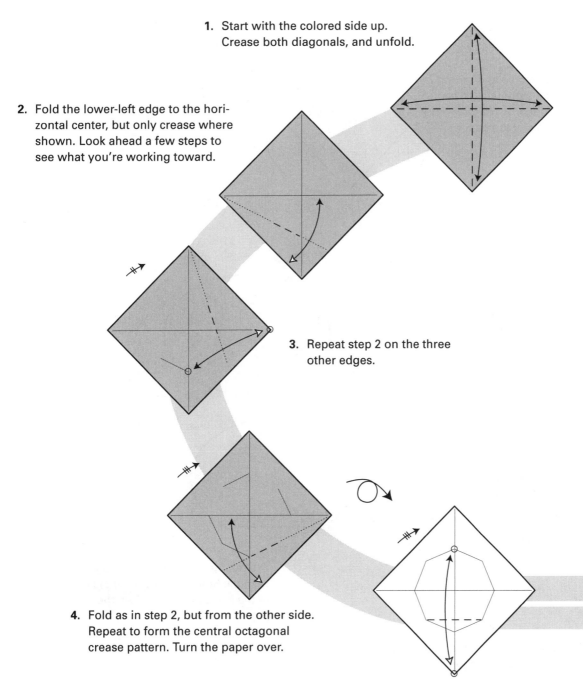

1. Start with the colored side up. Crease both diagonals, and unfold.

2. Fold the lower-left edge to the horizontal center, but only crease where shown. Look ahead a few steps to see what you're working toward.

3. Repeat step 2 on the three other edges.

4. Fold as in step 2, but from the other side. Repeat to form the central octagonal crease pattern. Turn the paper over.

5. Fold the lower corner to the opposite corner of the octagon, crease, and unfold. Repeat on each side.

continues

continued

10. Fold the outer edges to meet the most recent creases, which don't extend beyond the outer creases.

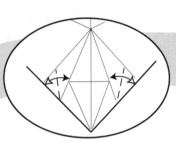

9. Reinforce and extend the mountain creases shown out to the edge of the paper.

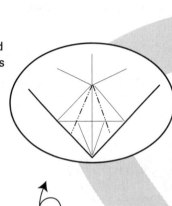

8. Fold the edges of the triangular section to the vertical center, crease, and unfold. Pull out the flap from underneath, and repeat steps 6 through 8 on each corner. Turn the paper over.

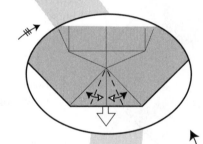

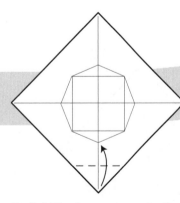

7. Fold along the edge of the colored triangle. Repeat on the other side of the same-color flap. Turn the paper over.

6. Fold the lower corner to the nearest corner of the octagon.

11. Turn the paper over. Lift up the corner, and form pleats as the paper becomes 3D. Don't flatten the paper! I recommend folding each corner to this stage before continuing.

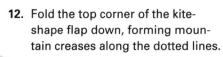

12. Fold the top corner of the kite-shape flap down, forming mountain creases along the dotted lines.

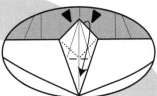

13. This is how your model should look. Tuck the colored edges behind using existing creases.

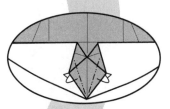

14. Lift the center area toward you, folding on a valley crease where the dotted line is. Repeat steps 11 through 14 on each corner.

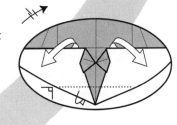

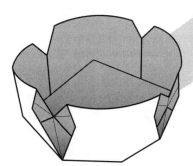

15. Complete.

Star Box   Difficulty level: 3

by Francesco Guarnieri

This design is appealing because it uses very standard geometry, yet produces a genuinely novel result. It's one of those designs that make creators think, *Why didn't I think of this?*

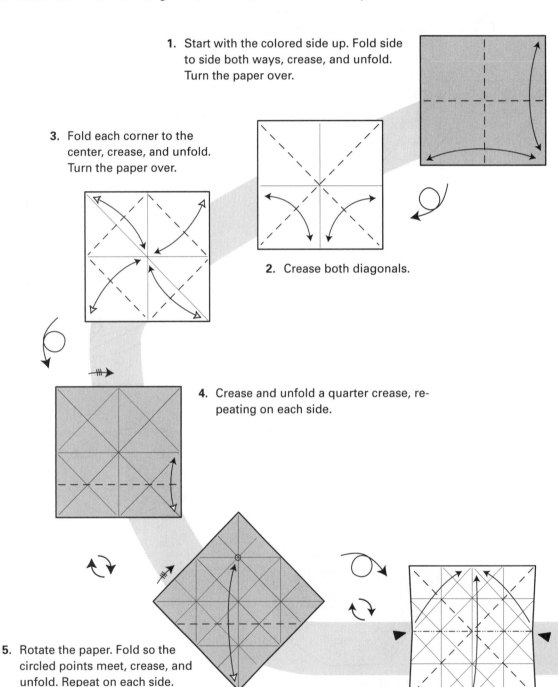

1. Start with the colored side up. Fold side to side both ways, crease, and unfold. Turn the paper over.

3. Fold each corner to the center, crease, and unfold. Turn the paper over.

2. Crease both diagonals.

4. Crease and unfold a quarter crease, repeating on each side.

5. Rotate the paper. Fold so the circled points meet, crease, and unfold. Repeat on each side. Turn the paper over.

6. Rotate and collapse the paper into an upside-down waterbomb base.

12. Make a small crease at right angles to the edge that starts at the end of the crease made in step 11.

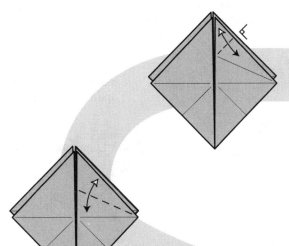

13. Fold the flap over, and tuck it into a pocket behind the layers. Repeat underneath. Repeat step 8 again as well as the move on the two remaining faces.

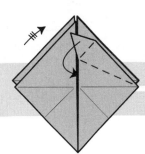

11. Fold the upper-right edge to the horizontal center, crease, and unfold.

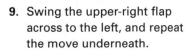

10. Make a move similar to step 8, repeating underneath.

9. Swing the upper-right flap across to the left, and repeat the move underneath.

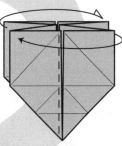

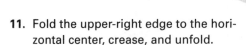

7. Fold the lower corner to the center, crease, and unfold.

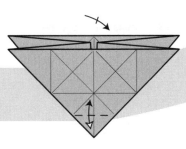

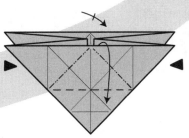

8. Fold the center of the upper edge to meet the bottom point, pressing in the sides. Repeat underneath.

continues

continued

14. Fold up the lower corner,
repeating on each face.

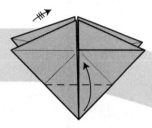

15. Gently press the triangular flap
inside. Repeat three times.

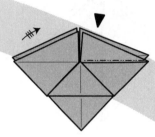

16. Place your fingers inside the model,
and ease it open into 3D. The base
opens into a square shape.

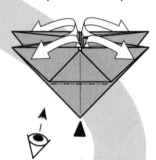

17. Fold the triangular
flaps out halfway.
Turn the paper over.

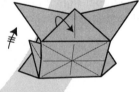

18. This is the top view.

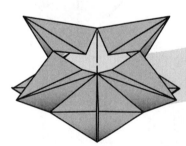

19. Complete.

Curly Box   Difficulty level: 3

Traditional design

This is a variation of the familiar *masu* box but has small petals on each corner. As a challenge, see if you can work out how to make the petals without the extra side creases. You'll have them on your model, but they're not shown in the final picture.

1. Start with the white side up. Crease both diagonals, and unfold.

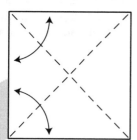

2. Fold all four corners to the center of the paper.

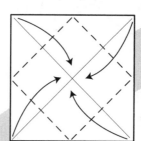

3. Fold the corners out to the center of each outside edge. Turn the paper over.

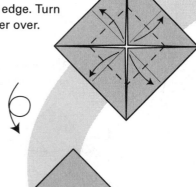

4. Fold a corner to the center.

6. Use the outer vertical creases to locate the center crease. If it helps, add diagonals in the center. (You don't need these for anything else.)

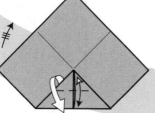

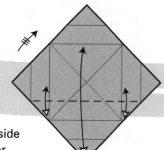

5. Fold the inside corner to the center of the outside edge, crease, and unfold. Unfold the triangular flap. Repeat on the other three corners.

continues

continued

12. Form the sides of the inner box into a circle by pressing with your thumbs and index fingers.

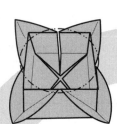

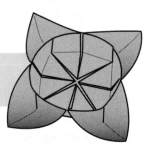

13. Complete.

11. Repeat the last three steps on the opposite side.

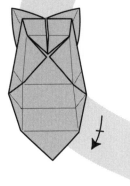

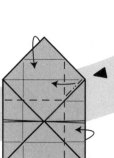

9. Repeat the last fold on the left side.

10. Fold the top corner in to the center, and crease firmly.

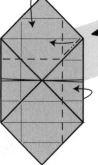

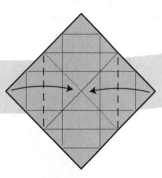

7. Fold the corners on either side to the center.

8. Lift up the right and top sides to form the corner of the box. Allow the loose flap underneath to hang out.

Lidded Box Difficulty level: 4

by Nick Robinson

This design uses a lot of center creasing, where the creases are added before the actual assembly. This enables you to fold very accurately, resulting in much more impressive results.

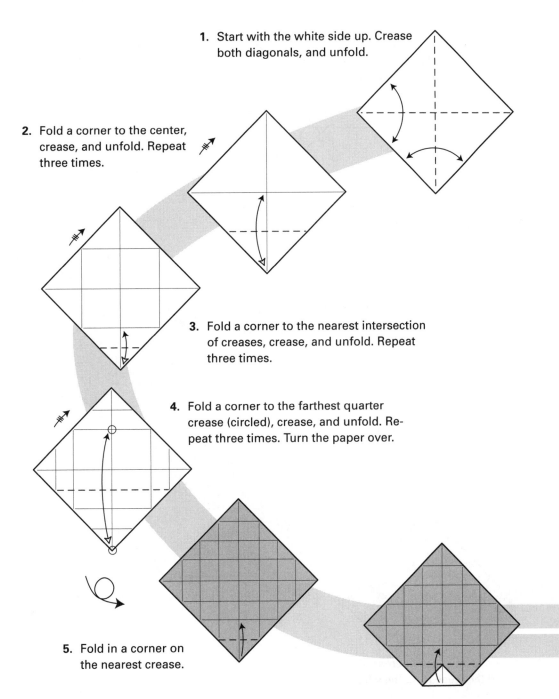

1. Start with the white side up. Crease both diagonals, and unfold.

2. Fold a corner to the center, crease, and unfold. Repeat three times.

3. Fold a corner to the nearest intersection of creases, crease, and unfold. Repeat three times.

4. Fold a corner to the farthest quarter crease (circled), crease, and unfold. Repeat three times. Turn the paper over.

5. Fold in a corner on the nearest crease.

6. Fold the same flap over again.

continues

continued

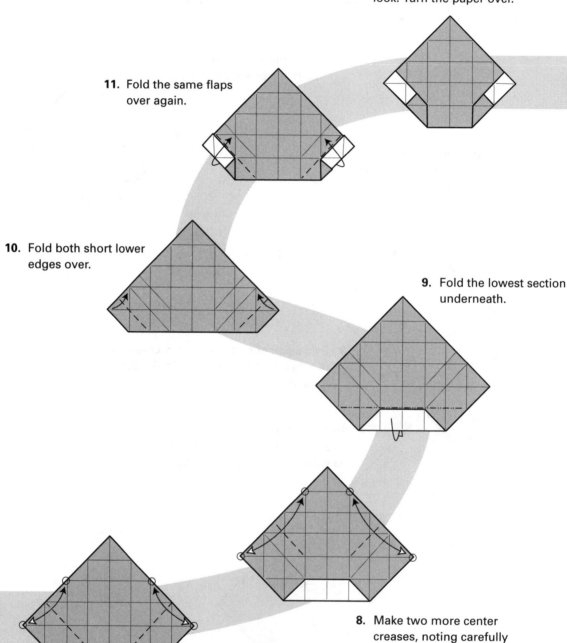

12. This is how your model should look. Turn the paper over.

11. Fold the same flaps over again.

10. Fold both short lower edges over.

9. Fold the lowest section underneath.

8. Make two more center creases, noting carefully where they should lie.

7. Make matching center creases. Don't extend the crease into the white paper.

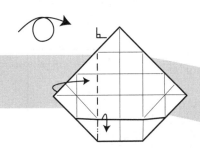

13. Turn the paper over. Pull out the lower folded edge, lifting up the right side at right angles to the paper.

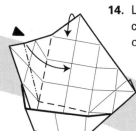

14. Lift up the top edge, folding the mountain crease over to meet it. Leave the right side of the paper as it is.

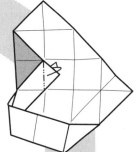

15. Fold the small triangular flap behind, and crease firmly.

20. Complete.

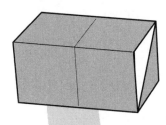

16. Repeat steps 14 and 15 on the right side.

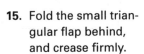

19. Tuck the flap into the pocket to close the box.

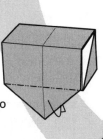

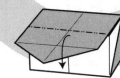

18. Fold the lid over the edge.

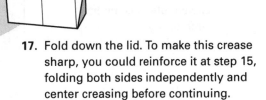

17. Fold down the lid. To make this crease sharp, you could reinforce it at step 15, folding both sides independently and center creasing before continuing.

Classic Bowl Difficulty level: 4

by Florence Temko

This is a classic design nearly 45 years old and utilizes logical creases throughout. Temko was one of the most prolific origami authors of all time and has inspired countless people to take up the hobby.

1. Start with the white side up. Center crease both diagonals.

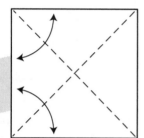

2. Fold in half, side to opposite side both ways, crease, and unfold. Turn the paper over.

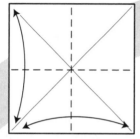

3. Fold through the center so the lower vertical crease lies along the upper-right diagonal.

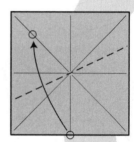

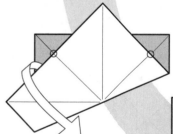

4. This is how your model should look. Note the circled reference points. Unfold.

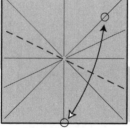

6. Now repeat on the other axis.

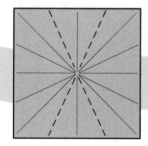

5. Repeat on the right side.

12. Using the existing creases shown, collapse the paper into an inverted triangular form.

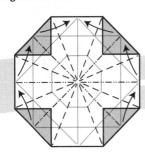

11. Fold the lower edge to the center, crease only here shown, and unfold. Repeat steps 9 through 11 seven more times.

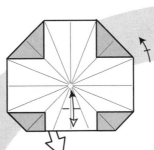

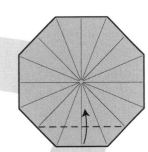

10. This is how your model should look. Turn the paper over.

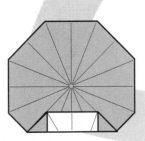

9. Fold the lower edge in between two diagonal creases.

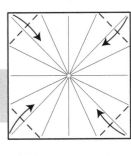

8. This is how your model should look. Turn the paper over.

7. Turn the paper over. Fold all four corners in between the most recent creases.

continues

continued

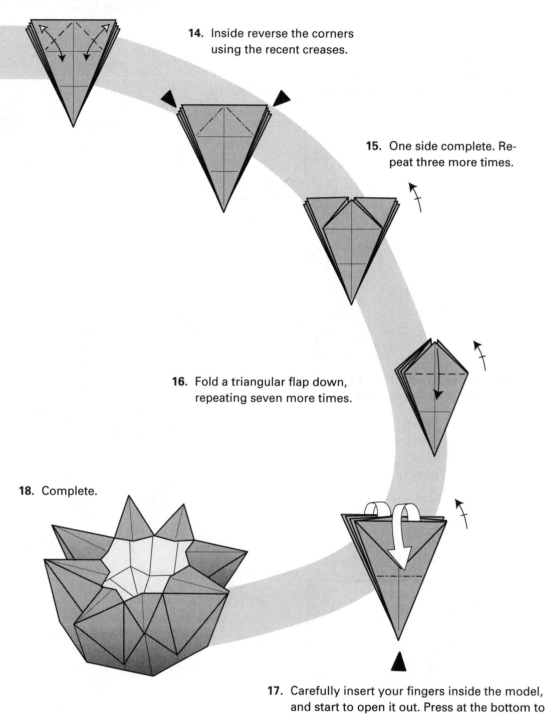

13. Fold the corners in between the top center and the ends of the horizontal crease, and unfold.

14. Inside reverse the corners using the recent creases.

15. One side complete. Repeat three more times.

16. Fold a triangular flap down, repeating seven more times.

18. Complete.

17. Carefully insert your fingers inside the model, and start to open it out. Press at the bottom to eventually form an octagonal base. Shape the model so it's symmetrical.

Bristol Box   Difficulty level: 4

by Dan Mason

Sadly, Mason died in his 20s, but he's well remembered for his inventive designs and lively personality. This model is 25 years old, but it still seems modern and stylish. Take special care to make the final corner as neat as the others.

1. Start with the white side up. Crease in half side to side both ways, and unfold.

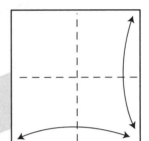

2. Fold each corner to the center, crease, and unfold.

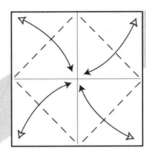

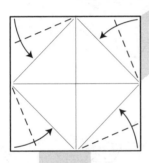

3. Fold half the length of each side to lie on the most recent creases.

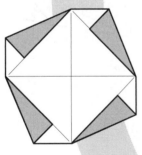

4. This is how your model should look. Turn the paper over.

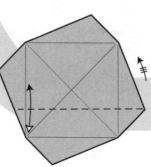

6. Wrap the sides underneath, using existing creases.

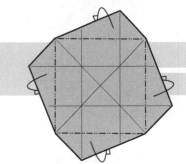

5. Be sure your paper is oriented exactly as shown. Make a horizontal valley crease that starts at the point farthest to the right. Crease, unfold, and repeat three more times.

continues

continued

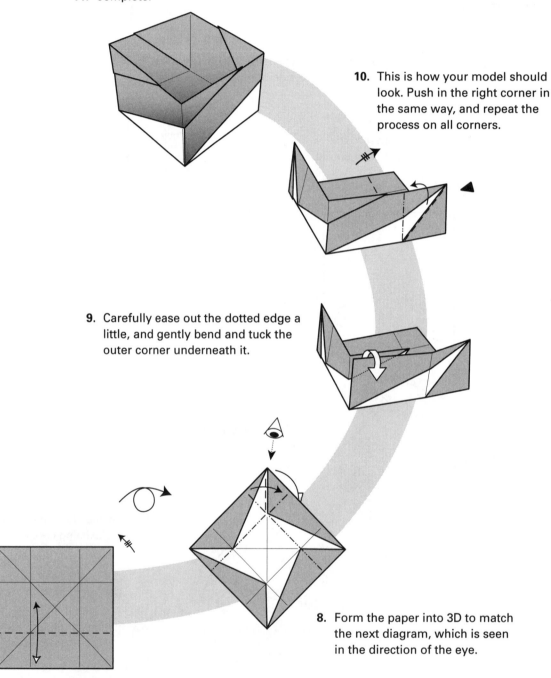

11. Complete.

10. This is how your model should look. Push in the right corner in the same way, and repeat the process on all corners.

9. Carefully ease out the dotted edge a little, and gently bend and tuck the outer corner underneath it.

8. Form the paper into 3D to match the next diagram, which is seen in the direction of the eye.

7. Reinforce this crease, passing it through the extra layers underneath. Repeat on each side. Turn the paper over.

Chapter 7
Geometric

Geometry is at the heart of all origami, yet with most subjects, you're trying to disguise it! A kitten with sharp corners and edges just wouldn't have the "cute" factor. The models in this chapter have been chosen because they emphasize rather than hide the geometry. In the following pages, you'll find puzzles, cubes, Pythagoras, even DNA!

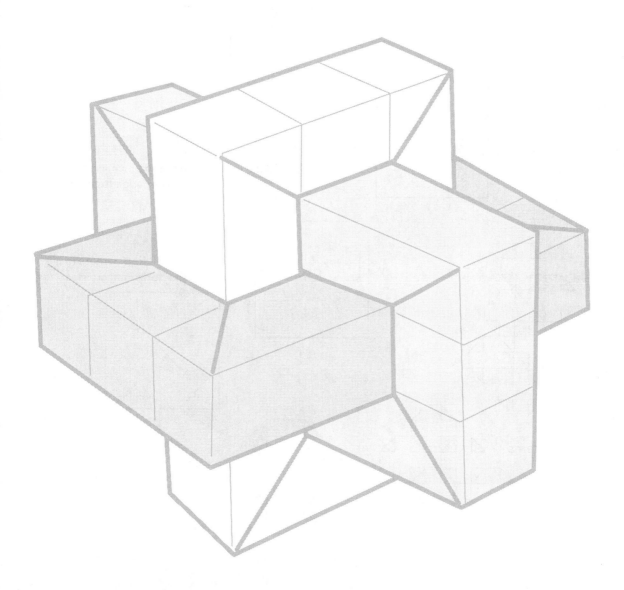

Tessellating Cross Difficulty level: 1

Traditional design

This simple design is primarily an exercise in dividing a square into thirds, but it can also form a pattern that can be tessellated, or tiled, to fill a space. The first three steps locate the point on the left side where one third of the height lies. Robert Lang discovered this elegant method using his *ReferenceFinder* origami software. To make a clean final unit (that is, one with minimal creasing), make the first cross, and have it serve as a template. Simply place it on a fresh square, and use it as a reference to fold in the corners.

1. Start with the white side up. Crease and unfold a diagonal.

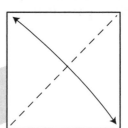

2. Fold the right edge to lie on the diagonal, crease, and unfold.

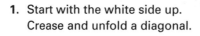

3. Fold the left edge to meet the recent crease, but make a pinch mark only at the left end of the crease. This marks one third.

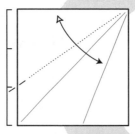

4. (A) Fold the upper edge to the pinch, crease, and unfold. (B) Fold the lower edge to the recent crease, and unfold.

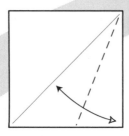

5. Fold in all four corners to lie on the horizontal creases.

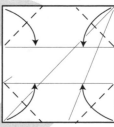

Some possible tessellated patterns are shown.

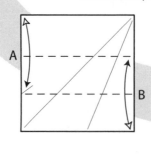

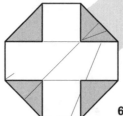

6. Complete.

Squared Square   Difficulty level: 2

by Robert Neale

This simple design celebrates the square by creating one within another. You can also use this design to form a Squared Square Cube (see Chapter 8). This design encompasses another design with it—a butterfly by Thoki Yenn. In origami, many creative minds find similar paths.

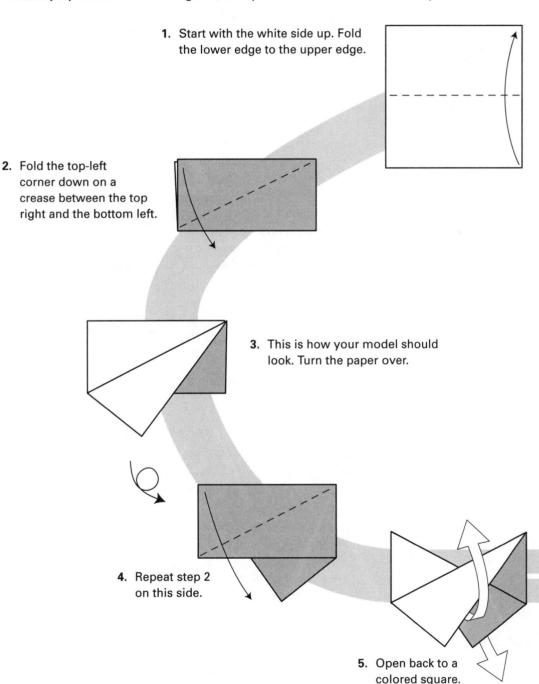

1. Start with the white side up. Fold the lower edge to the upper edge.

2. Fold the top-left corner down on a crease between the top right and the bottom left.

3. This is how your model should look. Turn the paper over.

4. Repeat step 2 on this side.

5. Open back to a colored square.

continues

continued

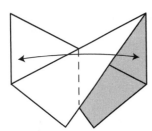

If you stop the folding at the start
of step 5 and add a vertical crease
instead, you have a butterfly!

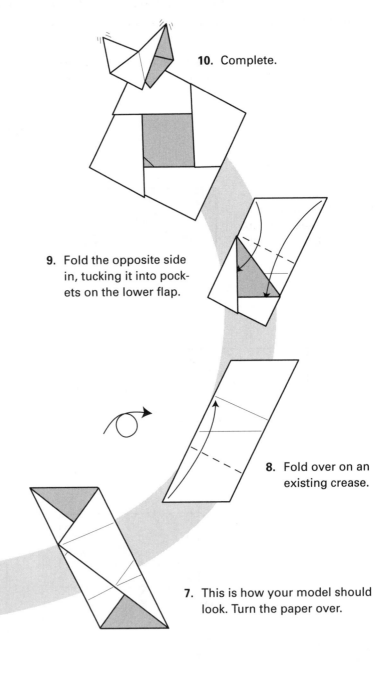

10. Complete.

9. Fold the opposite side
in, tucking it into pock-
ets on the lower flap.

8. Fold over on an
existing crease.

7. This is how your model should
look. Turn the paper over.

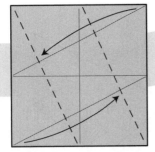

6. Fold the opposite sides in
on existing creases.

Proving Pythagoras Difficulty level: 2

by Mick Guy

This clever design creates modules you can combine to produce a visual representation of the famous Pythagorean theorem: the sum of the areas of the two squares on the shorter sides equals the area of the square on the hypotenuse. It requires some work and patience, but the assembled result is worthy of framing and displaying!

Module 1A

This requires 6.5-inch/16.8cm squares:

1. Start with a square divided into five both ways (see the Tent in Chapter 10). Make an incomplete crease by folding between the two circled points.

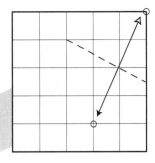

3. Fold in opposite corners to the corners of the central section.

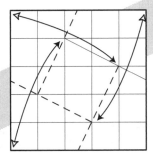

2. Repeat step 1 on the other three sides.

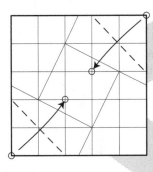

4. Fold the lower-right corner behind, and fold the upper and lower sections behind.

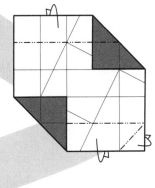

5. Precrease, and inside reverse the top-left corner.

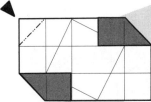

6. Fold in twice using existing creases.

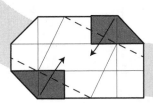

7. Fold over on an existing crease.

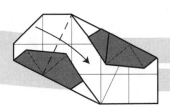

continues

continued

8. Fold over on an existing crease,
   tucking the flap under a loose layer.

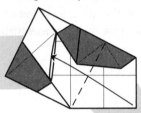

9. Tuck the loose trian-
   gular point under the
   layer beneath it.

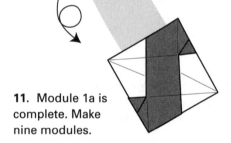

10. This is how your
    model should look.
    Turn the paper over.

11. Module 1a is
    complete. Make
    nine modules.

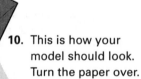

Module 1B

This requires 3-inch/7.5cm squares:

1. Start with a square, white side up.
   Pinch the midpoints on either side.

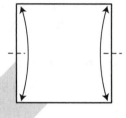

2. Fold the top-left corner
   down on a crease between
   the top-right corner and
   the left midpoint.

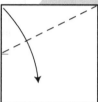

3. Repeat with the
   lower-right corner.

4. This is how your
   model should look.
   Turn the paper over.

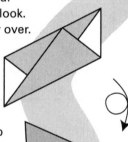

5. Module 1b
   is complete.

6. Complete Module 1 by sliding
   Module 1b inside Module 1a.

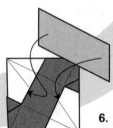

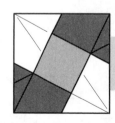

7. Module 1 is complete.
   Make nine modules.

Module 2

This requires 6-inch/15cm squares:

1. Start with the white side up. Crease in half from side to side. Fold in half up.

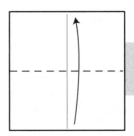

2. Make a crease between the top-right and bottom-left corners on the upper layer only. Unfold and repeat this move three times. Turn the paper over.

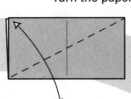

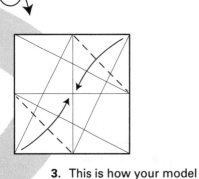

3. This is how your model should look. Fold opposite corners to the center.

4. Fold opposite corners behind on existing creases.

5. This is how your model should look. Turn the paper over.

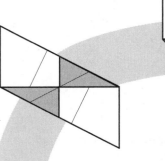

6. Fold over on an existing crease.

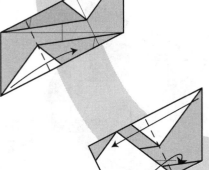

7. Fold over on an existing crease, tucking the white corner into a small pocket.

8. Tuck the remaining white corner into a small pocket. Turn the paper over.

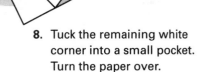

9. Here is the completed Module 2. Make nine modules.

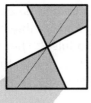

Module 3

This requires 3-inch/7.5cm squares:

1. Begin at the start of step 3 of Module 2. Fold in one corner.

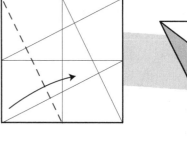

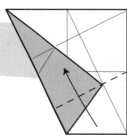

2. Fold in the next corner.

3. Guess what? Fold in the next corner!

6. Module 3 is complete. Make nine modules, four of one color and five of another.

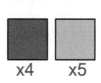

x4   x5

4. Fold in the final corner, tucking the first layer of the bottom-left corner into a small pocket.

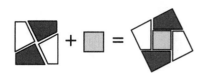

5. This is how your model should look. Turn the paper over.

The Proof

By now, you should be able to see how rearranging and combining Modules 1 and 3 produces Module 2. Therefore, the area of the larger square is, in fact, the sum of the areas of the smaller squares, or $A^2 + B^2 = C^2$!

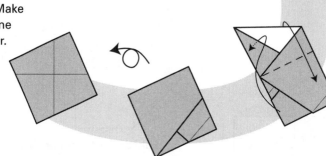

Flexagon Difficulty level: 2

by Arthur Stone

Flexagons were first created in 1939 and have fascinated folders ever since. This variation is a tri-hexaflexagon—a six-sided shape with three faces. Origami purists balk at cutting and gluing, but that's easily forgiven when you play with this finished model. The final diagram shows how you could use colors (or shading) instead of numbers. For some extra fun, check out *Foto-TriHexaFlexagon,* a free software program that enables you to divide and print three photographs on the initial strip.

1. Start with a strip of paper at least 7×1. Precrease in half at the left end. The crease should be about as long as the strip is high.

2. Starting the crease at the top left, fold the lower-left corner to lie on the halfway crease.

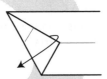

3. This is how your model should look. Unfold.

5. Fold the upper edge to meet the most recent crease, and unfold. Continue to the end of the strip.

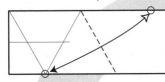

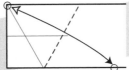

4. Fold the left side over so the recent crease lies along the lower edge. Crease and unfold.

6. Cut off the ends to leave two sets of five equilateral triangles on both sides.

8. Fold the strip down on the fourth crease from the top. Tuck the strip under the lower section.

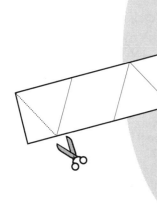

7. Fold the strip up on the third crease from the left.

continues

continued

15. A third side is revealed!

14. When the paper is flat, carefully ease open layers at the top.

13. This is how your fold should look in progress.

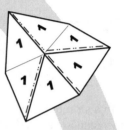

16. Write the number 3 on each of the triangles.

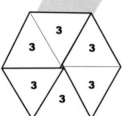

12. Form three mountain creases and one valley crease, and collapse the paper flat.

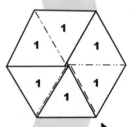

11. Turn the paper over, and write the number 1 on each of the triangles.

9. Fold the small triangle on the lower left back over the upper layer, and (*gasp!*) glue together the shaded areas.

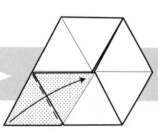

10. This is how your completed model should look. Write the number 2 on each of the triangles.

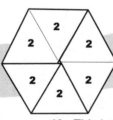

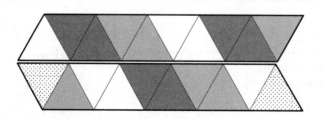

Tower Difficulty level: 2

Traditional design

This regular origami crease pattern reveals interesting 3D shapes when formed into a tower. With the following directions, you make a four-sided tower, but you can easily experiment with other configurations and heights.

1. Start with a square divided each way into 5 (see the Tent in Chapter 10). Fold upper and lower sections in. Turn the paper over.

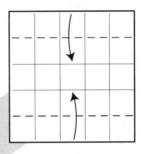

2. Following the patterns shown, add diagonal creases across the whole sheet, in both directions.

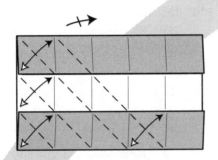

3. This is the result. Turn the paper over.

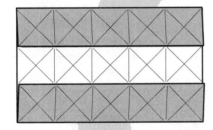

5. Add these precreases.

4. Reinforce these creases.

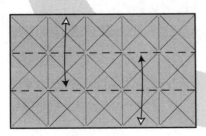

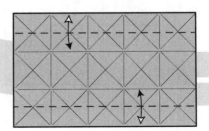

continues

continued

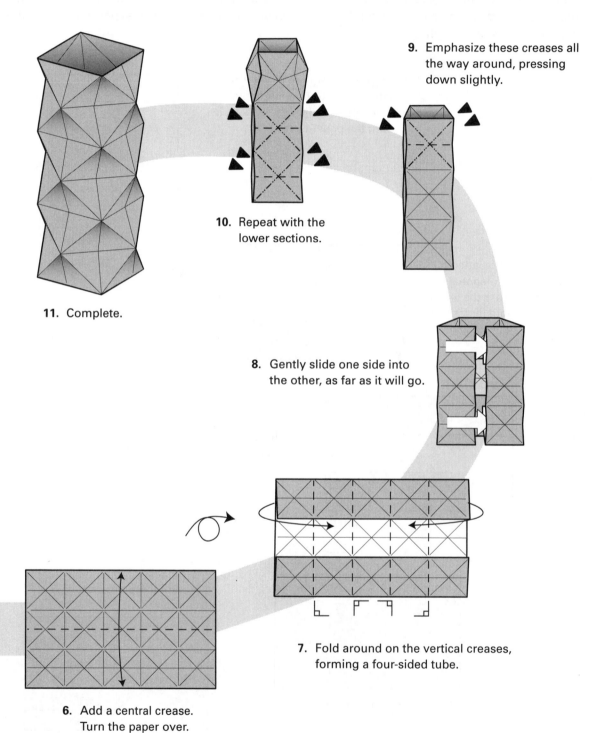

9. Emphasize these creases all the way around, pressing down slightly.

10. Repeat with the lower sections.

11. Complete.

8. Gently slide one side into the other, as far as it will go.

7. Fold around on the vertical creases, forming a four-sided tube.

6. Add a central crease. Turn the paper over.

8-Point Star   Difficulty level: 3

by Wayne Brown

To fold this model, you need to do some precise locating of the crease you make in step 4. This is another model that looks better clean, without any extra creases. I recommend you first fold a template, and use the template to create clean final pieces.

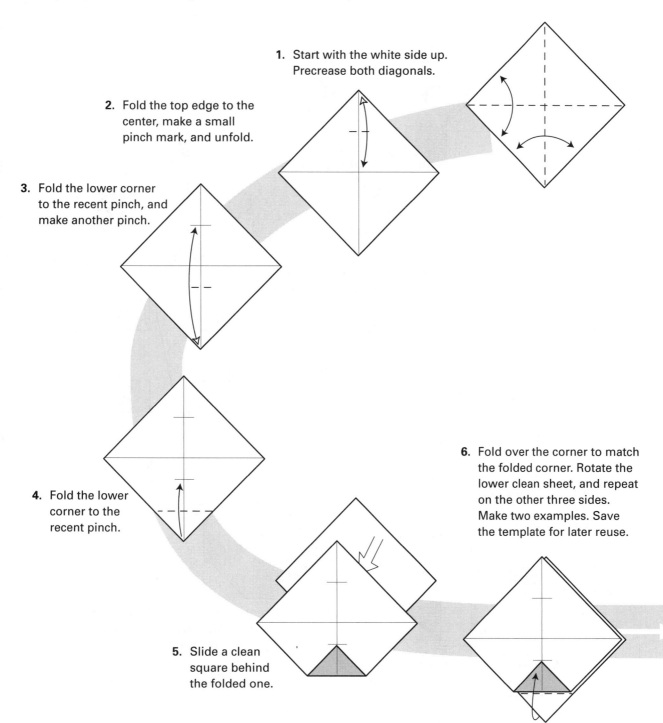

1. Start with the white side up. Precrease both diagonals.

2. Fold the top edge to the center, make a small pinch mark, and unfold.

3. Fold the lower corner to the recent pinch, and make another pinch.

4. Fold the lower corner to the recent pinch.

5. Slide a clean square behind the folded one.

6. Fold over the corner to match the folded corner. Rotate the lower clean sheet, and repeat on the other three sides. Make two examples. Save the template for later reuse.

continues

continued

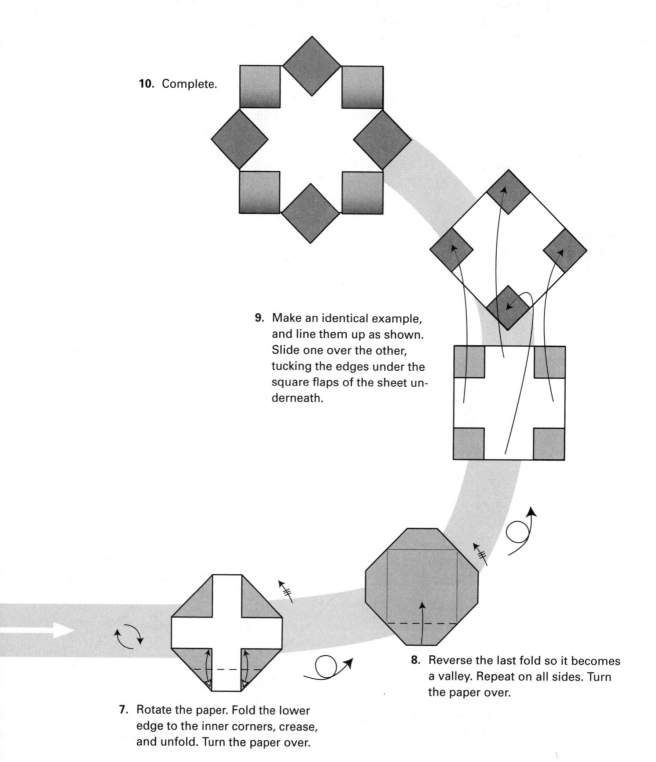

10. Complete.

9. Make an identical example, and line them up as shown. Slide one over the other, tucking the edges under the square flaps of the sheet underneath.

8. Reverse the last fold so it becomes a valley. Repeat on all sides. Turn the paper over.

7. Rotate the paper. Fold the lower edge to the inner corners, crease, and unfold. Turn the paper over.

Tri-Puzzle Difficulty level: 3

by David Petty

This origami puzzle produces four shapes, three of which are different. The idea is to combine the shapes to form an equilateral triangle as well as a square. This design is based on a wooden version produced by Henry Dudeney in 1907. (Find the solution to the puzzle on the last page of this chapter.)

Module 1

1. Start with the white side up, precreased into quarters in both directions. Fold the top-left corner to the center.

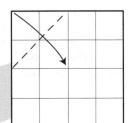

2. Fold so the circled points meet crease where shown, and unfold.

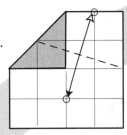

3. Make a similar move using the left edge.

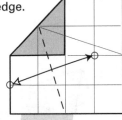

4. Fold the lower edge to the angled crease, and unfold.

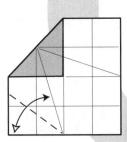

5. Fold down on an existing crease.

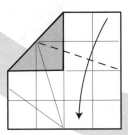

6. Make a crease between the circled corners.

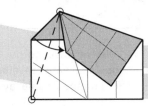

continues

continued

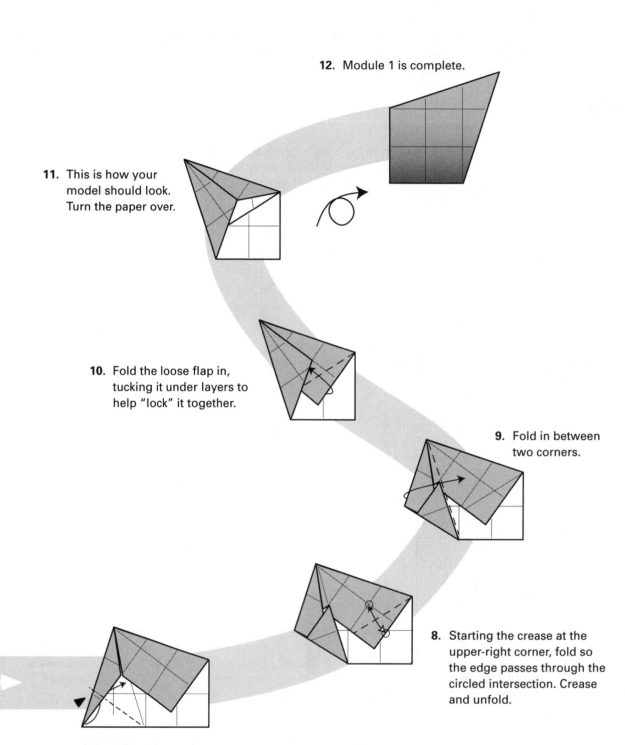

12. Module 1 is complete.

11. This is how your model should look. Turn the paper over.

10. Fold the loose flap in, tucking it under layers to help "lock" it together.

9. Fold in between two corners.

8. Starting the crease at the upper-right corner, fold so the edge passes through the circled intersection. Crease and unfold.

7. Fold the lower corner in, making a small reverse fold on the double layer.

Module 2

1. Start with the white side up, precreased into quarters in both directions. Fold up the lower quarter.

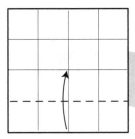

2. Fold the upper corners in between the circled points. Crease and unfold both.

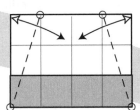

3. Fold the upper corners to lie along the angled creases. Tuck in the lower colored corners.

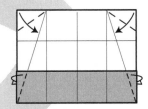

5. Fold in half from left to right.

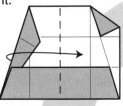

4. Fold in the left edge, tucking it under the lower flap.

6. Precrease, and inside reverse the top-left corner.

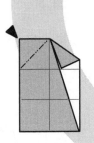

8. Module 2 is complete. Make two modules.

7. Tuck the right edge into a pocket directly underneath the top layer and above any inner layers.

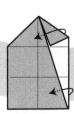

Module 3

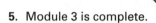

5. Module 3 is complete.

4. Fold on a diagonal,
   interlocking the layers
   to lock it together.

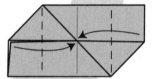

3. Fold the left and right
   edges to the center.

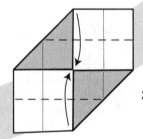

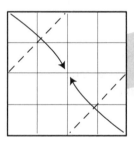

2. Fold the upper and lower
   edges to the center.

1. Start with the white side up, precreased
   into quarters in both directions. Fold the
   opposite corners to the center.

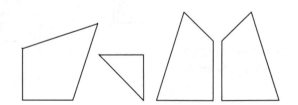

Now see if you can figure out how the four pieces fit together. The solution is on the last page of the chapter when you're ready to check your results.

Pinwheel Tato   Difficulty level: 3

Traditional design

A *tato* is a traditional Japanese patterned design. Here, you use an origami base, known as the windmill, to form the pattern in the center. If you feel like experimenting, you can make the flat tato into a 3D design.

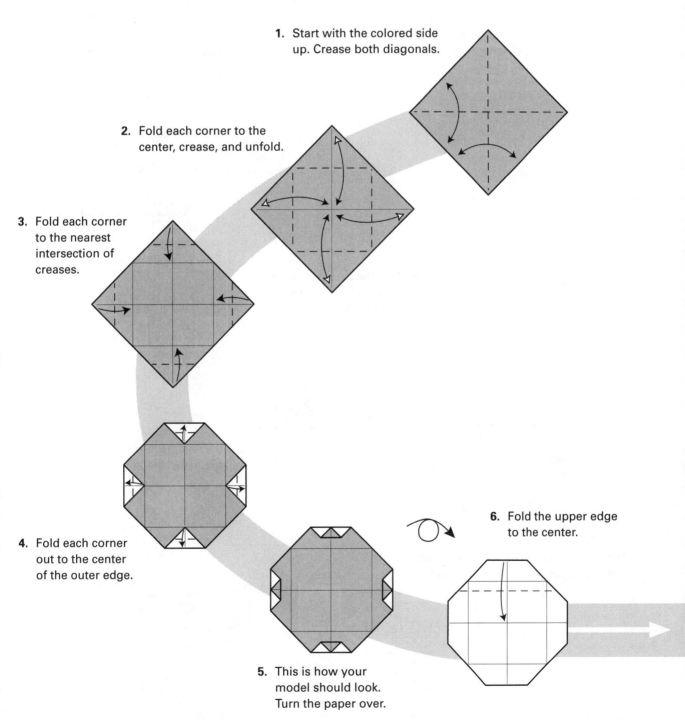

1. Start with the colored side up. Crease both diagonals.

2. Fold each corner to the center, crease, and unfold.

3. Fold each corner to the nearest intersection of creases.

4. Fold each corner out to the center of the outer edge.

5. This is how your model should look. Turn the paper over.

6. Fold the upper edge to the center.

continues

continued

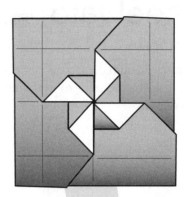

11. Complete.

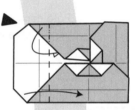

10. Fold the lower half in as before, and tuck the upper half underneath.

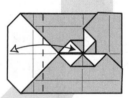

9. Fold the left edge to the center, crease firmly, and unfold.

7. Fold the right edge to the vertical center.

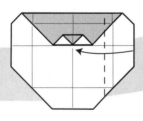

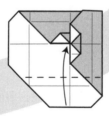

8. Now fold the lower edge to the center.

If you add these creases underneath each edge, you can form the tato into 3D.

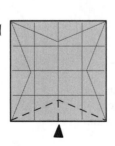

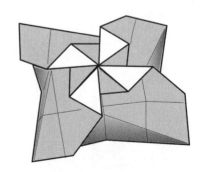

Cross Puzzle   Difficulty level: 3

by David Petty

This is an origami version of a dissection puzzle. The idea is to make four identical units, and assemble them to produce a cross and then a square. The most efficient way is to divide the model into thirds (see the technique used in the Reverse Pinwheel in Chapter 10), and divide each third in half. The slightly quicker and easier method is to divide a square into eighths each way, and cut off two eighths in each direction. That's the method used here. (Find the solution to the puzzle on the last page of this chapter.)

1. Start with a 6×6 grid on a square of paper, white side up.

2. Fold in half from right to left.

3. Fold the lower-right corner in to the first intersection of creases, and unfold.

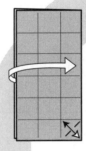

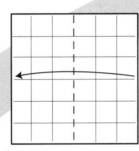

4. Fold up the lowest section.

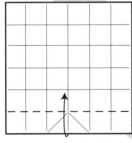

5. Make a pleat at the top.

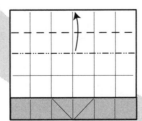

6. Fold in both upper corners (all layers) to the first creases, and unfold.

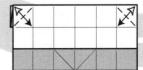

continues

continued

12. Rearrange the layers in the lower-
left corner so the layer currently
underneath moves on top.

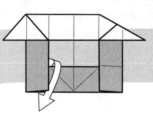

11. Fold up the lower half
of the white section.

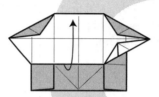

10. Fold over three corners
on diagonal creases
within 2×1 sections.

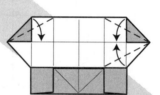

9. Fold in the top two corners to the first creases.

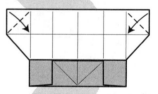

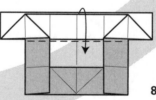

8. Fold down the
top section.

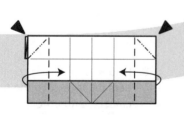

7. Fold in the left and right
sides, squashing the top
corners into triangles.

13. Start to fold the left side to the right. At the same time, pull the lower-left flap down.

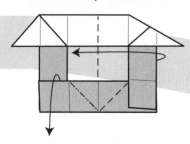

14. This is how your fold should look in progress.

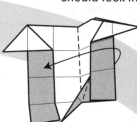

19. Complete. Make three more.

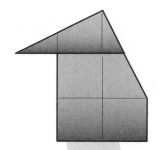

15. Make a valley crease between the opposite corners of the upper-right 2×1 section.

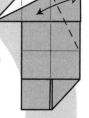

16. Inside reverse the same section.

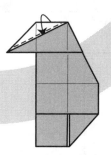

18. Fold the lower section in to close that end as well.

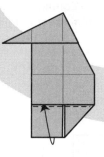

17. Tuck the top section into a pocket to lock it closed.

Now see if you can figure out how the pieces fit together. The solution is on the last page of the chapter when you're ready to check your results.

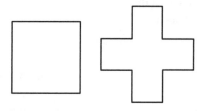

Classic Cube Difficulty level: 3

by Shuzo Fujimoto

Many of the world's leading origami designers and folders consider this model an absolute classic. It has perfect use of the paper (nothing's wasted), and the sequence is elegant and satisfying. To the unenlightened, it may be "just a cube," but it represents far more than that.

1. Start with a square, white side up. Fold in half from top to bottom.

2. Crease in half from side to side.

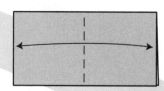

3. Add quarter creases.

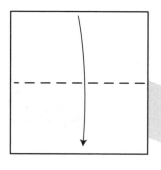

4. Fold in half from top to bottom, through both layers. Unfold.

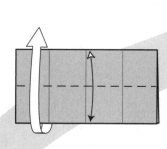

5. Add a diagonal valley in each of the bottom sections.

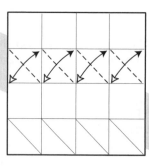

6. Add similar creases in the upper-middle sections. Turn the paper over.

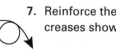

7. Reinforce the parts of the creases shown as valley folds.

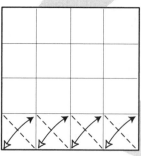

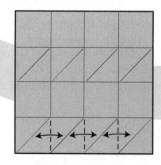

13. This is how your model should look.

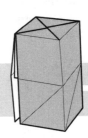

12. When you have achieved this shape, bring the layer out from behind the white section.

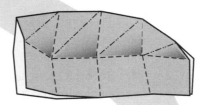

11. This is how your model should look in progress. What was the upper-right corner in step 9 tucks behind the white section facing you.

10. Note the creases you need to encourage your model into position.

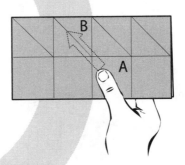

8. Turn the paper over. Fold in half from top to bottom.

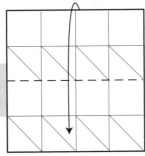

9. Hold the paper in the air. Your aim is to slide section A of the colored layer so it overlaps section B of the layer underneath. If you've creased carefully, this should happen quite easily.

continues

continued

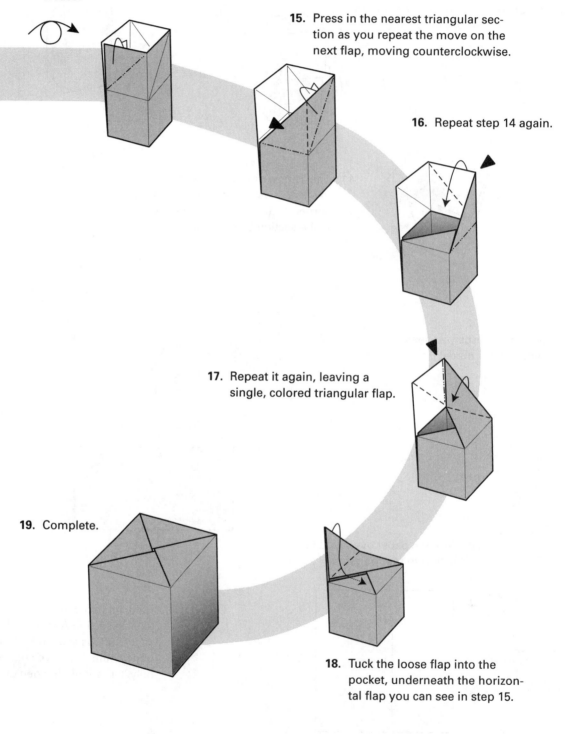

14. Turn the paper over. Fold the loose colored corner inside on an existing crease.

15. Press in the nearest triangular section as you repeat the move on the next flap, moving counterclockwise.

16. Repeat step 14 again.

17. Repeat it again, leaving a single, colored triangular flap.

19. Complete.

18. Tuck the loose flap into the pocket, underneath the horizontal flap you can see in step 15.

Double Cube   Difficulty level: 3

by Nick Robinson

This design, created in 1985, uses a technique known as the twist. Originally developed in the 1970s by Shuzo Fujimoto, the technique is now a central method of many origami designs. The two pieces slot into each other and hold their place due to the tension in the paper.

1. Start with the colored side up. Precrease in half both ways.

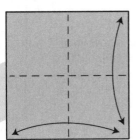

2. Add quarter creases at the top and bottom.

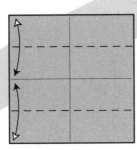

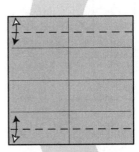

3. Add the outer eighth creases.

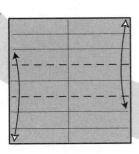

4. Add the inner eighth creases. Repeat steps 2 through 4 on the other side of the square.

5. Fold so the circled points meet, crease, and unfold. Repeat on each corner.

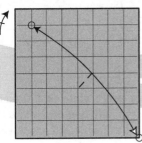

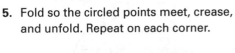

continues

continued

11. Reinforce these creases.

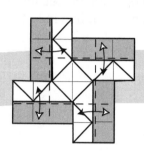

10. This is how your model should look. Repeat three times.

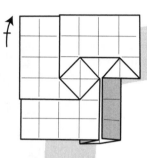

9. Fold the edge in, squashing the corner.

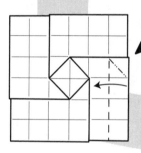

8. Fold over the corner, crease, and unfold. Repeat three times.

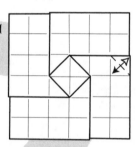

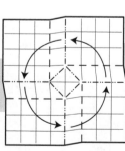

7. This is how your move should look in progress.

6. Turn to the white side. Crease as shown, and begin to rotate the center of the paper counterclockwise.

12. Turn the paper over. Reinforce these creases. Turn the paper over again.

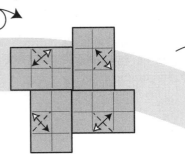

13. Fold up two sides, forming a 3D corner.

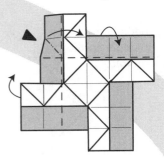

14. Pull out the layer from behind to hold the corner in place.

17. Complete.

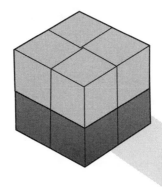

15. This is how your model should look. Repeat three times.

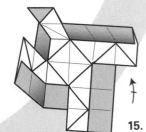

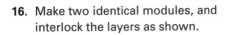

16. Make two identical modules, and interlock the layers as shown.

Tri-Coaster   Difficulty level: 4

by Nick Robinson

This design produces a simple triangular coaster, but in folding terms, it requires much accuracy and control, so it's a valuable benchmark for your developing abilities! Use a finger to hold the layers in place toward the end.

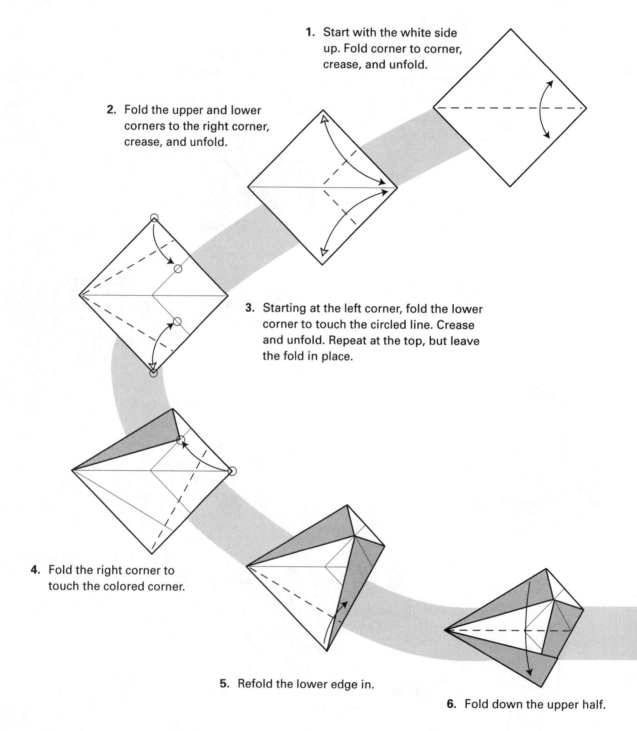

1. Start with the white side up. Fold corner to corner, crease, and unfold.

2. Fold the upper and lower corners to the right corner, crease, and unfold.

3. Starting at the left corner, fold the lower corner to touch the circled line. Crease and unfold. Repeat at the top, but leave the fold in place.

4. Fold the right corner to touch the colored corner.

5. Refold the lower edge in.

6. Fold down the upper half.

13. Continue to hold the layers in place at the circled area, and ease out the lowest layer on the right so it becomes the top layer.

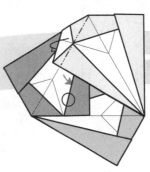

12. Slide in the next unit, holding the lower units firmly at the circled area.

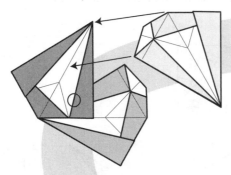

11. Tuck the small flap underneath the left end of the underside colored flap.

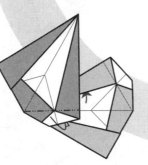

10. Slide one unit over the next.

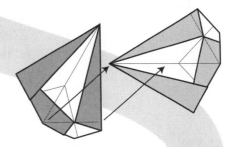

9. The unit is complete. Make two more, of contrasting colors or patterns.

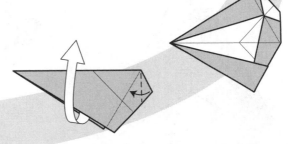

8. Fold the same short edge to the recent crease. Unfold the first layer up.

7. Fold the short edge over to the long colored edge, crease, and unfold.

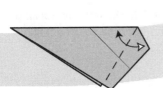

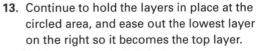

continues

continued

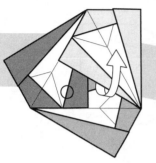

14. Move the holding point slightly more central. Fold the small flap underneath.

15. Fold up the lower flap.

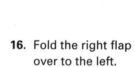

16. Fold the right flap over to the left.

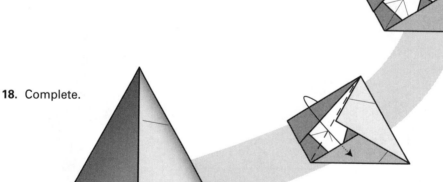

18. Complete.

17. Fold in the left flap, tucking it under the colored flap.

DNA Strand   Difficulty level: 5

by Thoki Yenn

Thoki was a magical folder from Denmark who loved mathematical puzzles and magic. This design looks very complex, but, in fact, it only requires fairly straightforward (and accurate!) creasing. Try to find crisp paper that holds creases well.

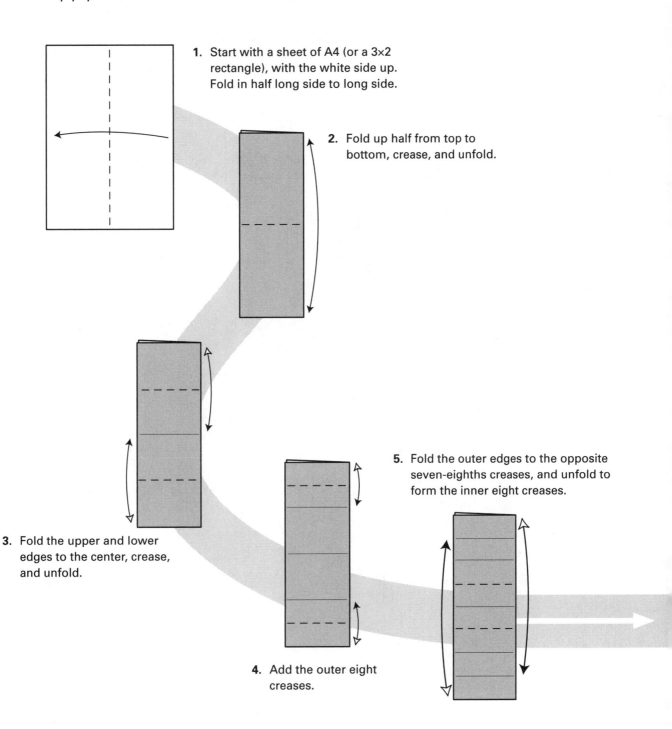

1. Start with a sheet of A4 (or a 3×2 rectangle), with the white side up. Fold in half long side to long side.

2. Fold up half from top to bottom, crease, and unfold.

3. Fold the upper and lower edges to the center, crease, and unfold.

4. Add the outer eight creases.

5. Fold the outer edges to the opposite seven-eighths creases, and unfold to form the inner eight creases.

continues

continued

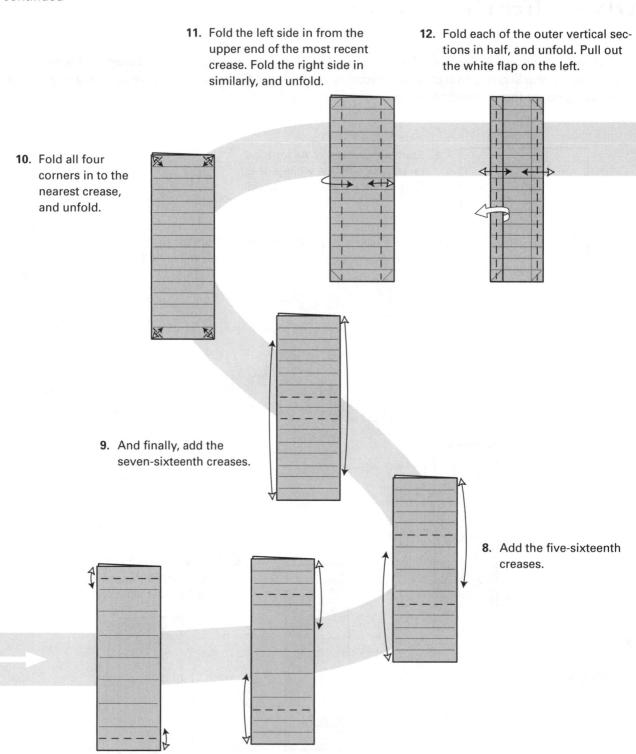

11. Fold the left side in from the upper end of the most recent crease. Fold the right side in similarly, and unfold.

12. Fold each of the outer vertical sections in half, and unfold. Pull out the white flap on the left.

10. Fold all four corners in to the nearest crease, and unfold.

9. And finally, add the seven-sixteenth creases.

8. Add the five-sixteenth creases.

6. Add the outer one-sixteenth creases.

7. Add the three-sixteenth creases.

13. Be sure the central horizontal sections are all valley folds. Turn the paper over.

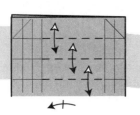

14. Add creases going from the upper-left to the lower-right corners of each central section. Turn the paper over again.

15. Open out both ends.

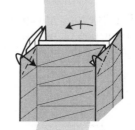

16. Fold over the four corners at either end, creasing firmly. These lock the layers together.

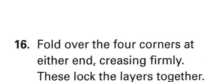

19. Complete.

17. Start to encourage the creases by twisting the paper gently in a clockwise direction.

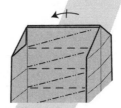

18. If you hold both ends, twist, and gently press in at either end, you can do this in one movement—if your creases are sharp enough! The idea is to form a spiral.

Umulius Rectangulum   Difficulty level: 5

by Thoki Yenn

In this model, L-shape units join together to form an apparently impossible set of interlocking magic rings. Fold very accurately to create perfect right-angled corners. You need half of an A4 rectangle, but a 3×1 rectangle works as well.

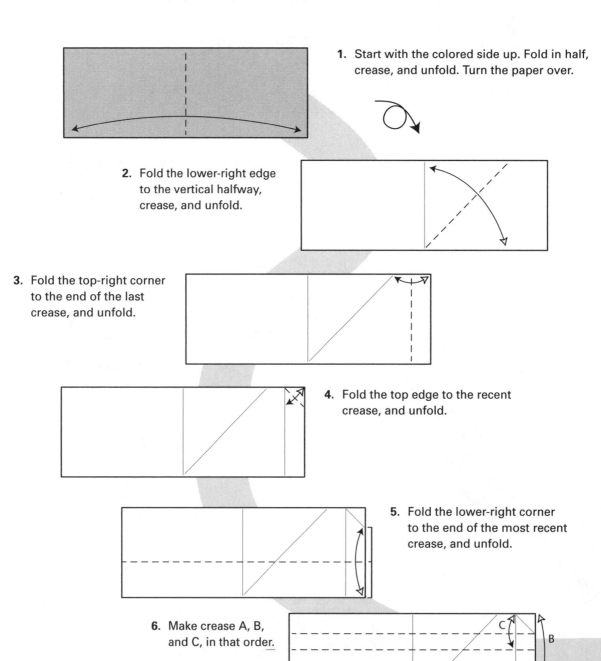

1. Start with the colored side up. Fold in half, crease, and unfold. Turn the paper over.

2. Fold the lower-right edge to the vertical halfway, crease, and unfold.

3. Fold the top-right corner to the end of the last crease, and unfold.

4. Fold the top edge to the recent crease, and unfold.

5. Fold the lower-right corner to the end of the most recent crease, and unfold.

6. Make crease A, B, and C, in that order.

12. Crease two diagonals, but leave the central section clear.

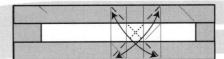

11. Fold the upper and lower edges toward the center.

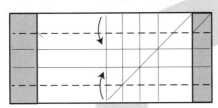

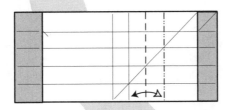

10. Use the most recent crease to form a new valley crease.

9. Fold the left edge to the most recent crease. Fold the right edge to the central vertical crease on the underside, crease, and unfold.

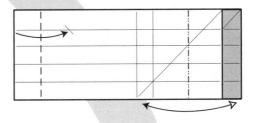

8. Make a fold similar to step 2, but only crease where it passes through the highest horizontal crease.

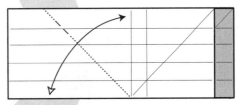

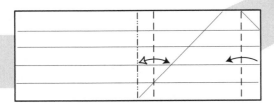

7. Make two vertical creases. (Look carefully at the diagram for the reference points.)

continues

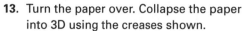

continued

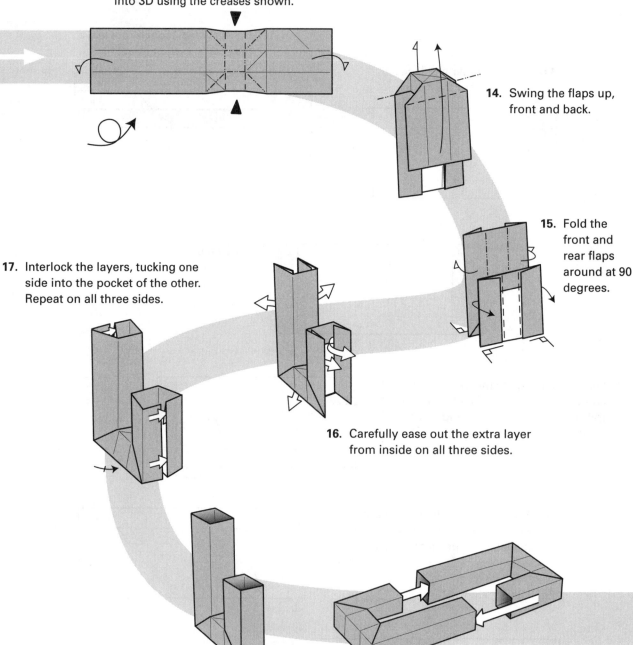

13. Turn the paper over. Collapse the paper into 3D using the creases shown.

14. Swing the flaps up, front and back.

15. Fold the front and rear flaps around at 90 degrees.

16. Carefully ease out the extra layer from inside on all three sides.

17. Interlock the layers, tucking one side into the pocket of the other. Repeat on all three sides.

18. The completed unit. Make six identical units, using three colors or patterns.

19. Using two of the same-color units, carefully slide the shorter end into the matching long end.

25. You can make a variation by cutting the paper where shown and folding four units instead of six.

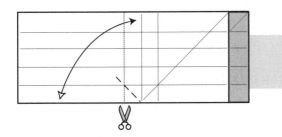

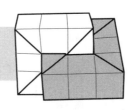

26. Complete.

23. Slide the two remaining units between the gaps and into each other. Try not to force the paper.

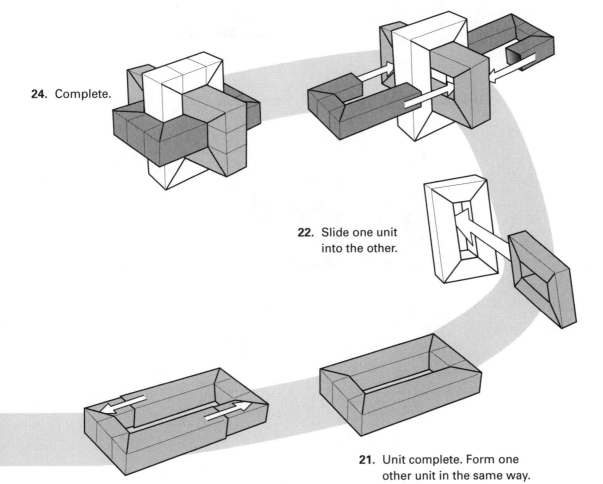

24. Complete.

22. Slide one unit into the other.

21. Unit complete. Form one other unit in the same way.

20. This is how the move should look in progress.

Tri-Puzzle and Cross Puzzle Solutions

How'd you do with the Tri-Puzzle and Cross Puzzle models? Did you figure out the puzzle? Here are the solutions:

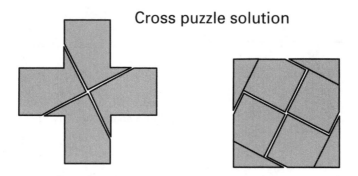

Cross puzzle solution

Tri-Puzzle solution

Chapter 8
Modular

Modular origami (known in Japan as "unit origami") describes models assembled from several identical smaller models, known as modules. Each generally has a "flap" and a "pocket," allowing them to be tucked into each other to form a geometric polyhedron (or polygon).

Extremely accurate folding is required to ensure the final model holds together well. Make all creases as sharp as possible. Try to be patient during assembly, when you may find two hands seem inadequate for the job. You may find small paperclips help hold modules in place as you assemble the model.

Hexahedron　Difficulty level: 2

by Molly Khan

This clever model makes very efficient use of the available paper. Try to use crisp paper, and make your creases sharp. The assembly might seem tricky to begin with, but you'll soon get the idea. Can you make a crown using four modules?

1. Start with the white side up.
   Fold in half from top to bottom.

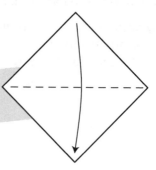

2. Fold the upper corners to the lower corner, crease firmly, and unfold.

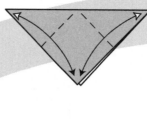

3. Fold in half from left to right to complete one module. Make two more modules in different colors.

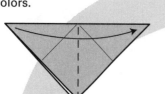

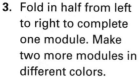

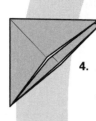

4. Arrange the three modules as shown, tucking the loose flaps into the pockets on the adjacent module.

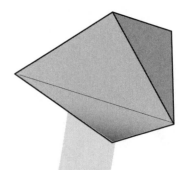

6. Complete. Here is the top view and a side view.

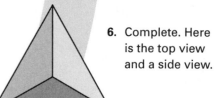

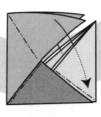

5. Form the model into 3D (bearing in mind what you're making!), and bend both loose flaps, tucking them into the pockets. Slide gently into place, making sure all flaps are fully inserted.

Squared Square Cube   Difficulty level: 2

by Robert Neale

For this design, Neale took a simple model and found a way to join multiples of it together to make a cube. Try to use crisp paper, and make all your creases sharp and accurate. You may need to ease the modules apart slightly to insert the others.

1. Start with Squared Square model in Chapter 7, folded to step 9 and unfolded to step 7. Make five more identical modules.

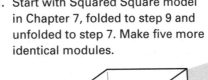
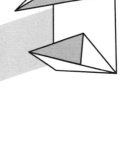

2. Arrange two modules opposite each other, and slide the flaps into the pockets on either side.

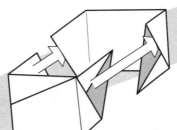

3. Fold two more modules, and arrange them as shown. Slide one carefully inside the other.

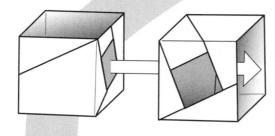

6. Complete.

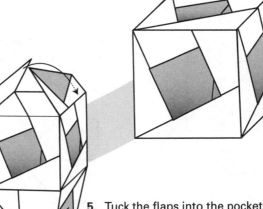

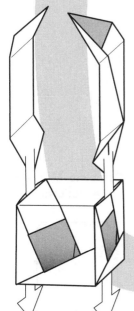

5. Tuck the flaps into the pockets as you did in step 2. Tighten up all modules.

4. Slide two more modules down inside the model.

Modular Twist   Difficulty level: 2

by Nick Robinson

This is a relatively simple modular design so you can get used to maneuvering several modules into position and locking them together. The first time you make it, it may be slightly scruffy. The next time, you'll—hopefully!—understand the method and can concentrate on folding and joining as neatly as possible.

Module

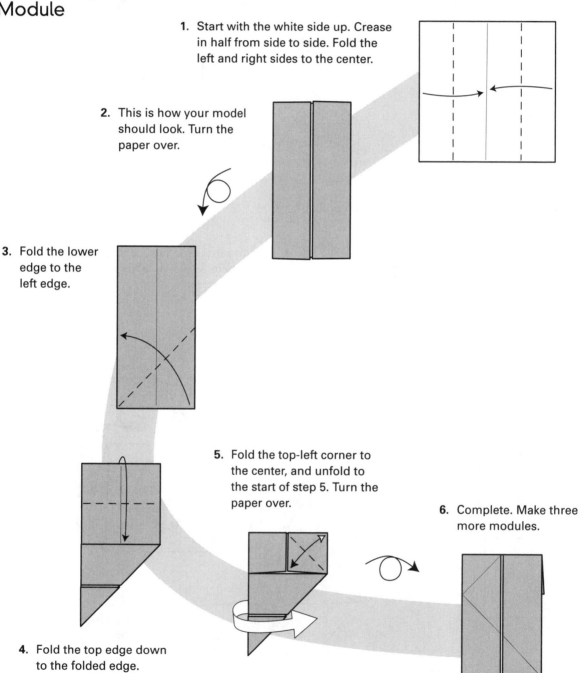

1. Start with the white side up. Crease in half from side to side. Fold the left and right sides to the center.

2. This is how your model should look. Turn the paper over.

3. Fold the lower edge to the left edge.

4. Fold the top edge down to the folded edge.

5. Fold the top-left corner to the center, and unfold to the start of step 5. Turn the paper over.

6. Complete. Make three more modules.

Assembly

1. Arrange two different-color modules as shown. Slide the flap of the upper module under the colored flap of the lower one.

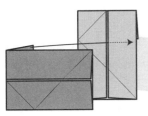

2. Fold the triangle underneath to lock the modules together.

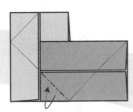

3. Fold over the lower-left corner, and tuck it under a layer.

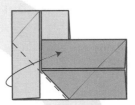

4. Tuck the lower flap of the lighter module into the pocket of the lowest module.

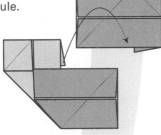

5. Repeat steps 2 and 3.

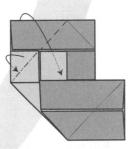

6. Slide the underneath flap of the final module into a pocket. Fold the flap on the highest module above the last inserted module and into a pocket.

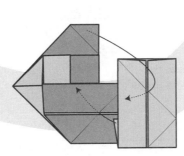

7. Repeat steps 2 and 3.

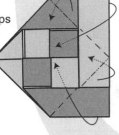

8. Complete.

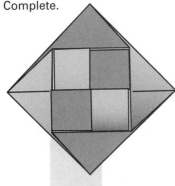

Pyramid Difficulty level: 2

by Javier Cabablanco

A good origami designer always explores the creative potential of any ideas he or she has. Compare this model with Javier's Hungry Chick (see Chapter 2), and you'll see the connection. The results, however, are dramatically different!

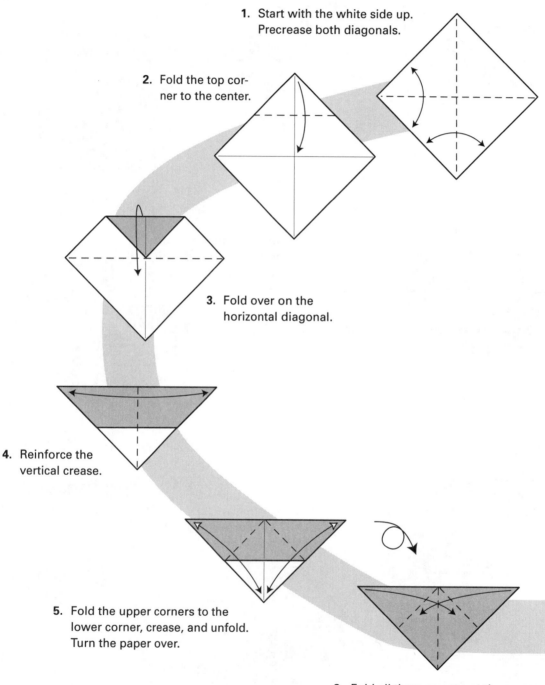

1. Start with the white side up. Precrease both diagonals.

2. Fold the top corner to the center.

3. Fold over on the horizontal diagonal.

4. Reinforce the vertical crease.

5. Fold the upper corners to the lower corner, crease, and unfold. Turn the paper over.

6. Fold all three creases at the same time, overlapping the edges with the right side on top.

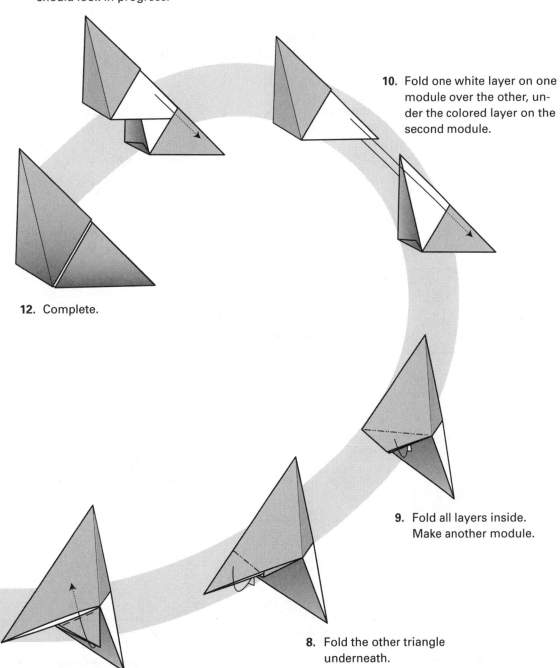

11. This is how the move should look in progress.

10. Fold one white layer on one module over the other, under the colored layer on the second module.

12. Complete.

9. Fold all layers inside. Make another module.

8. Fold the other triangle underneath.

7. Fold the lower triangle over the edge, and tuck it into the pocket.

Windmill Cube Difficulty level: 2

by Kunihiko Kasahara

This is a variation of the classic module designed by Mitsonobu Sonobe. You need modules to make a square, but you can join 3 to form a hexahedron; 30 to form a stellated icosohedron; or even more to form larger, more complicated polyhedra. If you look at one face of the cube, you can see a white windmill rotating in one direction and a colored windmill rotating in the other.

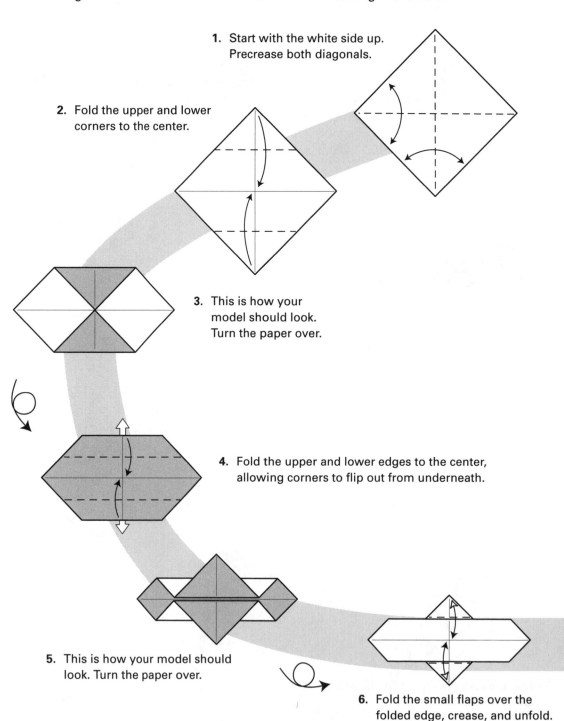

1. Start with the white side up. Precrease both diagonals.

2. Fold the upper and lower corners to the center.

3. This is how your model should look. Turn the paper over.

4. Fold the upper and lower edges to the center, allowing corners to flip out from underneath.

5. This is how your model should look. Turn the paper over.

6. Fold the small flaps over the folded edge, crease, and unfold.

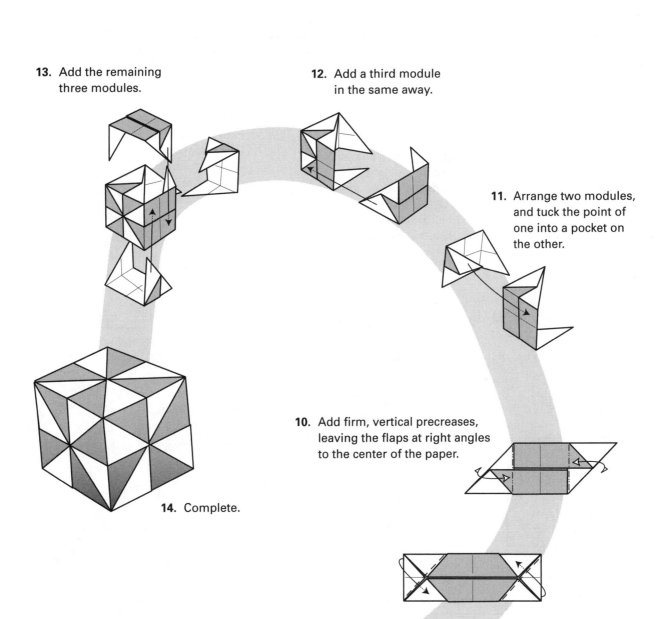

13. Add the remaining three modules.

12. Add a third module in the same away.

11. Arrange two modules, and tuck the point of one into a pocket on the other.

10. Add firm, vertical precreases, leaving the flaps at right angles to the center of the paper.

14. Complete.

9. Fold over the lower-right and upper-left corners, and tuck them under a layer of paper.

8. Fold in the left and right corners.

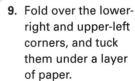

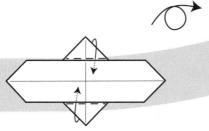

7. Refold the flaps, tucking them under the white layer. Turn the paper over.

Tri-Module Unit Difficulty level: 3

by Nick Robinson

This classic module can be combined in several ways to make different polyhedra. It will keep you amused for hours—if you have the patience to stick with it! As ever, accuracy is paramount.

Hexahedron

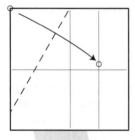

1. Start with the white side up. Crease in half both ways, and add a quarter crease on the right side. Starting the crease at the top center, fold the top-left corner to lie on the quarter crease. It will be slightly above halfway.

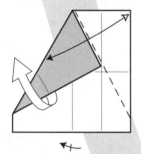

2. This is how your model should look. Fold the upper-right corner over the colored edge, crease, and unfold. Unfold to a square again. Repeat steps 1 and 2 on the lower half.

3. Fold the upper-right and lower-left corners to meet the recent creases, and unfold.

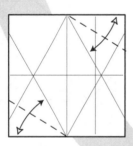

4. Fold the same corners to the recent creases.

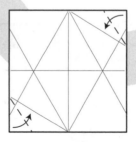

5. Using the existing creases, fold the corners over twice.

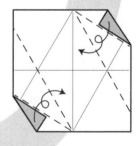

6. This is how your model should look. Turn the paper over.

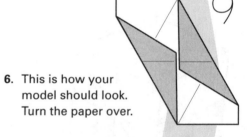

7. Fold the upper and lower edges to the nearest "diamond" creases, and unfold.

8. Reinforce these creases so they're sharp. The module is complete. Make two more modules.

9. Arrange the two modules as shown. Wrap the white flap from the upper module underneath the other, tucking it behind a colored layer of the second module.

10. Form the model into 3D using mountain creases, and tuck the white flap on the left module into the pocket on the right module.

I've included a diagram of a hexahedron for guidance.

11. Using the diagram as reference, add the third module in the same way.

12. Complete.

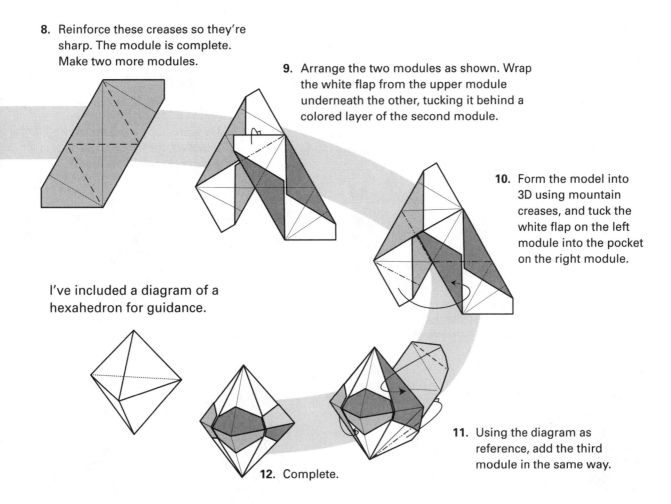

Tetrahedron

For this, you need to make two modules, but one must be a mirror image of the other, so from step 3 on, make all folds on the opposite corners. Join in the same way.

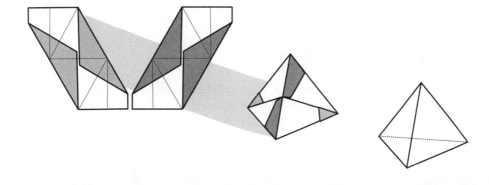

Spiked Models

To form these, alter the basic crease pattern slightly.

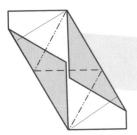

1. Reinforce these three creases.

2. This is how your model should look for assembly.

3. Here are three modules as-sembled, forming a three-sided pyramid in the center.

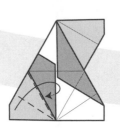

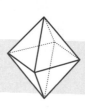

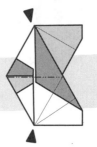

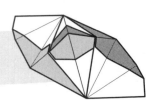

5. Here is a spiked icosahedron, requiring 30 modules.

4. Here is a dual tetrahedron, requiring 12 modules.

Four-Sided Pyramid

You can combine two modules to make a four-sided configuration.

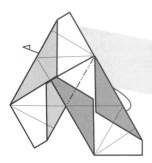

1. Start at step 10 of the hexahedron, but wrap the paper un-derneath as shown.

2. Wrap the lower corner around and into the pocket.

3. Gently press the sides together, opening into 3D.

4. Here is a four-sided "spike," which you can join with other three- or four-sided modules to form a huge variety of shapes.

For Real Enthusiasts

Finally, you can create a dodecahedron with pentagonal pyramids on all faces and inverted spikes on pyramids' side faces—a mere 90 modules in all! See if you can figure it out over a long weekend.

Snowflake Module Difficulty level: 3

by David Petty

This module shows one of the possibilities for using simple bases, in this case a preliminary base, as a module. See if you can combine waterbomb bases using the same principle. Make the creases in steps 3 and 4 firmly and accurately.

1. Start with the colored side up.
Fold in half from top to bottom.

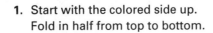

2. Fold the left corner to the bottom
corner. Fold the right corner behind
to the bottom corner.

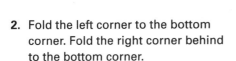

3. Fold the lower-right edge
to the horizontal center,
crease, and unfold.
Turn the paper over.

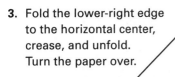

4. Repeat step 3. Unfold the
paper to the white side.

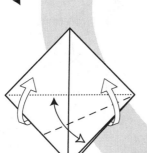

5. Press in the center, and fold
the side corners down to
form a preliminary base.

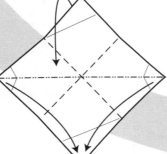

6. This is how your model should look.
Make three more modules in the same
color and four more in a different color.

continues

continued

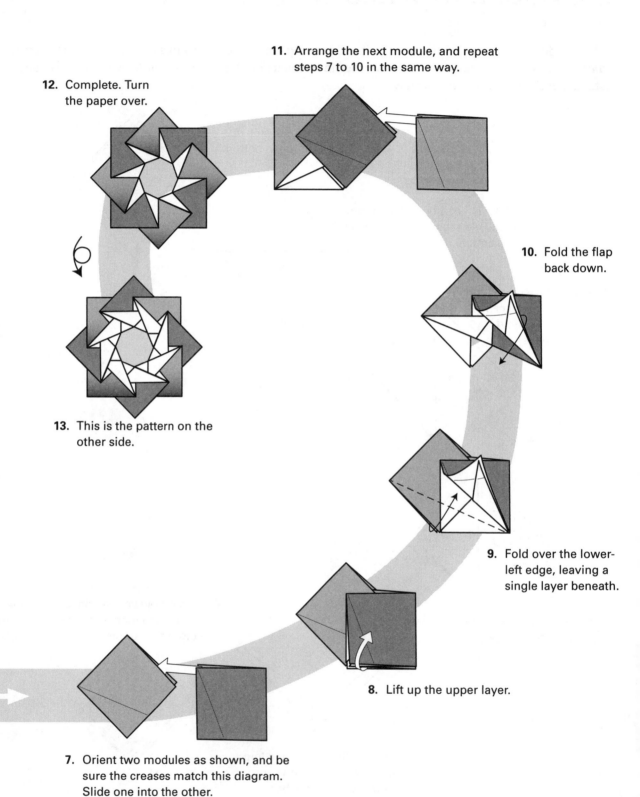

11. Arrange the next module, and repeat steps 7 to 10 in the same way.

12. Complete. Turn the paper over.

10. Fold the flap back down.

13. This is the pattern on the other side.

9. Fold over the lower-left edge, leaving a single layer beneath.

8. Lift up the upper layer.

7. Orient two modules as shown, and be sure the creases match this diagram. Slide one into the other.

Snow Cube   Difficulty level: 3

by Nick Robinson

Modular designs can sometimes be very delicate affairs, requiring a lot of subtlety to assemble. This one is less demanding! The smaller picture shows a combination of 12 modules. Other possibilities exist; can you find them? Try starting with three. For the cube, you need six modules. Try three lots of two colors. This was created during the worst snowfall in England for 30 years, hence the name.

1. Start with the white side up. Make light pinch marks to show the half-way points on two adjacent sides.

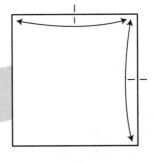

2. Fold outside quarter creases on all four sides.

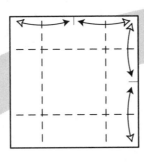

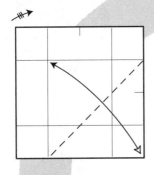

3. Fold each corner to the opposite intersection of the quarter creases.

4. Fold in the top-right and bottom-left corners to the nearest creases. Turn the paper over.

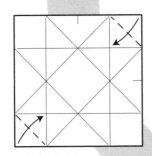

6. Fold the top and bottom quarters underneath.

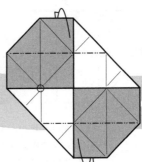

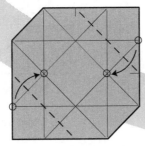

5. Fold in the corners so the circled points meet.

continues

continued

11. This is how your three joined modules
    should look. Add the other three in the
    same way. The eye shows the point of
    view of the next picture.

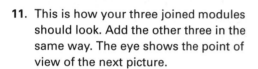

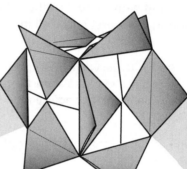

12. Complete.

10. Add a third module
    at the bottom, sliding
    the white flaps into the
    colored pockets.

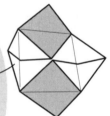

9. Arrange two modules as
   shown. Slide a white flap
   of one module inside the
   pocket at the back of the
   colored triangular flap on
   the second module.

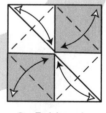

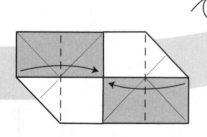

8. Fold each corner to the center, crease firmly, and unfold.
   Make five more modules.

7. Fold the left and right
   sides to the center. Turn
   the paper over.

Goldfinch Star   Difficulty level: 3

by Nick Robinson

This design makes use of 60-degree geometry. Fortunately for us, origami gives us a number of ways to create a perfect 60-degree angle. Using a variety of different colors, you can produce some spectacular results with this design. If you're feeling confident, see if you can join five units to form a 3D flower!

1. Start with the white side up. Fold in half, crease, and unfold.

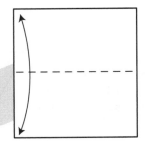

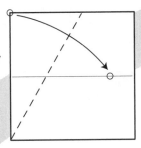

2. Starting at the lower-left corner, fold the top-left corner to lie on the halfway crease.

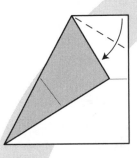

3. Fold the upper white edge to the colored edge.

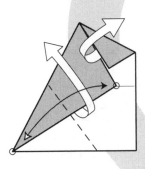

4. Fold the lower-left corner to the inner colored corner, crease, and unfold. Unfold back to the square.

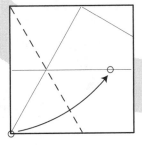

5. Fold over the lower-left corner. Half of this crease is already in place.

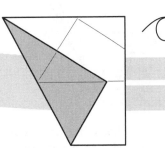

6. This is how your model should look. Turn the paper over.

continues

continued

12. Refold step 8. The paper goes over the top of the light-colored unit.

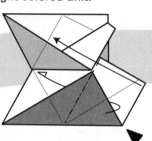

11. Fold over a flap on one module, tucking it under a layer of a second module.

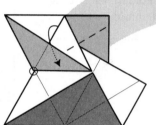

10. Unfold one module to the start of step 8. Orient as shown, and slide it into the pocket of the next so the circled points coincide.

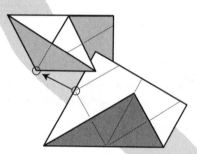

9. The module is complete. Make five more, using two different colors.

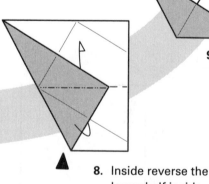

8. Inside reverse the lower half inside.

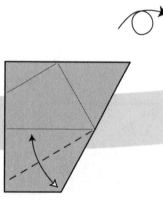

7. Fold the lower half of the right edge to the horizontal, crease, and unfold. Turn the paper over.

13. Slide in the next module in the same way.

14. Lock together as in step 11. Continue with the other three modules.

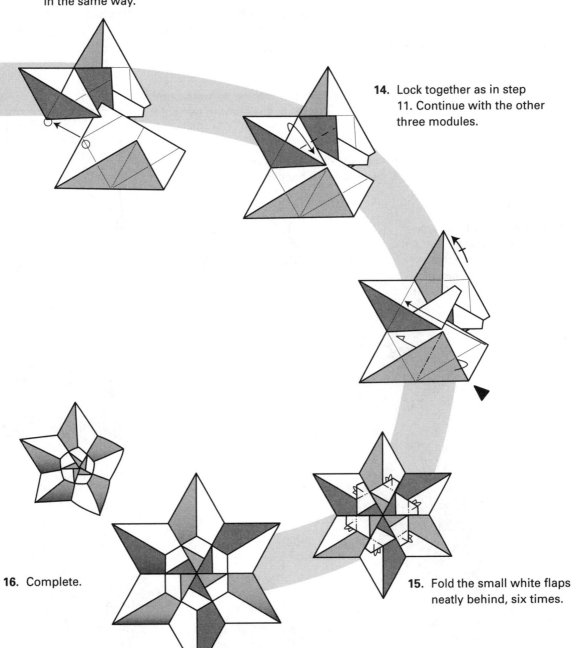

15. Fold the small white flaps neatly behind, six times.

16. Complete.

Octahedron Difficulty level: 3

by Robert Neale

This cunning design is very logical—it's quite easy to see what *should* be happening, but you'll need all your patience to *make* it happen! To begin with, use smaller squares so it's easier to hold them. Use crisp paper, and make every crease as sharp as possible.

1. Start by making six waterbomb bases in three sets of two colors.

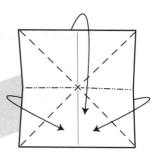

2. Arrange the flaps so they're all at 90 degrees to each other.

3. Arrange two of the same-color modules so they face away from each other. Slide the lighter module into the upper pockets of the darker module.

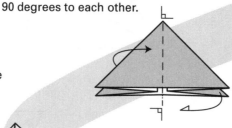

7. Complete.

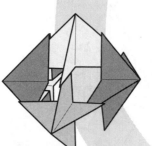

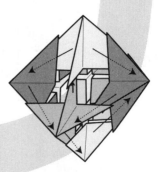

4. Slide the wide flaps of a mid-colored module with the center toward you outside the darker modules. Slide the upper point into a light-colored module.

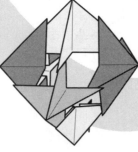

6. Place the mid-colored module into the final position. Every module should have flaps going first into a packet and then outside a flap. Carefully slide the modules toward each other, working your way around bit by bit.

5. Check everything before going any further. Arrange another light-colored module at the bottom so it matches the module at the top.

Chapter 9
Practical

Origami is often seen as a decorative and sometimes artistic hobby. However, many models can serve a useful (if not always serious) purpose. That's what's included in this chapter—cups, envelopes, caps, and other practical folds.

The life span of your model largely depends on the material you use to make it. I recommend using a slightly thicker paper for this reason. However, origami envelopes wing their way round the world every day, and many are made from standard photocopy paper.

Wallet   Difficulty level: 1

Traditional design

Simple and practical, you can actually use this wallet if you want to! To make the wallet big enough to hold your paper money, you need a square that's just more than twice the length of the bill. To make it last, choose a strong or slightly thicker paper.

1. Start with the white side up. Fold in half, side to opposite side, and unfold. Repeat in the other direction.

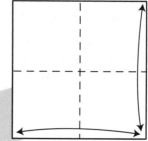

2. Fold the upper and lower edges to the center.

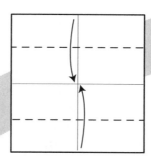

3. This is how your model should look. Turn the paper over.

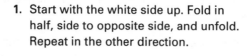

4. Fold the left and right (short) edges to the center.

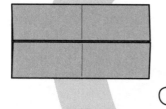

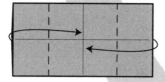

5. Fold in half from top to bottom.

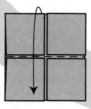

6. Complete.

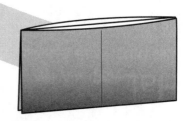

Cup Difficulty level: 1

Traditional design

This well-known design is a really useful model to have in your repertoire because you never know when you'll need a drink—and an impromptu cup! A typical paper cup lasts for about 2 minutes—after which it might well spontaneously empty itself through a hole in the base—so drink quickly!

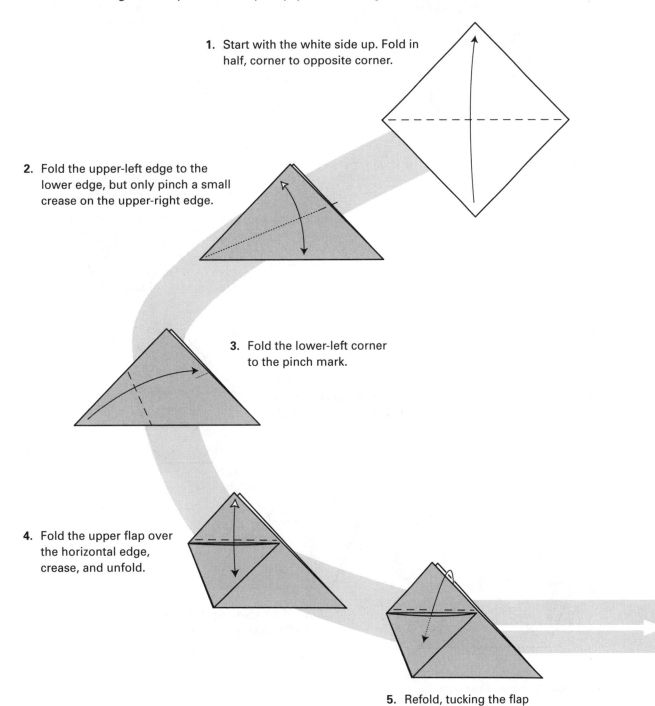

1. Start with the white side up. Fold in half, corner to opposite corner.

2. Fold the upper-left edge to the lower edge, but only pinch a small crease on the upper-right edge.

3. Fold the lower-left corner to the pinch mark.

4. Fold the upper flap over the horizontal edge, crease, and unfold.

5. Refold, tucking the flap fully into the pocket.

continues

continued

11. Complete.

10. Open the cup slightly, and make a gentle curve in the base to keep the cup open.

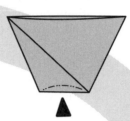

9. Refold the flap, tucking it into the pocket.

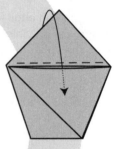

8. Fold the upper triangular flap down over the horizontal edge, crease, and unfold.

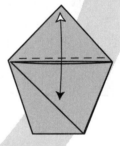

7. Fold the lower-right corner to the opposite corner.

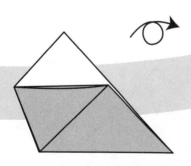

6. This is how your model should look. Turn the paper over.

Booklet   Difficulty level: 2

Traditional design

This design uses a small cut, but I hope you'll forgive this because the result is so neat and practical. Different shapes of paper produce booklets of different proportions. It's also possible to make more folds and cuts to produce more pages—can you work this out?

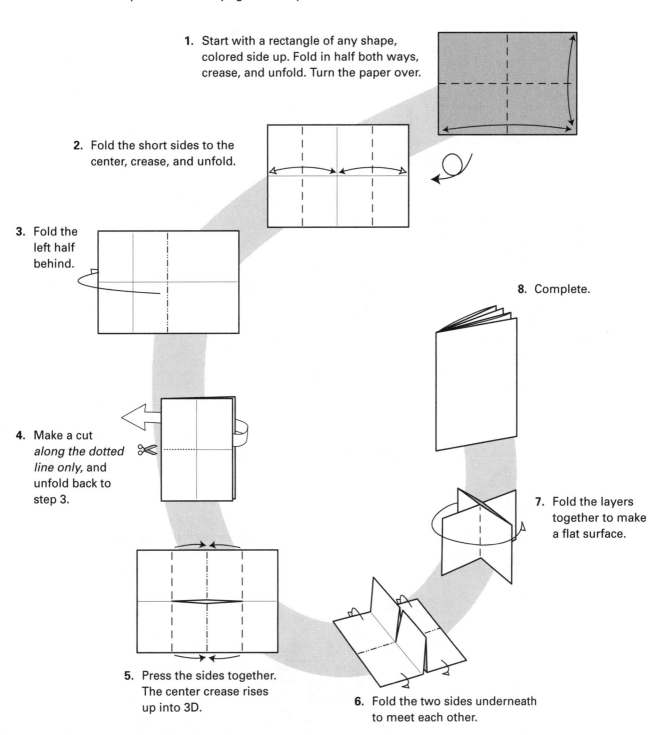

1. Start with a rectangle of any shape, colored side up. Fold in half both ways, crease, and unfold. Turn the paper over.

2. Fold the short sides to the center, crease, and unfold.

3. Fold the left half behind.

4. Make a cut *along the dotted line only,* and unfold back to step 3.

5. Press the sides together. The center crease rises up into 3D.

6. Fold the two sides underneath to meet each other.

7. Fold the layers together to make a flat surface.

8. Complete.

Envelope from Bonn   Difficulty level: 2

by Doris Lauinger

Envelopes are great models to experiment with and try creating your own designs. They simply have to hold together in some way. This model is delightfully simple, and it's perfect for mailing (yep, it's legal!), or passing love notes to your nearest and dearest.

1. Start with a sheet of letter paper. (If you use A4 paper, skip step 2.) Fold both short edges to the lower long edge, crease, and unfold.

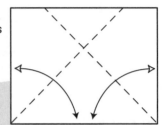

2. Fold the top edge to the intersection of creases. Turn the paper over.

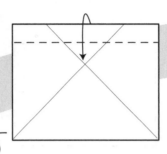

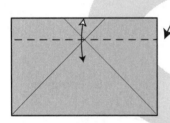

3. Make a valley crease that passes through the intersection of creases. Crease and unfold. Turn the paper over.

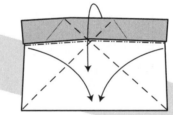

4. Collapse the paper using the creases shown.

5. Fold the lower corners to the top corner, crease, and unfold.

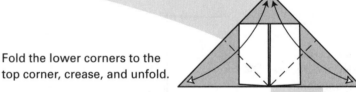

8. Complete.

6. Refold the corners, but tuck them under the top triangular pocket.

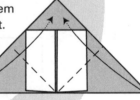

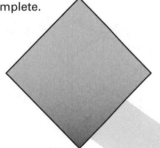

7. This is how your model should look. Turn the paper over.

Party Hat Difficulty level: 2

by David Neale (1972) / Nick Robinson (2010)

To make a life-size, wearable hat, you need a large sheet of paper: the diagonal of the initial square is just over twice the width of the final hat. Try to find brightly colored paper with different patterns on each side.

1. Start with an unfolded preliminary or waterbomb base. Fold the lower-left corner to the center.

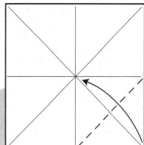

2. Fold in half from top to bottom.

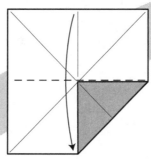

3. Fold in half from left to right.

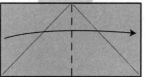

4. Fold two layers from the bottom right to the top left.

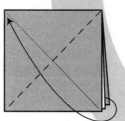

5. Fold a single layer from the top and the bottom to the center.

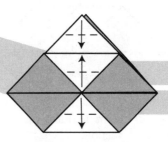

6. Fold the corner of each white triangle to the opposite side.

continues

continued

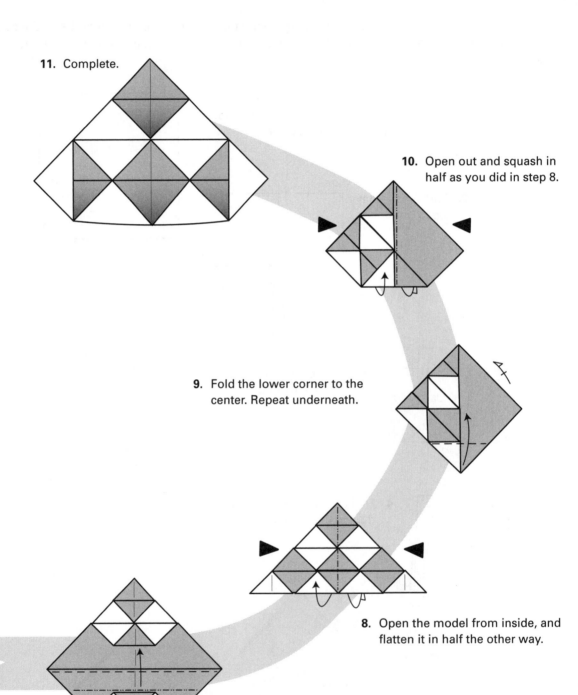

11. Complete.

10. Open out and squash in half as you did in step 8.

9. Fold the lower corner to the center. Repeat underneath.

8. Open the model from inside, and flatten it in half the other way.

7. Pleat up the lower section.

French Fries Bag   Difficulty level: 2

Traditional design

I learned this design in an English chip shop, where the model was made out of newspaper. It's a very quick and simple way of creating a boat-shape container for French fries, candies, and much more.

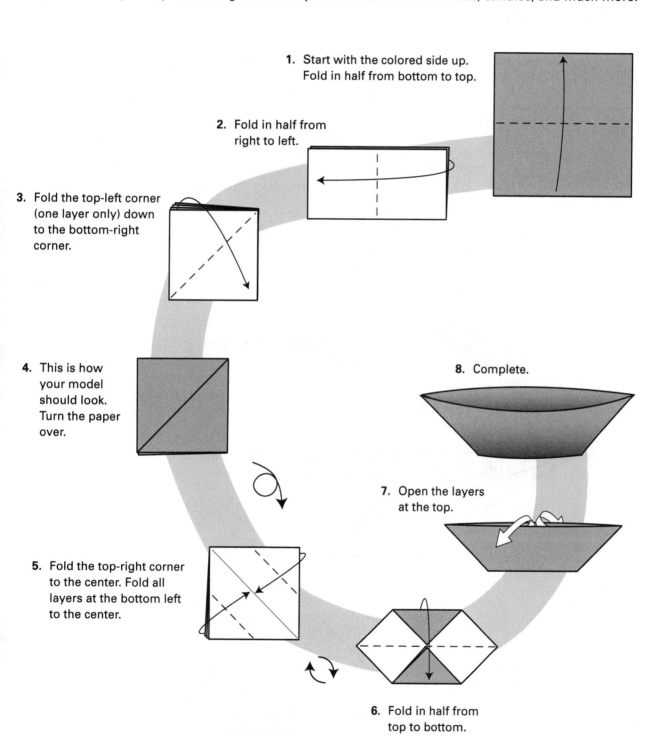

1. Start with the colored side up. Fold in half from bottom to top.

2. Fold in half from right to left.

3. Fold the top-left corner (one layer only) down to the bottom-right corner.

4. This is how your model should look. Turn the paper over.

5. Fold the top-right corner to the center. Fold all layers at the bottom left to the center.

6. Fold in half from top to bottom.

7. Open the layers at the top.

8. Complete.

Set Square   Difficulty level: 2

by Nick Robinson

Here, you use a handy technique for folding a 30- or 60-degree angle. This produces a set square offering 30-, 60-, and 90-degree corners. Use a paper that's crisp and gives a sharp crease. And be sure to fold accurately!

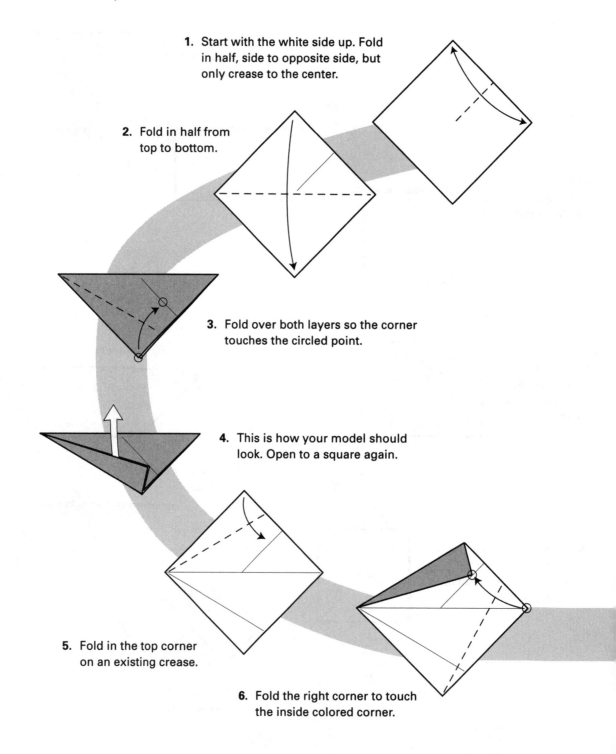

1. Start with the white side up. Fold in half, side to opposite side, but only crease to the center.

2. Fold in half from top to bottom.

3. Fold over both layers so the corner touches the circled point.

4. This is how your model should look. Open to a square again.

5. Fold in the top corner on an existing crease.

6. Fold the right corner to touch the inside colored corner.

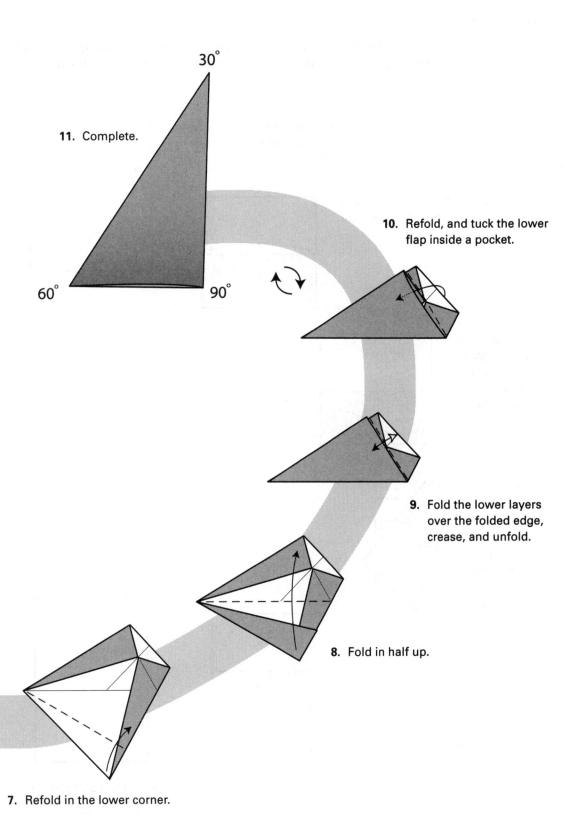

11. Complete.

30°

60°

90°

10. Refold, and tuck the lower flap inside a pocket.

9. Fold the lower layers over the folded edge, crease, and unfold.

8. Fold in half up.

7. Refold in the lower corner.

Pocket Fan Difficulty level: 2

by Sjaak Ariaanse

This model helps you keep cool in hot weather. And after you've cooled down, you can fold it neatly away and stick it in your pocket. Use slightly stiffer paper than normal for this one.

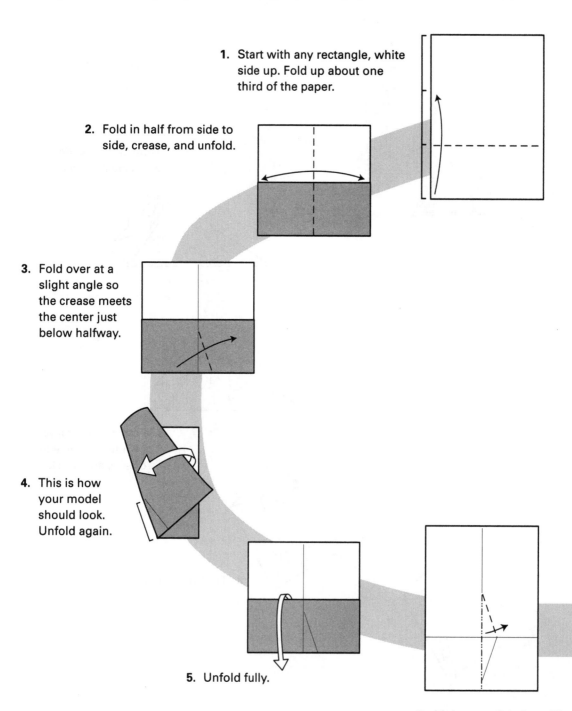

1. Start with any rectangle, white side up. Fold up about one third of the paper.

2. Fold in half from side to side, crease, and unfold.

3. Fold over at a slight angle so the crease meets the center just below halfway.

4. This is how your model should look. Unfold again.

5. Unfold fully.

6. Make a partial pleat. (The paper doesn't flatten.)

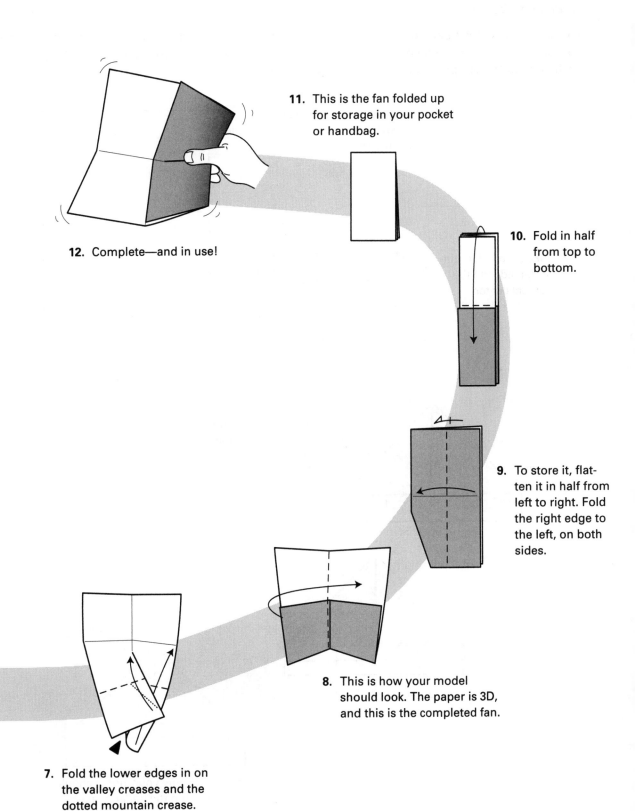

11. This is the fan folded up for storage in your pocket or handbag.

12. Complete—and in use!

10. Fold in half from top to bottom.

9. To store it, flatten it in half from left to right. Fold the right edge to the left, on both sides.

8. This is how your model should look. The paper is 3D, and this is the completed fan.

7. Fold the lower edges in on the valley creases and the dotted mountain crease.

Classic Cap

Difficulty level: 2

Traditional design

This simple cap has been around for many years and has adorned many heads around the world. You can practice with small paper first, or go straight in and make a full-size model! This cap is perfect if you're caught in the sun without protection.

1. Start with an unfolded sheet of newspaper or other large rectangle. Fold the short edges together.

2. Take each half of the folded edge to the vertical center.

3. Rotate the paper. Fold the upper layer at the bottom to meet the folded edges.

4. Fold the layer over once more.

5. This is how your model should look. Turn the paper over.

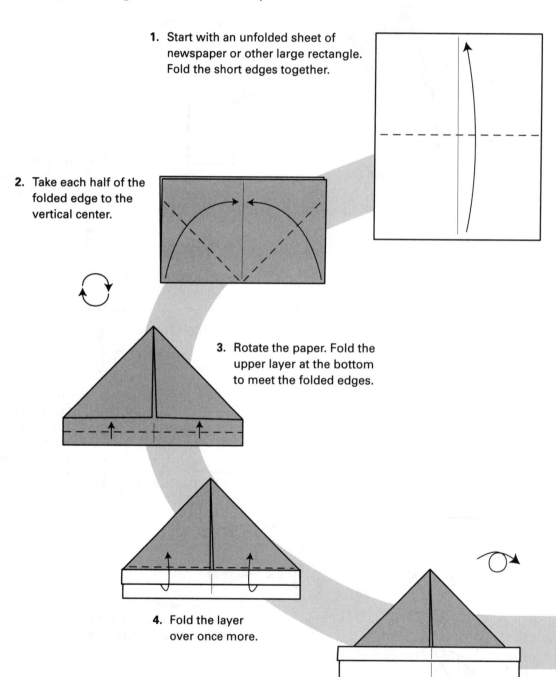

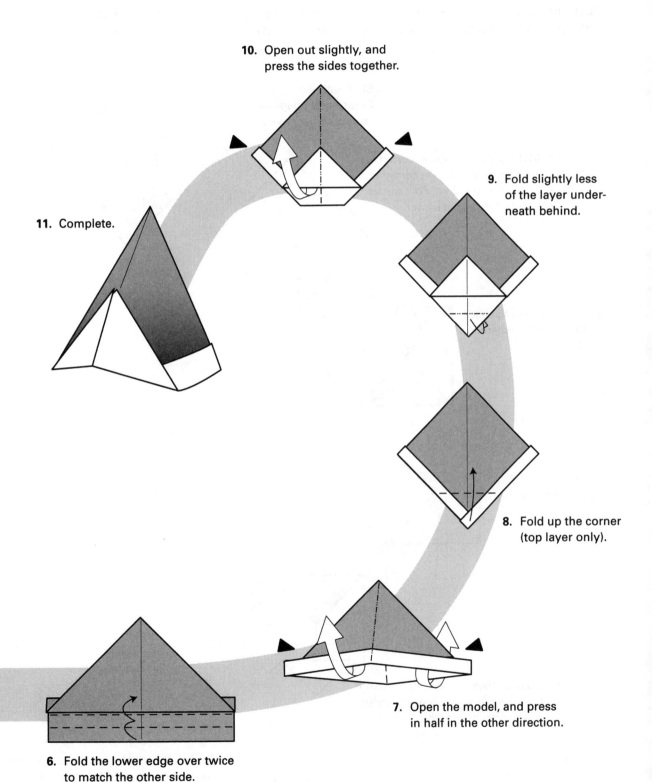

10. Open out slightly, and press the sides together.

9. Fold slightly less of the layer underneath behind.

11. Complete.

8. Fold up the corner (top layer only).

7. Open the model, and press in half in the other direction.

6. Fold the lower edge over twice to match the other side.

Sailboat Envelope   Difficulty level: 2

by Evi Binzinger

Evi from Germany enjoys creating simple origami designs. This envelope with a boat on it is typical of her work. Fold carefully at steps 5 and 6, where you rearrange the paper quite a bit.

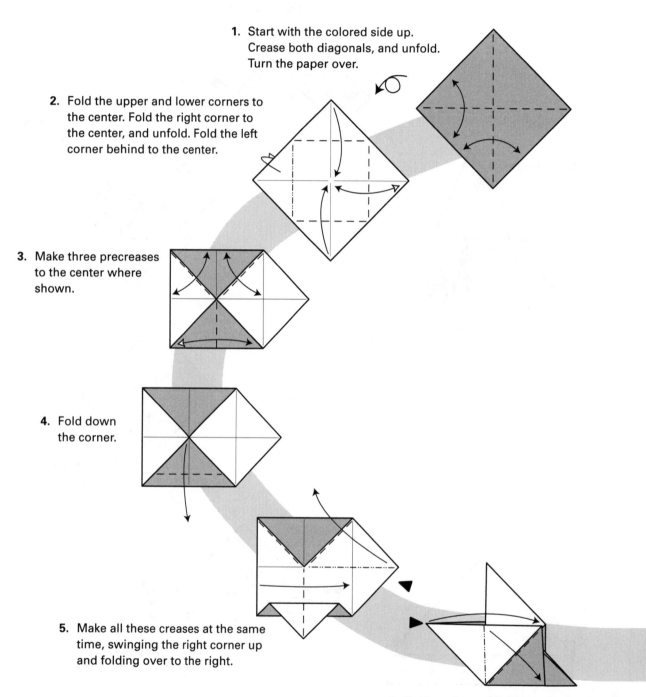

1. Start with the colored side up. Crease both diagonals, and unfold. Turn the paper over.

2. Fold the upper and lower corners to the center. Fold the right corner to the center, and unfold. Fold the left corner behind to the center.

3. Make three precreases to the center where shown.

4. Fold down the corner.

5. Make all these creases at the same time, swinging the right corner up and folding over to the right.

6. Fold on the small diagonal, allowing the corner on the left to fold to the right.

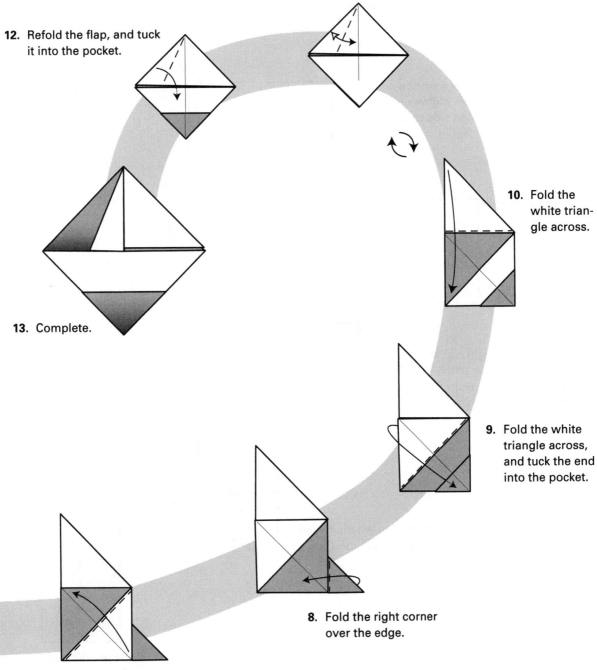

11. Rotate the paper. Fold the upper-right edge to the center, crease, and unfold.

12. Refold the flap, and tuck it into the pocket.

10. Fold the white triangle across.

13. Complete.

9. Fold the white triangle across, and tuck the end into the pocket.

8. Fold the right corner over the edge.

7. Fold the small white triangle across.

Elforia Envelope   Difficulty level: 3

by Sjaak Ariaanse

This is another simple yet practical envelope design that's neat and very satisfying to fold. I've written the instructions using an A4 rectangle of paper, but letter-size paper works just as well.

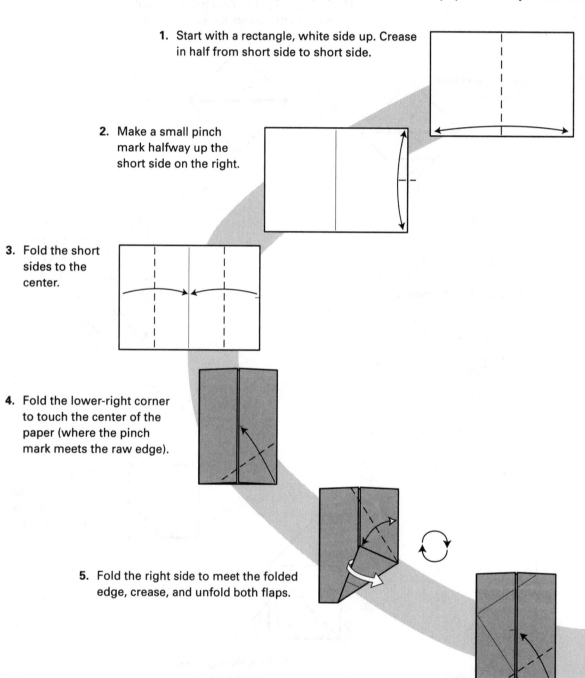

1. Start with a rectangle, white side up. Crease in half from short side to short side.

2. Make a small pinch mark halfway up the short side on the right.

3. Fold the short sides to the center.

4. Fold the lower-right corner to touch the center of the paper (where the pinch mark meets the raw edge).

5. Fold the right side to meet the folded edge, crease, and unfold both flaps.

6. Rotate the paper. Repeat step 4.

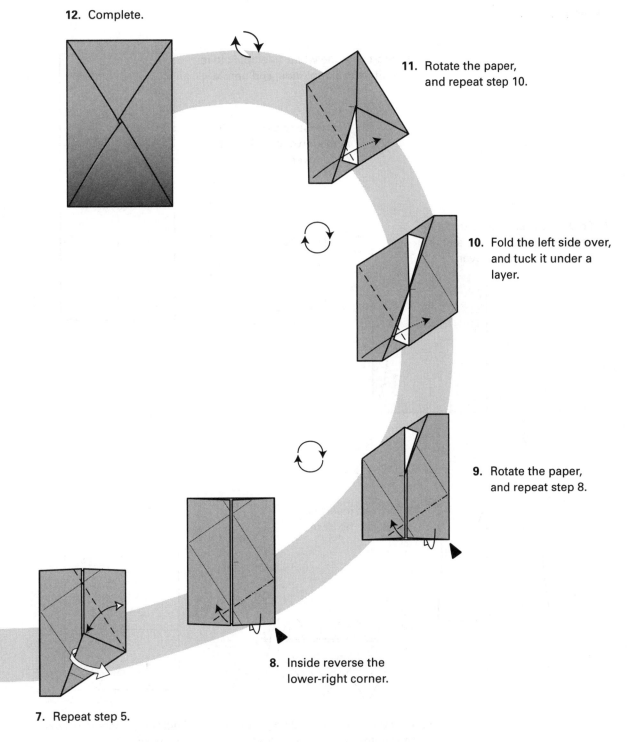

12. Complete.

11. Rotate the paper, and repeat step 10.

10. Fold the left side over, and tuck it under a layer.

9. Rotate the paper, and repeat step 8.

8. Inside reverse the lower-right corner.

7. Repeat step 5.

Holiday Card   Difficulty level: 3

by Doris Lauinger

For this holiday card, you need a rectangle with the proportions 1:2 plus about 2 inches (5cm)—for example, 8×17 inches (20×45 cm). Try to find paper that's green on one side and red or white on the other.

1. Start with the white side up. Fold in half from side to side, and unfold.

2. Precrease two diagonals at the lower end. Turn the paper over.

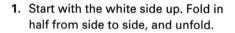

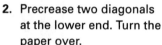

3. Fold the lower edge to the end of the diagonal, crease, and unfold. Turn the paper over.

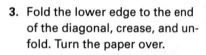

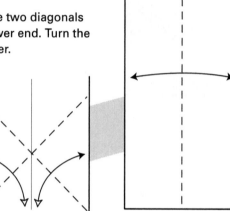

4. Form an inverted waterbomb base.

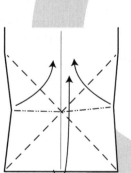

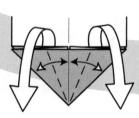

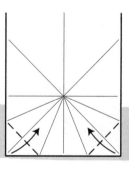

5. Fold the lower colored edges to the center, crease, and unfold. Open the paper out fully.

6. Fold the corners in between the existing creases.

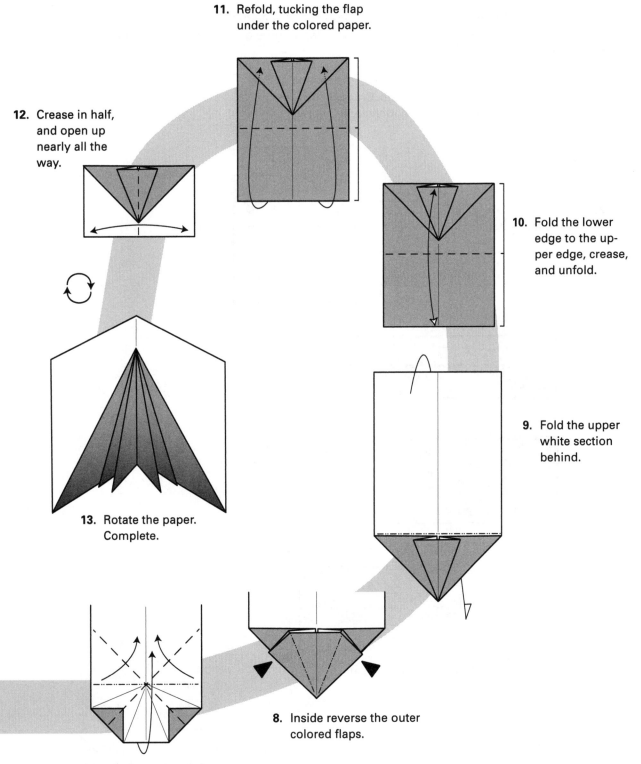

11. Refold, tucking the flap under the colored paper.

12. Crease in half, and open up nearly all the way.

10. Fold the lower edge to the upper edge, crease, and unfold.

9. Fold the upper white section behind.

13. Rotate the paper. Complete.

8. Inside reverse the outer colored flaps.

7. Reform the waterbomb base.

Ring   Difficulty level: 3

Traditional design

This model can be a large display ring or, if you can fold it small enough, make a life-size ring you can actually wear. If the loop slides apart, put a dab of glue on it—and hide from the outraged origamists!

1. Start with a 2×1 rectangle (half a square), white side up. Crease in half both from top to bottom, and unfold.

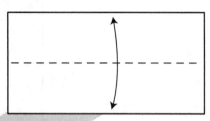

2. Fold the upper and lower sides to the center.

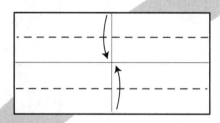

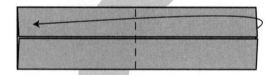

3. Fold in half from right to left.

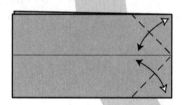

4. Fold each half of the right side to the center, crease firmly, and unfold.

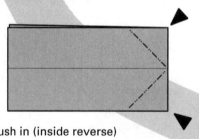

5. Push in (inside reverse) both corners.

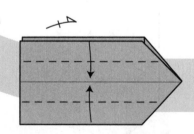

6. Fold the upper and lower sides to the center. Repeat underneath.

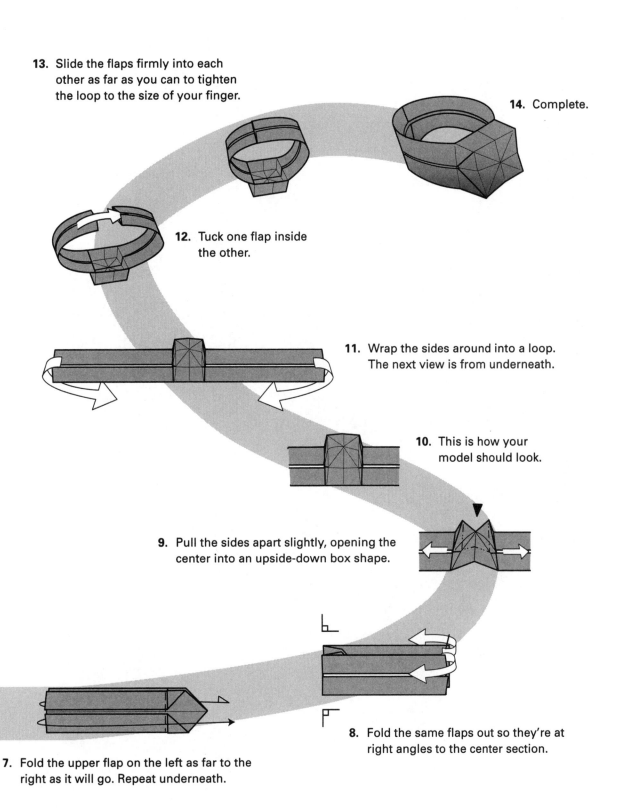

13. Slide the flaps firmly into each other as far as you can to tighten the loop to the size of your finger.

14. Complete.

12. Tuck one flap inside the other.

11. Wrap the sides around into a loop. The next view is from underneath.

10. This is how your model should look.

9. Pull the sides apart slightly, opening the center into an upside-down box shape.

8. Fold the same flaps out so they're at right angles to the center section.

7. Fold the upper flap on the left as far to the right as it will go. Repeat underneath.

Chapter 10
Fun

All origami is fun—or at least should be! However, some models aspire to be works of art, while others are meant to be enjoyed. This chapter gathers together some of the less-serious subjects, not just for children, but anyone who is young at heart.

These models reflect the wide range of things origami creators are inspired by, from a simple crown to a complex apple. These are also eminently suitable to give as gifts, guaranteed to put a smile on anyone's face!

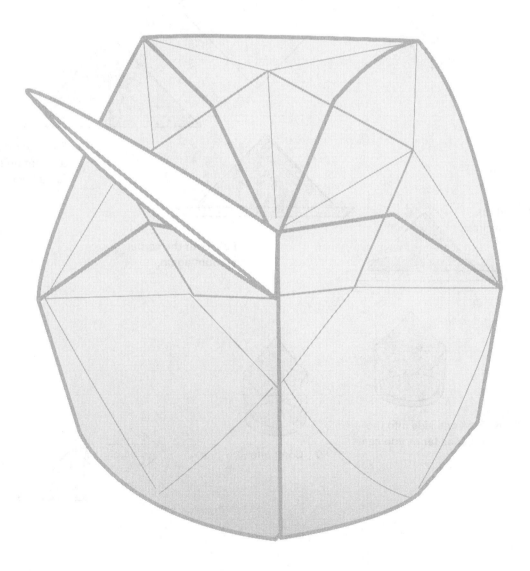

Gliding Hoop Difficulty level: 1

Traditional design

This is a very simple yet impressive aircraft. After you've folded it, smooth it into a circle by pinching all the way around with your thumb and index finger. Then, hold it by the longest corner with the hoop up, raise it above your head, and launch it with a gentle push.

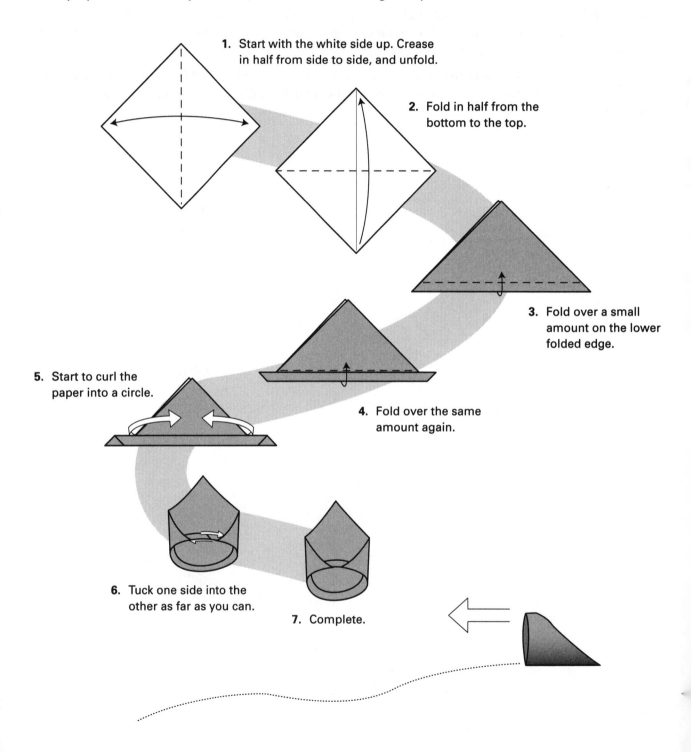

1. Start with the white side up. Crease in half from side to side, and unfold.

2. Fold in half from the bottom to the top.

3. Fold over a small amount on the lower folded edge.

4. Fold over the same amount again.

5. Start to curl the paper into a circle.

6. Tuck one side into the other as far as you can.

7. Complete.

Crown
Difficulty level: 1

by Nick Robinson

This is a very simple design requiring little skill to complete. Folding the edge inside in **step 9** should be enough to lock the paper together so you can wear the crown. The diagonal of the square should be half the diameter of your head.

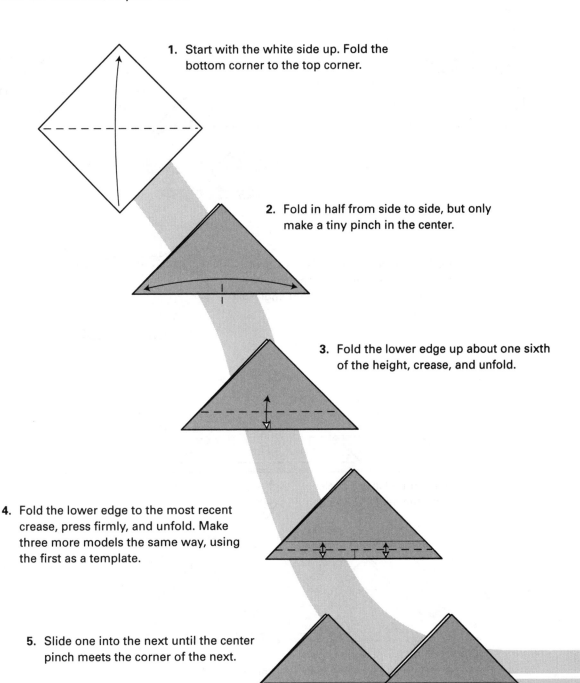

1. Start with the white side up. Fold the bottom corner to the top corner.

2. Fold in half from side to side, but only make a tiny pinch in the center.

3. Fold the lower edge up about one sixth of the height, crease, and unfold.

4. Fold the lower edge to the most recent crease, press firmly, and unfold. Make three more models the same way, using the first as a template.

5. Slide one into the next until the center pinch meets the corner of the next.

continues

continued

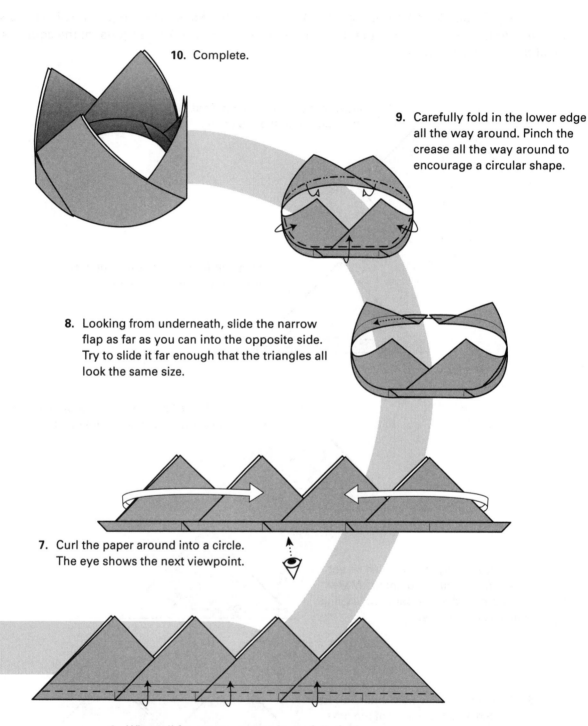

10. Complete.

9. Carefully fold in the lower edge all the way around. Pinch the crease all the way around to encourage a circular shape.

8. Looking from underneath, slide the narrow flap as far as you can into the opposite side. Try to slide it far enough that the triangles all look the same size.

7. Curl the paper around into a circle. The eye shows the next viewpoint.

6. When all four are connected, carefully fold them all up using the lower crease.

Sheffield Sailboat Difficulty level: 1

by Nick Robinson

This simple sequence results in a boat colored on one side and white on the other. You can use a number of different proportions and alter the distance of the creases in steps 4 and 11.

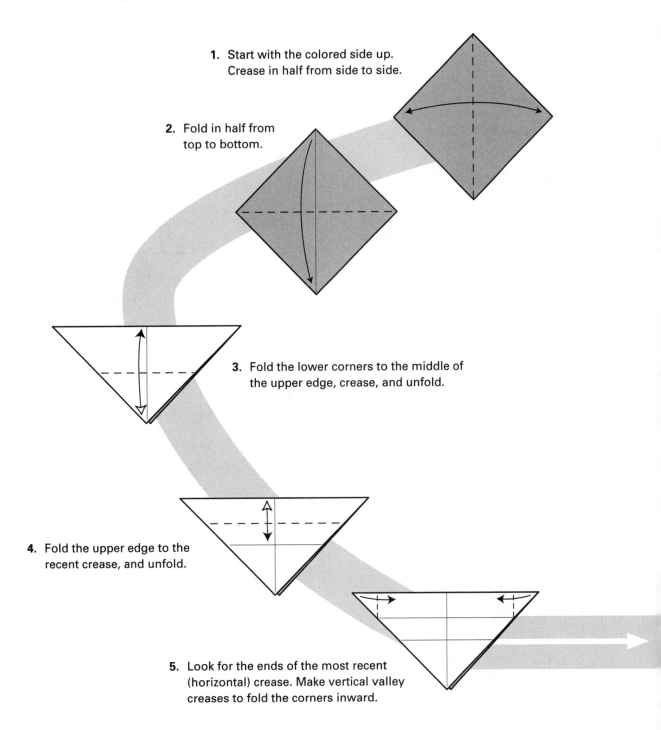

1. Start with the colored side up. Crease in half from side to side.

2. Fold in half from top to bottom.

3. Fold the lower corners to the middle of the upper edge, crease, and unfold.

4. Fold the upper edge to the recent crease, and unfold.

5. Look for the ends of the most recent (horizontal) crease. Make vertical valley creases to fold the corners inward.

continues

continued

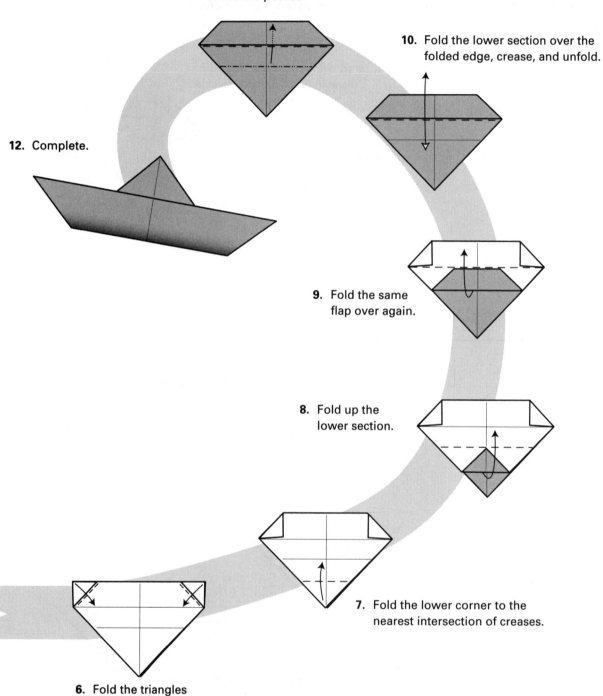

11. Make a pleat, and tuck it into the pocket.

10. Fold the lower section over the folded edge, crease, and unfold.

12. Complete.

9. Fold the same flap over again.

8. Fold up the lower section.

7. Fold the lower corner to the nearest intersection of creases.

6. Fold the triangles over on either side.

Word Dominoes Difficulty level: 1

by Mick Guy

Mick loves puzzles, especially origami puzzles. Here he's made a twist on dominoes, substituting letters for spots. Choose combinations of letters (with plenty of vowels), and add the letters in the positions shown in step 1. Fold as many as you can, distribute them among the players, and try to form words.

1. Start with the colored side up. Crease into quarters both ways. Fold the upper half behind.

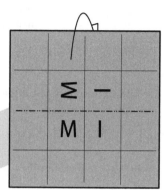

2. Fold in the upper corners.

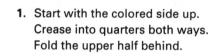

3. Fold the sides of the upper layer underneath.

8. Complete.

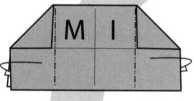

4. Tuck the lower half of the colored section underneath.

7. Fold the triangular flap up and into a pocket.

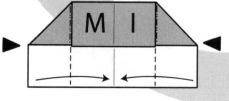

5. Inside reverse the two corners.

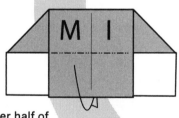

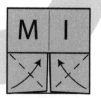

6. Fold in the lower corners.

Freising Plane   Difficulty level: 2

by Nick Robinson

The majority of paper planes are folded from rectangles. This one is made from a square and is designed to be folded from standard origami paper. I created this for Paulo, a very talented origami artist and friend who lives in a small town called Freising, in Germany.

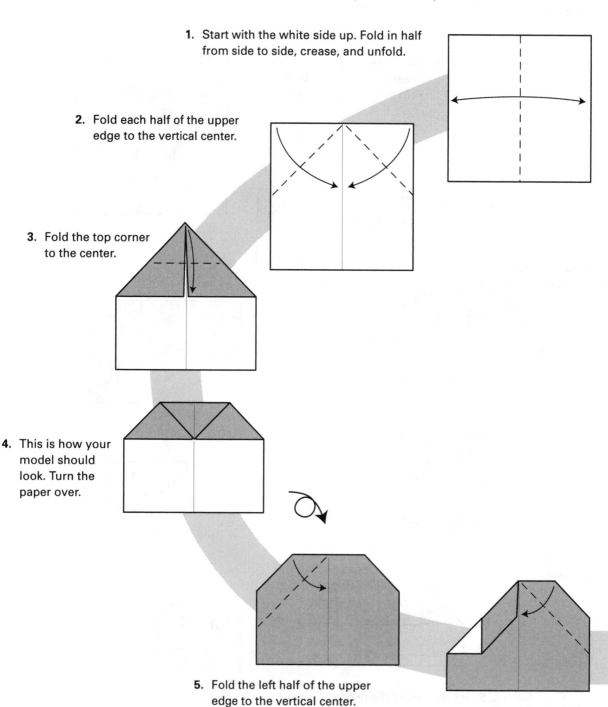

1. Start with the white side up. Fold in half from side to side, crease, and unfold.

2. Fold each half of the upper edge to the vertical center.

3. Fold the top corner to the center.

4. This is how your model should look. Turn the paper over.

5. Fold the left half of the upper edge to the vertical center.

6. This is how your model should look. Repeat on the right.

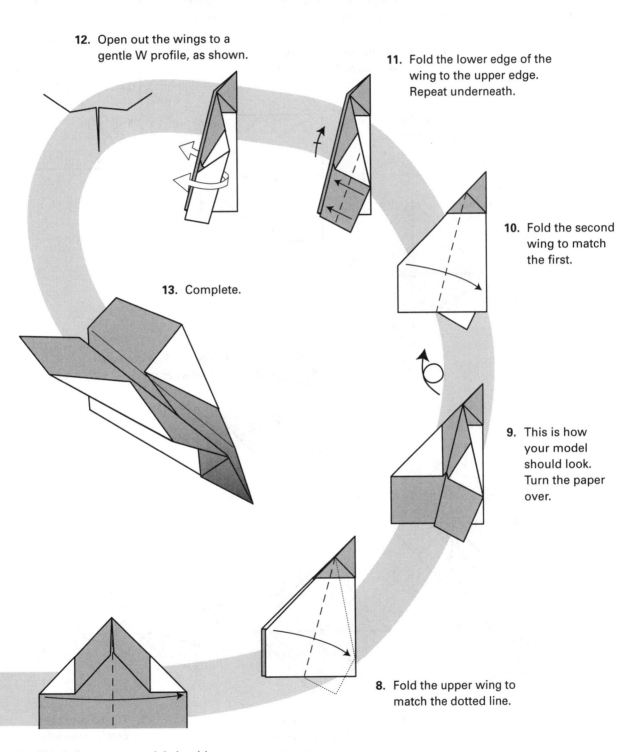

12. Open out the wings to a gentle W profile, as shown.

11. Fold the lower edge of the wing to the upper edge. Repeat underneath.

13. Complete.

10. Fold the second wing to match the first.

9. This is how your model should look. Turn the paper over.

8. Fold the upper wing to match the dotted line.

7. This is how your model should look. Fold in half from left to right.

Cart Difficulty level: 2

Traditional design

This two-piece design is very old and makes a perfect accompaniment to the horse, found in Chapter 3. Use slightly thicker paper for this one so the wheels stay in place.

1. Start with the white side up. Fold side to opposite side, both ways. Crease and unfold.

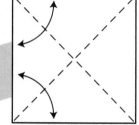

2. Fold all four corners to the center.

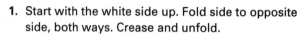

3. Fold each central corner to the center of the outer edge, crease, and unfold. Turn the paper over.

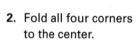

4. Fold all four corners to the center.

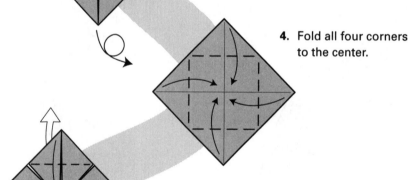

5. Fold the upper and lower corners to the center, allowing a flap of paper to flip out from underneath.

6. Fold the same flaps back 90 degrees to form the wheels. Turn the paper over.

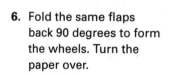

7. The base of the cart is complete.

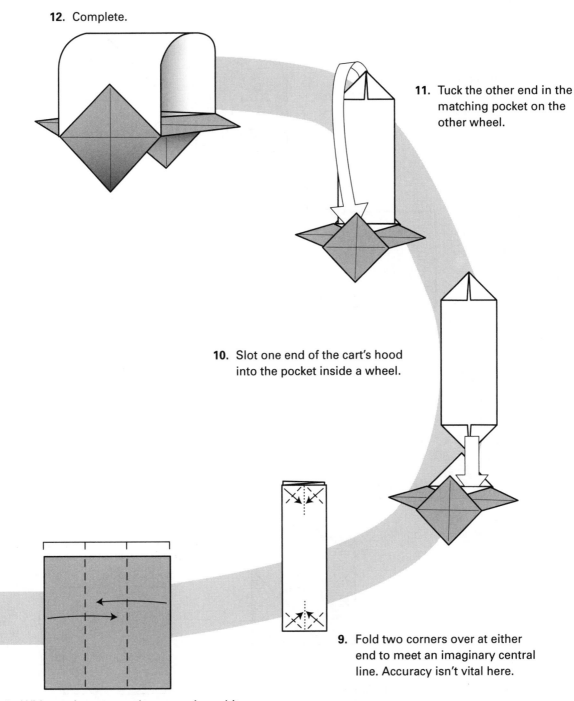

12. Complete.

11. Tuck the other end in the matching pocket on the other wheel.

10. Slot one end of the cart's hood into the pocket inside a wheel.

9. Fold two corners over at either end to meet an imaginary central line. Accuracy isn't vital here.

8. With another square the same size, white side up, fold the sides over about one third of the way so they overlap exactly.

Standing Heart   Difficulty level: 2

by Nick Robinson

This design uses two sheets to achieve the distinctive heart profile. In general, do you think it is easier to use two sheets for a simple sequence, or follow a slightly more complex sequence with a single sheet?

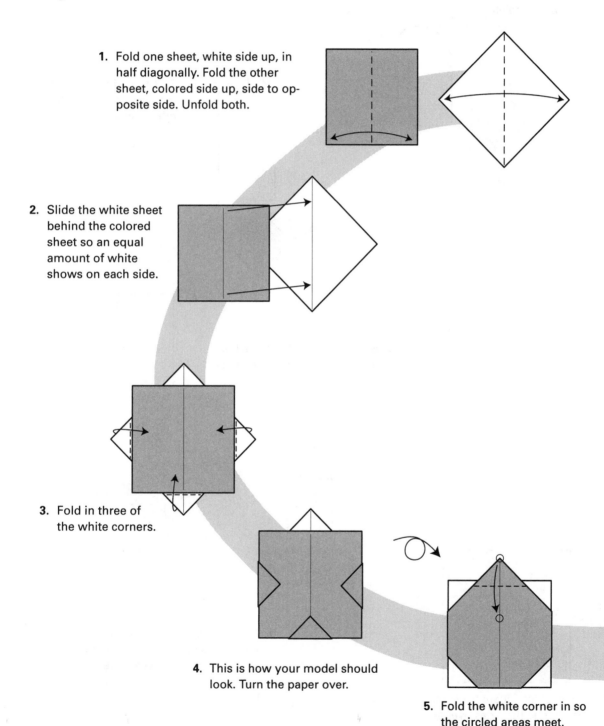

1. Fold one sheet, white side up, in half diagonally. Fold the other sheet, colored side up, side to opposite side. Unfold both.

2. Slide the white sheet behind the colored sheet so an equal amount of white shows on each side.

3. Fold in three of the white corners.

4. This is how your model should look. Turn the paper over.

5. Fold the white corner in so the circled areas meet.

12. Complete.

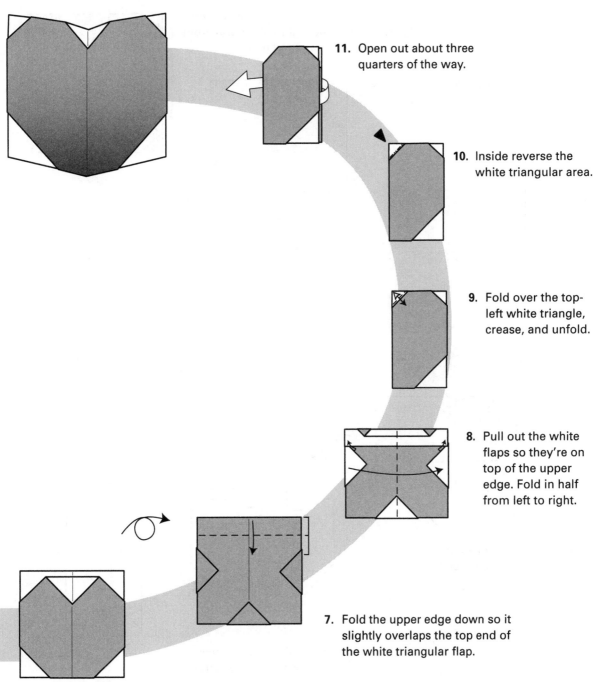

11. Open out about three quarters of the way.

10. Inside reverse the white triangular area.

9. Fold over the top-left white triangle, crease, and unfold.

8. Pull out the white flaps so they're on top of the upper edge. Fold in half from left to right.

7. Fold the upper edge down so it slightly overlaps the top end of the white triangular flap.

6. This is how your model should look. Turn the paper over.

Popsicle Difficulty level: 2

by Gilad Aharoni

Some objects are so familiar, we don't think of them as potential origami subjects. This Popsicle is a great example. When you've made it, see if you can create a stick, too.

1. Start with the colored side up. Fold the top edge to roughly one eighth of the way from the lower edge. Crease and unfold.

2. Fold the lower-left side to lie on the crease.

3. Fold the right side the same way.

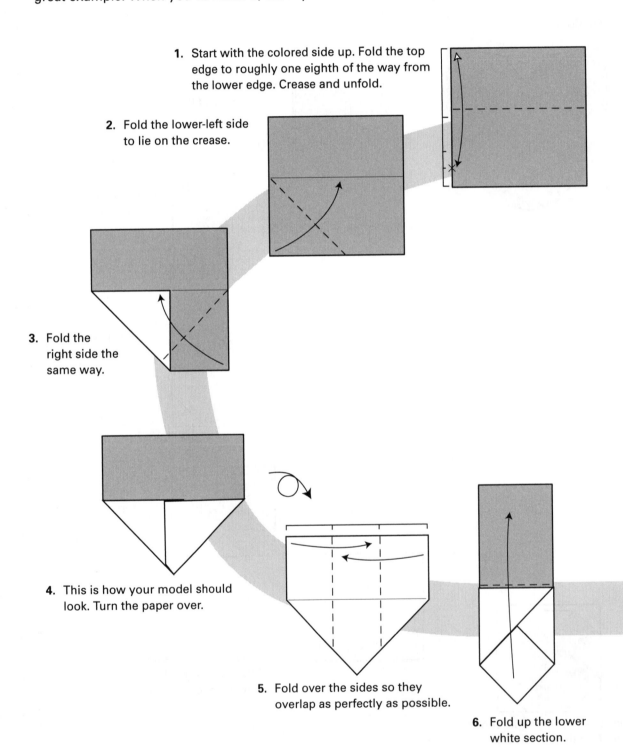

4. This is how your model should look. Turn the paper over.

5. Fold over the sides so they overlap as perfectly as possible.

6. Fold up the lower white section.

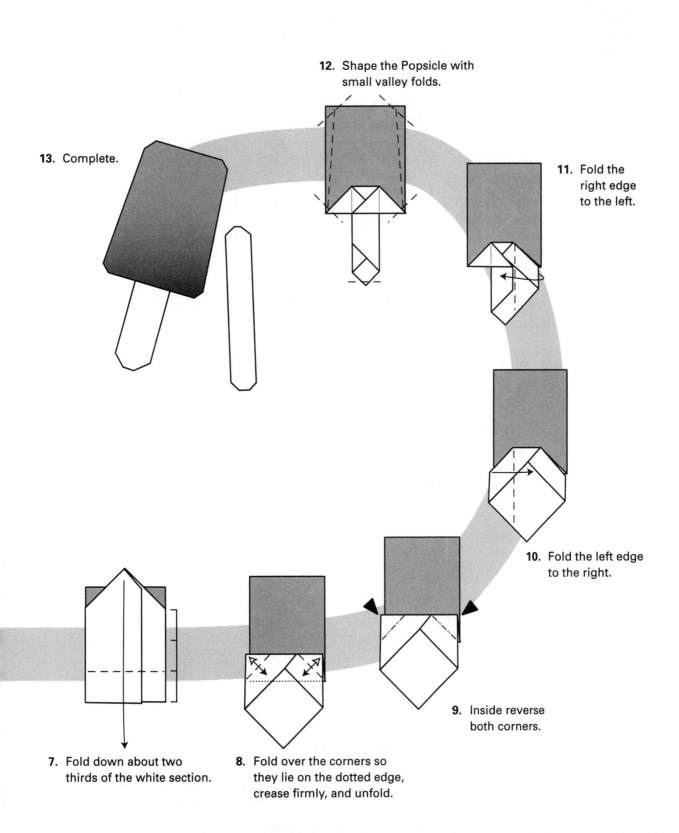

12. Shape the Popsicle with small valley folds.

13. Complete.

11. Fold the right edge to the left.

10. Fold the left edge to the right.

9. Inside reverse both corners.

7. Fold down about two thirds of the white section.

8. Fold over the corners so they lie on the dotted edge, crease firmly, and unfold.

Bug-Eye Glider   Difficulty level: 2

by Nick Robinson

This is an unusual take on the paper plane—it looks like some kind of alien insect! As with all planes, this flies better if the wings are angled up slightly (known as *dihedral*). Launch this one at medium speed with the nose slightly up.

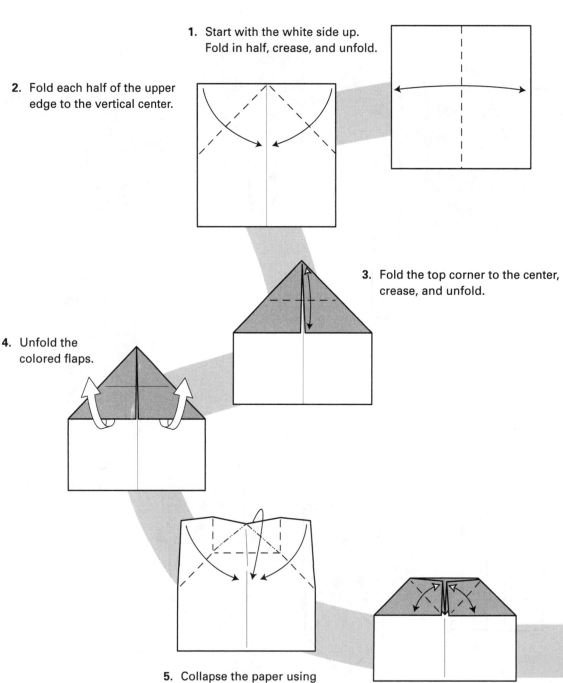

1. Start with the white side up. Fold in half, crease, and unfold.

2. Fold each half of the upper edge to the vertical center.

3. Fold the top corner to the center, crease, and unfold.

4. Unfold the colored flaps.

5. Collapse the paper using the creases shown.

6. Fold the loose corners at the center of the top edge down to the lower edge, crease, and unfold.

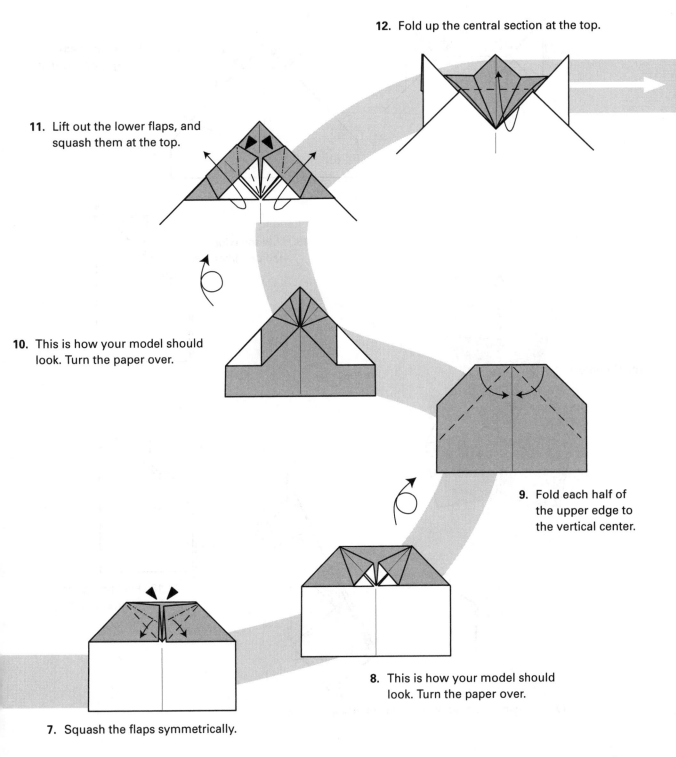

12. Fold up the central section at the top.

11. Lift out the lower flaps, and squash them at the top.

10. This is how your model should look. Turn the paper over.

9. Fold each half of the upper edge to the vertical center.

8. This is how your model should look. Turn the paper over.

7. Squash the flaps symmetrically.

continues

continued

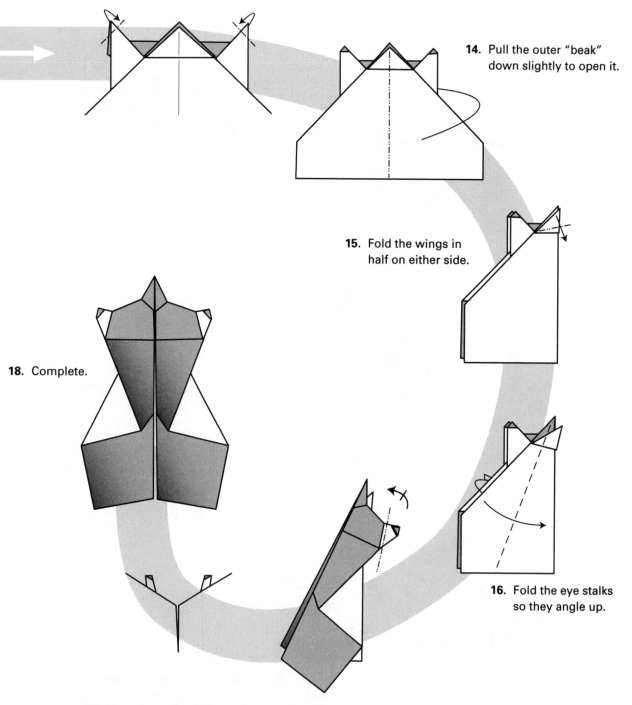

13. Wrap the ends of the pointed flaps around the outside to change the color.

14. Pull the outer "beak" down slightly to open it.

15. Fold the wings in half on either side.

16. Fold the eye stalks so they angle up.

17. The wings should be at these angles, slightly up.

18. Complete.

3D Heart   Difficulty level: 3

by Haui Boglarka

If you look, you can find probably hundreds of origami hearts out there, but most are flat, or 2D. This design has three dimensions and is a more geometric interpretation of a heart. The final model is held in place by the tension in the paper.

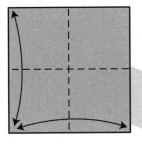

1. Start with the colored side up. Fold side to opposite side, crease and unfold. Repeat in the other direction. Turn the paper over.

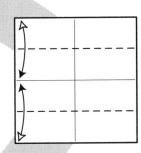

2. Fold the upper and lower edges to the center, crease, and unfold.

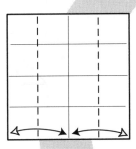

3. Repeat with the left and right edges.

4. Fold the lower corners to the circled points, creasing only where shown. Unfold.

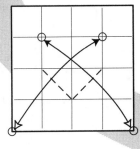

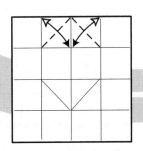

5. Make two small valley folds where shown.

continues

continued

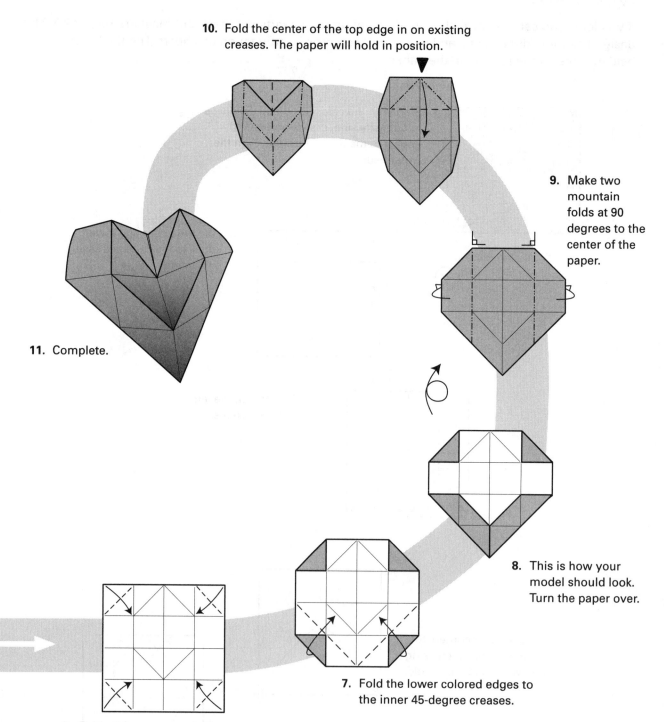

10. Fold the center of the top edge in on existing creases. The paper will hold in position.

9. Make two mountain folds at 90 degrees to the center of the paper.

11. Complete.

8. This is how your model should look. Turn the paper over.

7. Fold the lower colored edges to the inner 45-degree creases.

6. Fold all four corners to the nearest crease intersections.

Candle   Difficulty level: 3

by Nick Robinson

This model makes use of precreasing—almost every crease you need to assemble the model at the end is put in place earlier. Go slowly with steps 13 through 15. Like much of origami, it's easy to actually do, but harder to see what you're *trying* to do!

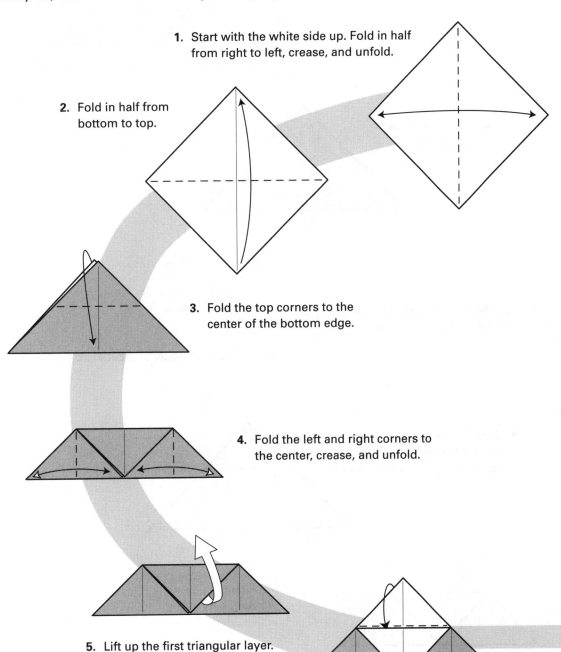

1. Start with the white side up. Fold in half from right to left, crease, and unfold.

2. Fold in half from bottom to top.

3. Fold the top corners to the center of the bottom edge.

4. Fold the left and right corners to the center, crease, and unfold.

5. Lift up the first triangular layer.

6. Tuck the same flap behind the other layers.

continues

continued

11. Fold about two thirds of the top corner back up.

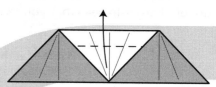

10. Fold the top corner back down.

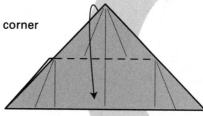

9. Fold the lower halves of the outer edges to the nearest creases, and unfold.

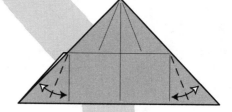

8. Fold the upper halves of the outer edges to the vertical center, creasing only where shown.

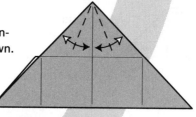

7. Lift up the single layer.

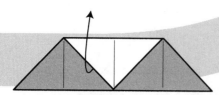

12. Fold the left corner over and over.

13. Curl the right side around.

14. Tuck the flap on the right underneath the angled flap on the left.

15. Fold the left flap over to form a tube.

16. Tuck the bottom triangle inside to lock it together. Shape the flame with an existing crease. Turn the paper over.

17. Complete.

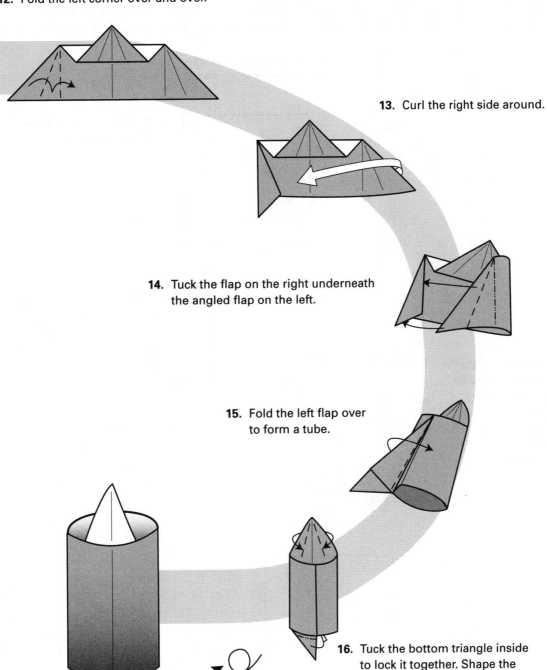

Reverse Pinwheel   Difficulty level: 4

by Florence Temko

This is a fun challenge for any creative paper-folder. You might recognize the standard pinwheel, but this multicolored variant is less obvious. The initial set of creases is to divide the paper into thirds. If you want a result with fewer visible creases, use the method to create a template given earlier.

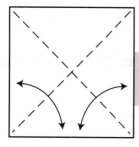

1. Start with the white side up. Precrease both diagonals.

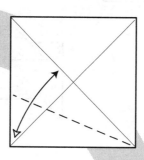

2. Fold the lower edge to the diagonal, crease gently, and unfold.

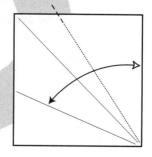

3. Fold the right edge to the most recent crease, but only crease at the very top.

4. (A) Fold the right corner to the pinch to make a valley crease on the right, and (B) fold the left side to the most recent crease.

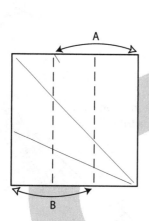

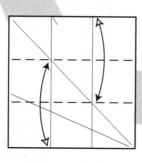

5. Add two more similar creases on the other axis.

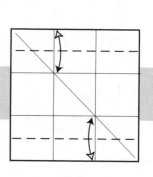

6. Add upper and lower one-sixth creases. Turn the paper over.

11. Fold over one sixth all the
way along the lower edge.

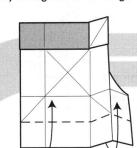

10. Pull out a layer at the
bottom-right corner.

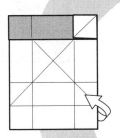

9. Fold one sixth behind
on the left.

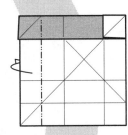

8. Fold down one
sixth at the top.

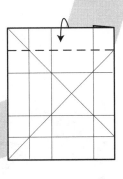

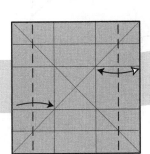

7. Precrease on the right,
and fold over on the left.
Turn the paper over.

continues

continued

12. This is how your model should look. Turn the paper over.

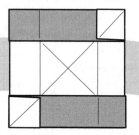

13. Fold each corner to the center, but only crease on the right half of the paper. Unfold, and turn the paper over.

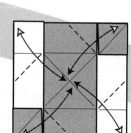

18. Complete.

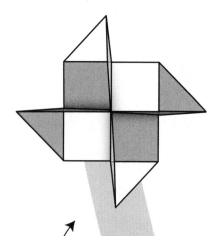

14. Collapse in using these creases.

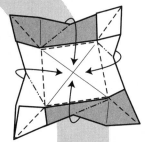

15. This is how your fold should look in progress.

17. Tuck the small colored triangles underneath a layer. Turn the paper over.

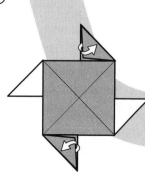

16. This is how your completed fold should look. Turn the paper over.

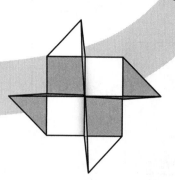

Kettle Difficulty level: 4

by Adolfo Cerceda

This design dates to the 1960s but still looks stylish. The move in step 25 is technically known as a "closed sink" and needs to be done with confidence! Use a slightly larger square for your first attempt.

1. Start with the colored side up. Precrease both diagonals. Turn the paper over.

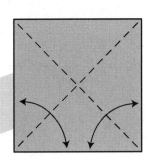

2. Fold in half from side to side, crease, and unfold.

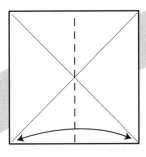

3. Fold both upper corners to the center.

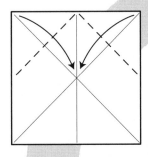

4. Fold the paper to the right so the circled areas meet.

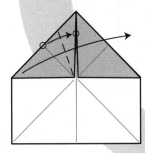

5. Note the folded edge is at right angles to the vertical center. Crease only where shown, and unfold.

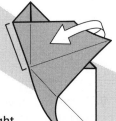

6. Repeat the last move on the other side.

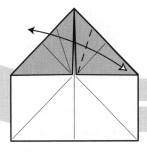

continues

continued

13. Fold the right corner to the circled point.

12. Fold left and right corners to the center, crease, and unfold.

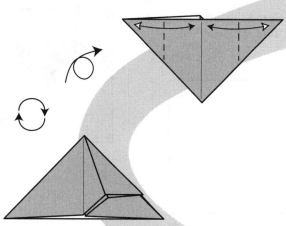

11. This is how your model should look. Turn the paper over and rotate.

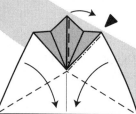

10. Collapse the paper to the right using the creases shown.

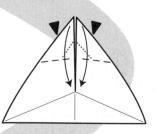

9. Fold the upper corners to the center, carefully squashing along the dotted edge underneath.

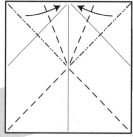

8. Form the paper into 3D using the creases shown.

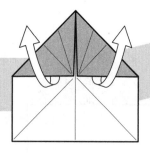

7. Unfold the two flaps.

14. Fold the corner to the vertical
crease, and unfold.

15. Inside reverse the corner on
the crease you just made.

16. Swing the central
flap down.

17. Fold the small
flap to the right.

18. Repeat steps 13 through 17
on the left side of the paper.
The vertical crease on the left
meets the center.

19. Fold the triangles to the center on the
left and the right. Fold the lower corner
to the center, crease, and unfold.

20. On the left, fold the horizontal edge up
to the nearest folded edge. Repeat on
the right, but unfold after creasing.

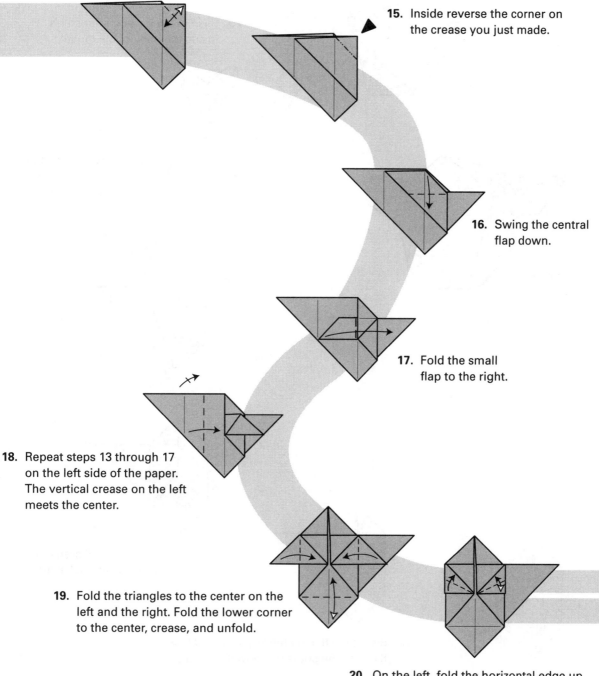

continues

continued

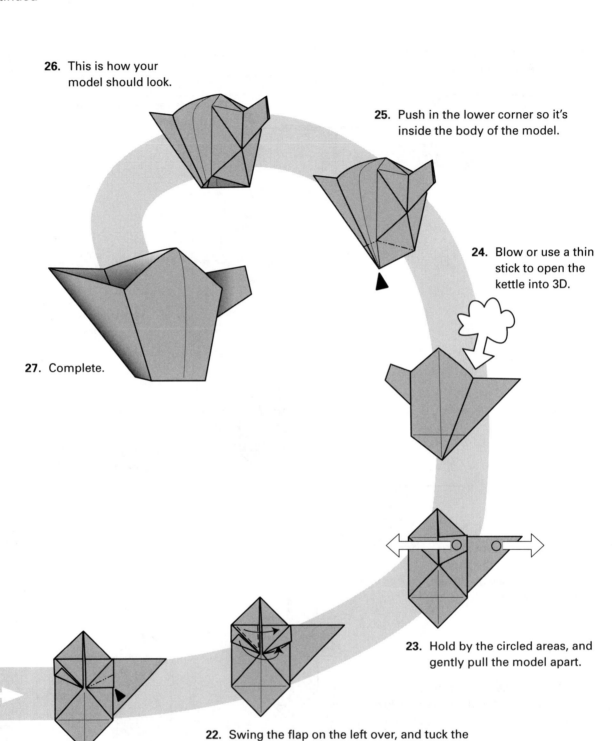

26. This is how your model should look.

25. Push in the lower corner so it's inside the body of the model.

24. Blow or use a thin stick to open the kettle into 3D.

27. Complete.

23. Hold by the circled areas, and gently pull the model apart.

22. Swing the flap on the left over, and tuck the flap into the pocket to form the handle.

21. Inside reverse on the most recent crease.

Tent Difficulty level: 4

by Francesco Guarnieri

This model may look simple, but it will certainly test your folding abilities. The opening sequence of folds is designed to divide the paper into fifths vertically. The move that forms the ridges (steps 14 through 16) is known as a "butterfly lock" and was first done by Philip Shen.

1. Start with the colored side up. Crease in half from side to opposite side, and unfold.

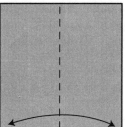

2. Add quarter creases. Turn the paper over.

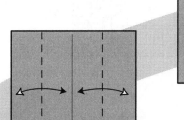

3. Take the top-right corner to the end of the right vertical quarter crease. *Do not flatten.* Just hold in place so the colored edge lies on the left vertical edge.

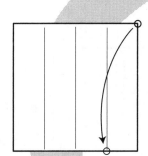

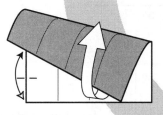

4. Fold the lower corner to the colored edge, starting a crease, and let the paper open out again.

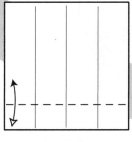

5. Extend the crease across the square.

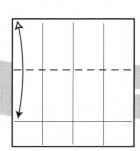

6. Fold the top edge to the recent crease, and unfold.

continues

continued

12. Repeat steps 10 and 11 on the other vertical creases. The first crease is shown for you.

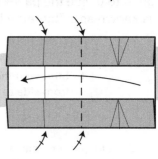

11. Fold the top-right corner in to meet the dotted halfway mark, crease firmly, and unfold. The crease starts at the right end of the upper horizontal crease. Repeat on the lower-right corner. Unfold.

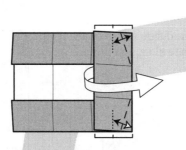

10. Fold the right quarter to the left.

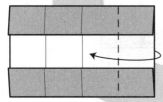

9. Refold the upper and lower edges in on the outer creases.

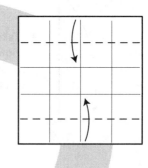

8. Fold the lower-edge crease to the uppermost crease, and unfold.

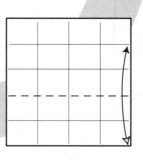

7. Fold the top edge to the nearest crease, and unfold.

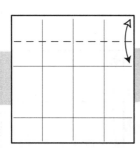

13. Unfold back to the square.

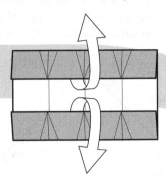

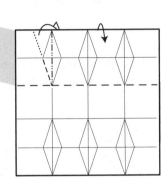

14. Folding the top section in slightly, form a pleat using the vertical mountain and partial valley. Don't flatten the paper.

15. Fold in the upper edge, flattening a crease where the dotted line lies. The paper will remain 3D.

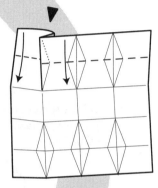

18. Complete.

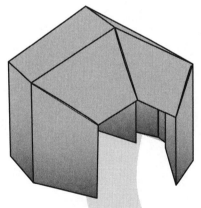

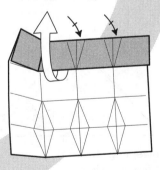

16. Partially unfold the paper, and repeat step 15 in three matching places. You will need to ease them all into place together firmly.

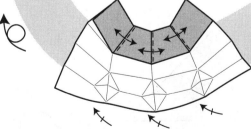

17. Reinforce the valley creases shown.

Take a deep breath, and repeat steps 15 through 17 on each of the matching lower sections. Turn the paper over.

Trees on a Hillside   Difficulty level: 4

by Eric Kenneway

The late Kenneway had a unique take on origami, both in terms of subject matter and technique. You might find the color change (steps 15 through 17) a challenge, but it's very logical once you see what's happening. The final diagram shows two models, one folded as a mirror image of the first one, so as you work the directions, swap "left" for "right." Another way to achieve this is to view the instruction through a mirror!

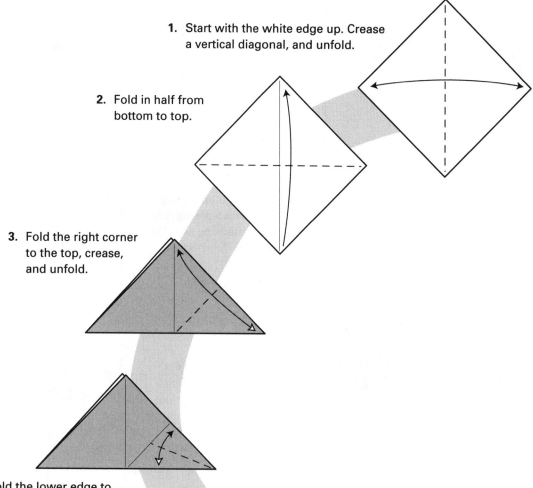

1. Start with the white edge up. Crease a vertical diagonal, and unfold.

2. Fold in half from bottom to top.

3. Fold the right corner to the top, crease, and unfold.

4. Fold the lower edge to the right edge, creasing only as far as the existing crease. Unfold.

5. Fold the right edge (both layers) to the vertical center, creasing where shown, and unfold.

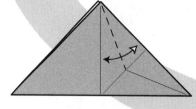

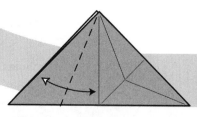

6. Fold the left edge to the vertical center, crease, and unfold.

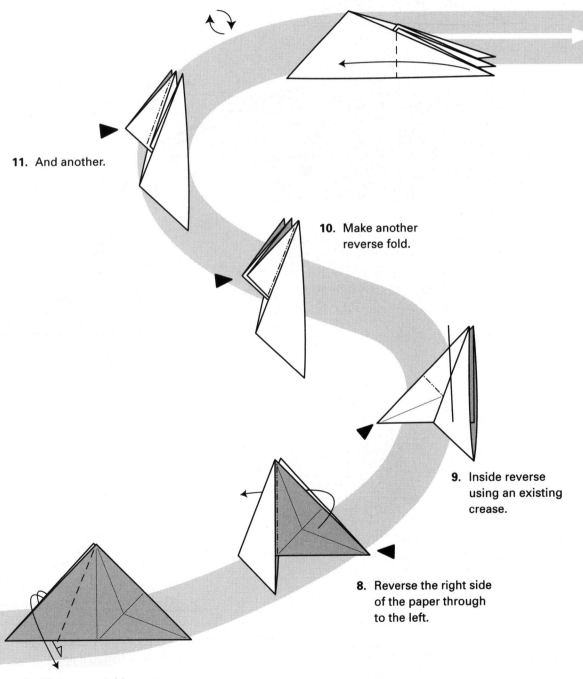

12. Rotate the paper. Swing the upper flap on the right across to the left.

11. And another.

10. Make another reverse fold.

9. Inside reverse using an existing crease.

8. Reverse the right side of the paper through to the left.

7. Make an outside reverse fold on the left.

continues

continued

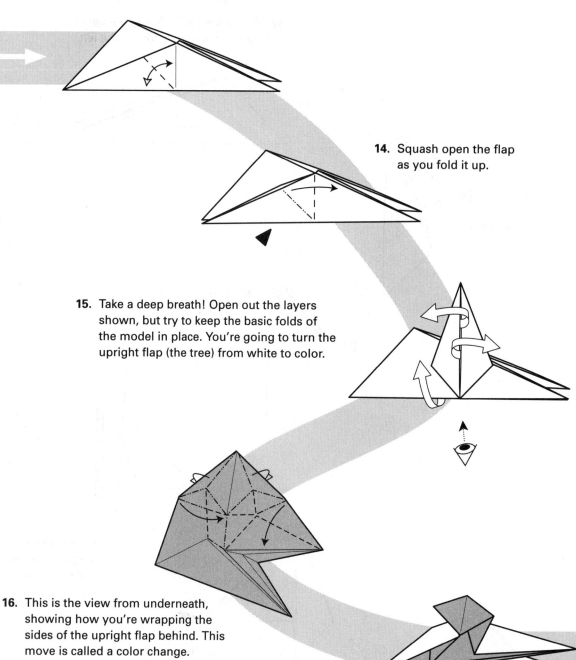

13. Fold the same flap to the vertical, crease, and unfold.

14. Squash open the flap as you fold it up.

15. Take a deep breath! Open out the layers shown, but try to keep the basic folds of the model in place. You're going to turn the upright flap (the tree) from white to color.

16. This is the view from underneath, showing how you're wrapping the sides of the upright flap behind. This move is called a color change.

17. This is how your model should look as you flatten it again.

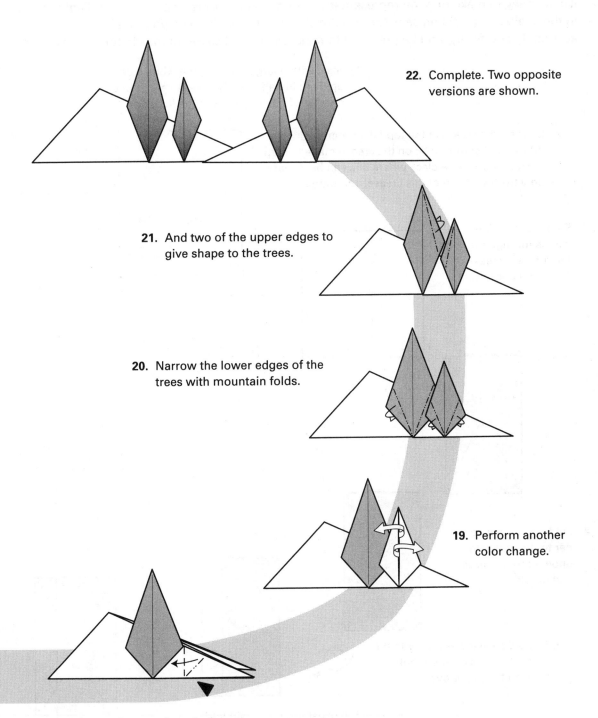

22. Complete. Two opposite versions are shown.

21. And two of the upper edges to give shape to the trees.

20. Narrow the lower edges of the trees with mountain folds.

19. Perform another color change.

18. Form another tree in a similar way.

Apple   Difficulty level: 5

by Shuzo Fujimoto

It's not easy to make origami representations of circular objects, like this apple. That fact is reflected in the challenging folding sequence you're about to tackle. Be sure you do all early precreasing accurately and firmly, and be prepared to make the model several times before it looks neat.

1. Start with a larger square, the white side up. Fold in half, but only crease about one quarter of the way in from the left edge.

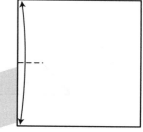

2. Starting the crease at the top-left corner, fold the bottom-left corner to lie on the crease made in step 1. There's only one place where this can be. Crease only the lower end of this crease, and unfold.

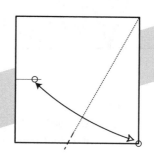

3. Fold the left edge across through the most recent crease. Turn the paper over.

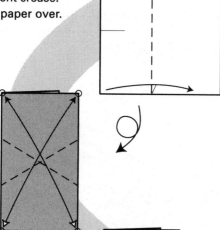

4. Fold each lower corner to the opposite upper corner, crease, and unfold.

5. Fold each lower corner to the center, crease, and unfold. Turn the paper over.

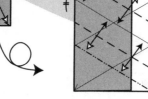

6. Fold the (existing) mountain fold to the center creases, crease, and unfold. Repeat three times.

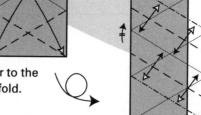

7. Add the "missing" creases to complete the pattern of 30-degree creases. Open out the paper.

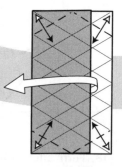

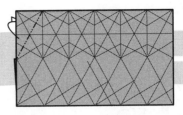

13. Fold the top-left corner behind on an existing crease.

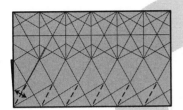
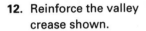

12. Reinforce the valley crease shown.

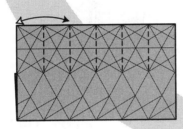

11. Add vertical valley creases.

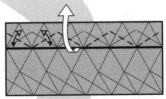

10. Add more precreases at the top in the same way. Open out the top flap. Turn the paper over.

9. At the bottom, fold the lower edge to the right edge of the creased triangles. Crease and unfold. At the top, fold each edge of the creased triangles to the horizontal. Crease and unfold.

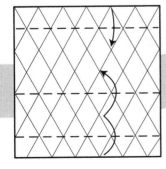

8. Fold the lower edge to the nearest crease intersections, and fold over again where shown. Fold the upper edge to meet the new lower folded edge.

continues

continued

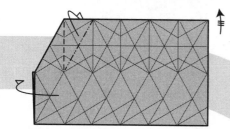

14. Fold the mountain and valley shown to form the paper into 3D. Continue along the top edge in the same way. The paper will form into a hexagonal tube.

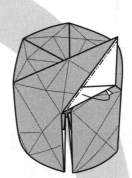

15. Fold the white section underneath.

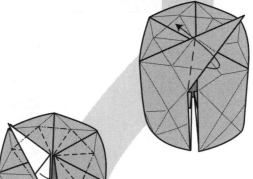

16. Fold back the pointed flap.

17. Slide the left edge into a pocket on the right. As it slides in, encourage the top to form a small dimple facing in.

18. The paper should now be a five-edge tube. Put your fingers inside, and gently reinforce the shape. Turn the paper upside down.

23. Complete.

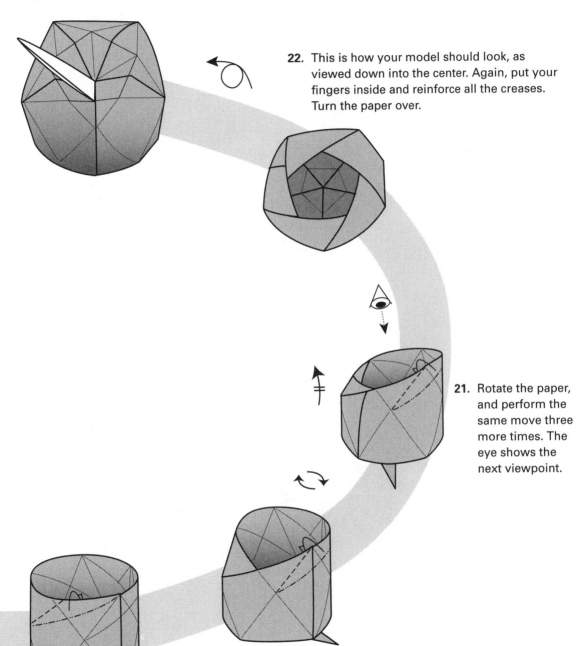

22. This is how your model should look, as viewed down into the center. Again, put your fingers inside and reinforce all the creases. Turn the paper over.

21. Rotate the paper, and perform the same move three more times. The eye shows the next viewpoint.

20. Repeat the previous move on the next set of creases, working counterclockwise.

19. Form the creases shown. The paper will start to move toward the center.

Index of Models

Numbers

3D Heart, 283-284
8-Point Star, 193-194

A

Angel, 146-149
animal models
   Cat's Head, 61-62
   Cricket, 58
   Dolphin, 73-75
   Elephant, 83-85
   Fantail Goldfish, 67-68
   Frog on a Window, 76-78
   Frog's Head, 63-64
   Horse, 69-70
   Howling at the Moon, 79-82
   Koala, 94-96
   Mad March Hare, 71-72
   Pig, 59-60
   Puma's Head, 86-89
   Squarosaurus, 90-93
   Whale's Tail, 65-66
Apple, 302-305

B

beginner (level 1) models
   Cricket, 58
   Crown, 267-268
   Cup, 243-244
   Girl's Head 1, 120
   Gliding Hoop, 266
   Long-Stemmed Rose, 101
   Pecking Bird, 30
   Pig, 59-60

Sheffield Sailboat, 269-270
Simple Tray, 152-153
Swan, 31-32
Tessellating Cross, 182
Tulip and Stem, 99-100
   Stem, 100
   Tulip, 99
Wallet, 242
Water Lily, 98
Word Dominoes, 271
bird models
   Bowing Bird, 48-51
   Fancy Swan, 52-55
   Fat Bird, 46-47
   Great-Horned Owl, 40-42
   Hungry Chick, 35
   Mother and Baby Penguin, 43-45
   Peacock, 33-34
   Pecking Bird, 30
   Perched Owl, 36-37
   Songbird, 38-39
   Swan, 31-32
Bluebell, 111-113
Booklet, 245
Boutonniere Blossom, 102-103
Bowing Bird, 48-51
Bristol Box, 179-180
Bug-Eye Glider, 280-282

C

Camellia, 108-109
Candle, 285-287
Cart, 274-275
Cat's Head, 61-62
Classic Bowl, 176-178
Classic Cap, 254-255

Classic Cube, 204-206
container models
  Bristol Box, 179-180
  Classic Bowl, 176-178
  Curly Box, 171-172
  Fox Dish, 165-167
  Lidded Box, 173-175
  Poppy Dish, 158-160
  Simple Tray, 152-153
  Spanish Box, 156-157
  Square Bowl, 154-155
  Star Box, 168-170
  Triangular Box, 161-164
    Desk Tidy, 164
Cricket, 58
Cross Puzzle, 201-203
Crown, 267-268
Crying Baby, 132-134
Cup, 243-244
Curly Box, 171-172

D

Desert Flower, 114-117
Desk Tidy (Triangular Box), 164
DNA Strand, 213-215
Dolphin, 73-75
Double Cube, 207-209

E

easy (level 2) models
  Booklet, 245
  Boutonniere Blossom, 102-103
  Bug-Eye Glider, 280-282
  Camellia, 108-109
  Cart, 274-275
  Cat's Head, 61-62
  Classic Cup, 254-255
  Envelope from Bonn, 246
  Flexagon, 189-190
  Freising Plane, 272-273

French Fries Bag, 249
Frog's Head, 63-64
Girl's Head 2, 121-122
Grumpy Alien, 127-128
Hexahedron, 222
Hungry Chick, 35
Modular Twist, 224-225
Napoleon, 125-126
Party Hat, 247-248
Peacock, 33-34
Perched Owl, 36-37
Pocket Fan, 252-253
Popsicle, 278-279
Proving Pythagoras, 185-188
  Module 1A, 185-186
  Module 1B, 186
  Module 2, 187
  Module 3, 188
  The Proof, 188
Pyramid, 226-227
Sailboat Envelope, 256-257
Set Square, 250-251
Simple Santa, 123-124
Snowdrop, 106-107
Spanish Box, 156-157
Square Bowl, 154-155
Squared Square, 183-184
Squared Square Cube, 223
Standing Heart, 276-277
Sunflower, 104-105
Tower, 191-192
Whale's Tail, 65-66
Windmill Cube, 228-229
Elephant, 83-85
Elforia Envelope, 258-259
Envelope from Bonn, 246
experienced (level 4) models
  Bird, 48-51
  Bristol Box, 179-180
  Classic Bowl, 176-178
  Dolphin, 73-75
  Elephant, 83-85

Frog on a Window, 76-78
Howling at the Moon, 79-82
Human Face, 138-141
Kettle, 291-294
Lidded Box, 173-175
Reverse Pinwheel, 288-290
Robot's Head, 135-137
Tent, 295-297
Trees on a Hillside, 298-301
Tri-Coaster, 210-212
expert (level 5) models
    Angel, 146-149
    Apple, 302-305
    Desert Flower, 114-117
    DNA Strand, 213-215
    Fancy Swan, 52-55
    Koala, 94-96
    Mr. Muppet, 142-145
    Puma's Head, 86-89
    Squarosaurus, 90-93
    Umulius Rectangulum, 216-219

F

Fancy Swan, 52-55
Fantail Goldfish, 67-68
Fat Bird, 46-47
Flexagon, 189-190
flower models
    Bluebell, 111-113
    Boutonniere Blossom, 102-103
    Camellia, 108-109
    Desert Flower, 114-117
    Long-Stemmed Rose, 101
    Orchid, 110
    Snowdrop, 106-107
    Sunflower, 104-105
    Tulip and Stem, 99-100
        Stem, 100
        Tulip, 99
    Water Lily, 98

Four-Sided Pyramid (Tri-Module Unit), 232
Fox Dish, 165-167
Freising Plane, 272-273
French Fries Bag, 249
Frog on a Window, 76-78
Frog's Head, 63-64
fun models
    3D Heart, 283-284
    Apple, 302-305
    Bug-Eye Glider, 280-282
    Candle, 285-287
    Cart, 274-275
    Crown, 267-268
    Freising Plane, 272-273
    Gliding Hoop, 266
    Kettle, 291-294
    Popsicle, 278-279
    Reverse Pinwheel, 288-290
    Sheffield Sailboat, 269-270
    Standing Heart, 276-277
    Tent, 295-297
    Trees on a Hillside, 298-301
    Word Dominoes, 271

G

geometric models
    8-Point Star, 193-194
    Classic Cube, 204-206
    Cross Puzzle, 201-203
    DNA Strand, 213-215
    Double Cube, 207-209
    Flexagon, 189-190
    Pinwheel Tato, 199-200
    Proving Pythagoras, 185-188
        Module 1A, 185-186
        Module 1B, 186
        Module 2, 187
        Module 3, 188
        The Proof, 188
    Squared Square, 183-184

Tessellating Cross, 182
Tower, 191-192
Tri-Coaster, 210-212
Tri-Puzzle, 195-198
    Module 1, 195-196
    Module 2, 197
    Module 3, 198
    Umulius Rectangulum, 216-219
Girl's Head 1, 120
Girl's Head 2, 121-122
Gliding Hoop, 266
Goldfinch Star, 237-239
Great-Horned Owl, 40-42
Grumpy Alien, 127-128

H

Hexahedron, 222
Hexahedron (Tri-Module Unit), 232
Holiday Card, 260-261
Horse, 69-70
Howling at the Moon, 79-82
Human Face, 138-141
Hungry Chick, 35

I–J

intermediate (level 3) models
    3D Heart, 283-284
    8-Point Star, 193-194
    Bluebell, 111-113
    Candle, 285-287
    Classic Cube, 204-206
    Cross Puzzle, 201-203
    Crying Baby, 132-134
    Curly Box, 171-172
    Double Cube, 207-209
    Elforia Envelope, 258-259
    Fantail Goldfish, 67-68
    Fat Bird, 46-47
    Fox Dish, 165-167
    Goldfinch Star, 237-239

Great-Horned Owl, 40-42
Holiday Card, 260-261
Horse, 69-70
Mad March Hare, 71-72
Mother and Baby Penguin, 43-45
Octahedron, 240
Orchid, 110
Pinwheel Tato, 199-200
Poppy Dish, 158-160
Ring, 262-263
Snow Cube, 235-236
Snowflake Module, 233-234
Songbird, 38-39
Star Box, 168-170
Triangular Box, 161-164
    Desk Tidy, 164
Tri-Module Unit, 230-232
    For Real Enthusiasts, 232
    Four-Sided Pyramid, 232
    Hexahedron, 230-231
    Spiked Models, 232
    Tetrahedron, 231
Tri-Puzzle, 195-198
    Module 1, 195-196
    Module 2, 197
    Module 3, 198
Vampyra, 129-131

K–L

Kettle, 291-294
Koala, 94-96

Lidded Box, 173-175
Long-Stemmed Rose, 101

M

Mad March Hare, 71-72
modular models
    Goldfinch Star, 237-239
    Hexahedron, 222

Modular Twist, 224-225
Octahedron, 240
Pyramid, 226-227
Snow Cube, 235-236
Snowflake Module, 233-234
Squared Square Cube, 223
Tri-Module Unit, 230-232
  For Real Enthusiasts, 232
  Four-Sided Pyramid, 232
  Hexahedron, 230-231
  Spiked Models, 232
  Tetrahedron, 231
Windmill Cube, 228-229
Modular Twist, 224-225
Mother and Baby Penguin, 43-45
Mr. Muppet, 142-145

N–O

Napoleon, 125-126

Octahedron, 240
Orchid, 110

P–Q

Party Hat, 247-248
Peacock, 33-34
Pecking Bird, 30
people models
  Angel, 146-149
  Crying Baby, 132-134
  Girl's Head 1, 120
  Girl's Head 2, 121-122
  Grumpy Alien, 127-128
  Human Face, 138-141
  Mr. Muppet, 142-145
  Napoleon, 125-126
  Robot's Head, 135-137
  Simple Santa, 123-124
  Vampyra, 129-131

Perched Owl, 36-37
Pig, 59-60
Pinwheel Tato, 199-200
Pocket Fan, 252-253
Poppy Dish, 158-160
Popsicle, 278-279
practical models
  Booklet, 245
  Classic Cap, 254-255
  Cup, 243-244
  Elforia Envelope, 258-259
  Envelope from Bonn, 246
  French Fries Bag, 249
  Holiday Card, 260-261
  Party Hat, 247-248
  Pocket Fan, 252-253
  Ring, 262-263
  Sailboat Envelope, 256-257
  Set Square, 250-251
  Wallet, 242
Proving Pythagoras, 185-188
  Module 1A, 185-186
  Module 1B, 186
  Module 2, 187
  Module 3, 188
  The Proof, 188
Puma's Head, 86-89
Pyramid, 226-227

R

Reverse Pinwheel, 288-290
Ring, 262-263
Robot's Head, 135-137

S

Sailboat Envelope, 256-257
Set Square, 250-251
Sheffield Sailboat, 269-270
Simple Santa, 123-124

Simple Tray, 152-153
Snow Cube, 235-236
Snowdrop, 106-107
Snowflake Module, 233-234
Songbird, 38-39
Spanish Box, 156-157
Spiked Models (Tri-Module Unit), 232
Square Bowl, 154-155
Squared Square, 183-184
Squared Square Cube, 223
Squarosaurus, 90-93
Standing Heart, 276-277
Star Box, 168-170
Sunflower, 104-105
Swan, 31-32

T–U–V

Tent, 295-297
Tessellating Cross, 182
Tetrahedron (Tri-Module Unit), 231
Tower, 191-192
Trees on a Hillside, 298-301
Triangular Box, 161-164
   Desk Tidy, 164
Tri-Coaster, 210-212
Tri-Module Unit, 230-232
   For Real Enthusiasts, 232
   Four-Sided Pyramid, 232
   Hexahedron, 230-231
   Spiked Models, 232
   Tetrahedron, 231
Tri-Puzzle, 195-198
   Module 1, 195-196
   Module 2, 197
   Module 3, 198
Tulip and Stem, 99-100
   Stem, 100
   Tulip, 99

Umulius Rectangulum, 216-219

Vampyra, 129-131

W–X–Y–Z

Wallet, 242
Water Lily, 98
Whale's Tail, 65-66
Windmill Cube, 228-229
Word Dominoes, 271